Economists and the Stock Market

This book is dedicated to our families for their enduring support.
Thank you Judy and Patrick; Marilyn, Colby, and Danni.

Economists and the Stock Market

Speculative Theories of Stock Market Fluctuations

J. Patrick Raines
Professor of Economics and F. Carlyle Tiller Chair in Business, University of Richmond, USA

and

Charles G. Leathers
Professor of Economics, University of Alabama, USA

Edward Elgar
Cheltenham, UK • Northampton, MA, USA

Published by
Edward Elgar Publishing Limited
Glensanda House
Montpellier Parade
Cheltenham
Glos GL50 1UA
UK

Edward Elgar Publishing, Inc.
136 West Street
Suite 202
Northampton
Massachusetts 01060
USA

Reprinted 2001

A catalogue record for this book
is available from the British Library

Library of Congress Cataloguing in Publication Data

Raines, J. Patrick, 1951–
    Economists and the stock market: speculative theories of stock
market fluctuations / by J. Patrick Raines, Charles G. Leathers.
    Includes bibliographical references.
    1. Speculation—United States. 2. Stocks—Prices—United States.
3. Investments—United States. 4. Stock exchanges—United States.
I. Leathers, Charles G., 1940– . II. Title.
HG6041.R33   1999
332.63'228'0973—dc21   98–53753
                                            CIP

ISBN 1 85898 564 1

Printed and bound in Great Britain by Biddles Ltd, www.Biddles.co.uk

Contents

Preface: The New Bull: Will the Market Still Fluctuate?

According to Wall Street legend, when asked what the stock market was going to do, Jay Gould replied, 'The market, sir, will fluctuate.' It did, and has continued to do so. Most of those fluctuations have been in the form of rather gradual rises over a number of months, sometimes for several years, followed by fairly gradual declines over a number of months or for several years. Stocks in the S&P 500, for example, lost 4.25 percent annually (after adjusting for inflation) over the decade after 1965, and a similar investment in 1972 lost 3.75 percent annually over the next decade.

But sometimes the price increases accelerated into trading frenzies that produced price bubbles that ended in sudden and sharp price declines usually described as crashes, panics and/or crises. The classic 'bubble and crash' scenario was the great bull market of the 1920s, which ended in the Great Crash of October 1929. After briefly seeming to be moving into a recovery phase, the market went into a long decline reaching a low in the summer of 1932. At that point, the value of stocks was only about 16 percent of the pre-1929 crash high, a level not regained for 25 years.

Another great bull market emerged in the 1980s, with the Dow Industrial Average rising from a low of around 800 in 1982 to a high of over 2700 in August 1987. In January 1987, John Kenneth Galbraith, author of *The Great Crash 1929*, noted parallels between the 1920s and 1980s, and warned of the possibility of another crash. Virtually on cue, the market crashed in October, as it is wont to do in that month. 'Black Monday', 19 October 1987, became the largest single-day crash in history as prices fell nearly 23 percent. Over a period of only a few days of trading, approximately one-third of the value of corporate stocks evaporated.

While the 1987 crash exhibited the characteristics of previous crashes, it was distinctively different in two ways. First, the 'official' explanation by the Brady Commission (appointed by the President to investigate the crash) laid the blame on an inability of the market mechanism to absorb a huge volume of selling that was allegedly generated by new computerized trading strategies. Popularly referred to as 'program trading', these strategies – dynamic hedging via portfolio insurance and stock index arbitrage – linked trading in stocks in stock markets with trading in the new stock index futures contracts in commodity markets.

According to this 'official' explanation, a 'cascade effect' occurred. First, several disturbing economic and political events caused a relatively small decline in stock prices. That decline in turn triggered a cascade-like wave of selling by the computerized programs as the two computerized trading strategies interacted. When the stock market was unable to absorb that selling, as revealed publicly by the ticker tape running late, many investors rushed to get out of the market. This created an episode of panic selling and prices plummeted.

The Brady Commission's recommended solution was to reform the market mechanism through institutional changes, including new regulations on program trading and stock index futures trading. While no governmental reforms have been instituted, the New York Stock Exchange (NYSE) in February 1988 implemented 'circuit breakers' or 'collars' to halt program trading temporarily when the Dow moved 50 points. In October 1988 the exchanges adopted rules that would stop all trading. The NYSE would stop trading for one hour (now 30 minutes) if the market falls 250 points and for another two hours if the market falls 400 points. In 1998, the circuit breaker restrictions were revised to allow the Dow to drop 10 percent before trading halts for the first time and additional halts (depending on the time of the day) after declines of 20 percent and 30 percent. Other exchanges, including futures exchanges, adopted related rules.

The second difference has been that the aftermath of the worst crash in history in 1987 has been very different from the aftermath of the 1929 crash. This has raised a number of questions about theories of investors' behavior and the importance of the risk of sudden and drastic declines in stock prices.

THE STOCK MARKET RECOVERS

The Dow Industrial Average closed on 19 October 1987 at 1739, but finished the year at 1940. The market moved up during 1988, closing at 2168. But in 1989, the market rose 25 percent, closing at 2753. A new high of 2791 was established in October. A 'mini-crash' on 13 October revived memories of the 1987 crash and stimulated new calls, especially from retail brokerage houses, for regulations on trading in stock index futures contracts.

The market closed lower at the end of 1990, primarily due to Iraq's invasion of Kuwait which produced fears of sharply rising petroleum prices.

But it very nearly broke the existing psychologically important 3000 mark in July before declining some 20 percent between August and mid October.

In 1991, the market broke the 3000 mark on the Dow Industrial Average, and rose 20 percent for the year. Another 'mini-crash' occurred on 15 November when the market dropped by 4 percent. The drop was initially blamed on fears that Congress would pass a bill putting ceilings on interest rates charged on credit card debt. Later, the Securities Exchange Commission (SEC) blamed institutional investors using esoteric market-trading strategies designed to lock in high profits and protect against losses. The SEC viewed this practice as a normal part of market activities.

FEARS OF A NEW SPECULATIVE MARKET

By June 1992, the Dow Industrial Average had risen to 3413, sparking warnings about a new speculative stock market. In April 1992, the market was described as being in the 'midst of a speculative buying panic', with stocks overpriced by some $800 billion (Baldwin 1992). According to one report, the market was being influenced by several popular delusions common to periods of speculative binges, including 'prosperity is around the corner', 'the market is rational' and 'it's different this time' (Baldwin 1992).

The performance of the market during the latter part of 1992, however, seemed to dispel any concerns about a new speculative market as the Dow Industrial Average closed at 3284, rising only 3.6 percent for the year. Yet in October, the *Wall Street Journal* headlined a review of the five years after the 1987 crash with the title 'Black Monday Taught Investors to Lose Fear'. Sease (1992) observed that the 1987 crash had taught small investors to lose their fear of declining stock prices. With the market's remarkable recovery, the 'average small investor' was willing to believe that the crash was due to a market mechanism failure as claimed by the Brady Commission.

The market rose nearly 14 percent in 1993, closing at 3794 on the Dow. A curious characteristic of this new bull market appeared to be emerging. While students graduating from college faced the worst job market in decades, stocks continued to rise. Seemingly, the worse the news on the employment front, the higher prices of stocks would go.

Concerns about Speculative Markets Don't Halt Advances

During 1994, the market was volatile, ending the year at 3834 on the Dow, for an annual gain of slightly over 2 percent. But 1995 was a boom year for the stock market as it soared above both the 4000 and 5000 levels on the

Dow to end the year with a 33 percent gain. Financial markets commentators were again asserting that the conventional stock market indicators were warning of an overvalued market. One such indicator was Tobin's Q Ratio. Based on complex calculations, the Q Ratio divides the price of all stocks in a country, excluding non-manufacturing companies such as banks, by the replacement value of companies' assets (not including intangibles such as knowledge). By using the replacement cost, the Q Ratio screens out the effects of inflation. If the Q Ratio equals 1, the stock market is valuing $1 worth of assets at $1. When Q falls below 1, the stock market is valuing $1 of assets at less than $1; if Q is greater than 1, $1 of assets is being valued at more than $1. In November 1995, the Q Ratio was 1.25, as against the post-World War II average of 0.7.

The boom in stocks continued in 1996, with the Dow posting a 26 percent gain for the year. Commentators continued to warn that the market was overvalued. In May, the Q ratio had shot up to 1.88. In June 1996, financial reporters were calling the stock market a 'launch pad', noting that individual investors and mutual-fund buyers had become so 'spell-bound' by the stocks of small, 'aggressive-growth' companies that hundreds of once-unknown stocks were experiencing triple-digit gains (Browning 1996). Wall Street professionals were warning that a broad speculative wave was gripping the stock market, with some evidence of a mania stage of the cycle.

During the summer of 1996, the market was clearly overpriced by historical standards. The reported price/earnings ratio was 24, compared with the historical norm of only 15. To get back to that norm, the Dow Industrial Average would have to fall by more than 2000 points. Similarly, the current dividend yield was 2.2 percent as compared with the historical norm of 4.3 percent. A decline in the Dow Industrial Average of some 2600 points would be required to return the dividend yield to the historical norm (McGeehan 1996).

In his *Wall Street Journal* commentary in September 1996, Lowenstein asserted that: 'Investing in stocks has become a national hobby and a national obsession. People may denigrate their government, their schools, their spoiled sports stars. But belief in the market is almost universal. To update Marx, it is the religion of the masses' (p. A11). While that religion was described as a calm and reassuring one, 'firstly concerned with providing security and a sense of control', investors were showing the signs of 'classic herd investing' in switching funds with little knowledge but simply based on watching prices. An important new factor noted by Lowenstein was that the internet was transforming people into ready-formed crowds.

Other market watchers, such as Kuhn (1996) were asking whether this was a healthy bull market running on sound economic fundamentals or a new market mania that would end with a thud. Fundamentalists were citing a low inflation rate, relatively low interest rates and increased corporate profits. But there was also the huge inflow of funds into mutual funds (averaging about $100 per month per citizen). Kuhn (1996) observed that 'the boomer obsession with stock and investing' had 'made mutual funds as much a part of the prosperous American family's profile as sport-utility vehicles or golden retrievers' (p. 80). But she noted a disquieting sense that the stock market had become more vulnerable than most people believed. The biggest source of worry was 'the very enthusiasm for stock that drives the market these days. It is said that a stock market mania, or any mania for that matter, is in full bloom when people are least inclined to heed the signs of trouble' (p. 81). In view of the speculative 'insanities' that were appearing in the market behavior of investors, a 'confidence-shattering crash' could occur (p. 83).

Kuhn's warning, however, was not destined to be the 1996 version of Galbraith's 1987 prescient warning of a stock market crash. October came and went, with the stock market climbing ever higher and no crash. With the stock market rising 8.2 percent in November, and world stock exchanges being described as in the midst of a liquidity boom fueled by central bank policies, Federal Reserve officials were reported to be concerned about an overvalued market. It was feared that some bad news would result in an exaggerated reaction, leading to a sharp plunge in prices that could turn into a rout if investors began a mass movement out of mutual funds (Wessel 1996).

Some commentators were suggesting that a headline speech by Alan Greenspan, Chairman of the Federal Reserve Board, about 'speculative excess', would shatter the market's complacency, although they thought it would be out of character with Greenspan's usual optimism. Kaufman (1996, A18) described the current situation as one in which 'the exaggerated financial euphoria is increasingly conspicuous', and drew an analogy with the 1920s, citing (as others over the years have done) Irving Fisher's inaccurate assurance that stocks had reached a new high permanent plateau. Kaufman argued that a wide variety of monetary policy measures could be used to head off an unsustainable financial bubble, ranging from simple reminders by Greenspan of the risks to investors in a bull market to greater restrictions on leverage in buying stocks and considering the state of the financial markets in determining monetary conditions.

The market continued its upward projection through much of 1997 and 1998. Each time as new highs in the Dow Industrial Average were reached and surpassed, pundits and prognosticators warned that stock prices did not reflect estimates for corporate profits and a sizeable correction in the market was imminent.

THE PUBLIC INTEREST IN THE NEW BULL MARKET

There is always public concern over stock market fluctuations of the magnitudes that occurred in the 1980s and 1990s. Yet, the public interest in the new bull market is especially strong for several reasons. In part, the behavior of investors has been influenced by public policies. The Federal Reserve played a key role in restoring the confidence of investors in the market after the 1987 crash. On 20 October 1987, the day after the largest stock market crash in history, Federal Reserve officials announced that 'The Federal Reserve, consistent with its responsibility as the nation's central bank, affirmed today its readiness to serve as a source of liquidity to support the economic and financial system' (Brady Commission 1989, 169). The lowering of short-term interest rates to record lows in the post-World War II era by the Fed in the early 1990s was a factor in the movement of funds from money market funds to equity funds.

Moreover, the government bailout of failing depository institutions was instrumental in keeping investors' confidence in the financial system, including the stock market, at a high level. The low federal funds and discount rates allowed banks to enhance their profits. Tax laws that shelter contributions to 401(k) accounts increased investor interest in stocks. The prospect that part of social security contributions may in the future be invested in stocks (see Tanner 1996) introduces an additional reason for social concern over the stock market. Specifically, investors must be concerned that a market that can experience the worst crash in history and then bounce back into a soaring bull market is a speculative market.

A major factor in the new bull market has been the inflow of money into mutual stock funds. The inflow to mutual funds continued to run very strong, surpassing $200 billion in the first 11 months of 1996. For the first time employees, lured by higher returns, put more 401(k) money into stocks than into fixed income investments. In 1992, stock funds accounted for 25 percent of all 401(k) money. In 1996, that figure was 40 percent.

GREENSPAN AND THE STOCK MARKET

In December 1996, Greenspan began to hint of concern about the level of stock prices. In a dinner address to the American Enterprise Institute on 5 December, Greenspan asked the rhetorical question: 'How do we know when irrational exuberance has unduly inflated asset values, which then become subject to unexpected and prolonged contractions as they have in Japan over the past decade?' (Crutsinger 1996, A1). Many traders interpreted Greenspan's remarks as expressing concern over speculative stock markets in America. While stock prices initially dipped sharply, the

Dow ended the following day down only 55 points. Leading senators and representatives of the administration hastened to reassure the public that all was sound.

Stock prices were volatile over the next several weeks, and Republican Senate Leader, Trent Lott, criticized Greenspan for expressing concern about speculation in the market. In the early part of January 1997, the market was showing no impact from Greenspan's implied warning of 'irrational exuberance'. In fact, Greenspan's implied warning of 'irrational exuberance' had no lasting effects. Between 1 January and 18 February 1997, the Dow Industrial Average rose 9.6 percent, with a record amount pouring into stock mutual funds in the month of January.

In February, as the market moved above 7000 on the Dow, Greenspan spoke again, this time to Congress. In delivering his semi-annual 'Humphrey Hawkins' address, he suggested that stock prices remained at unnaturally high levels (Cnnfn.com. 26 February 1997). He told the Senate Banking Committee on 27 February that the recent upward run in stock prices posed an inflationary threat. Greenspan stated that 'History demonstrates that participants in financial markets are susceptible to waves of optimism which ... foster a general process of asset price inflation that can feed through into markets for goods and services. Excessive optimism sows the seeds of its own reversal in the form of imbalances that tend to grow over time' (USAToday.com. 27 February 1997). He seemed to be suggesting that the rises in stock prices might encourage workers to demand higher wages, which would be regarded by the Fed as inflationary and hence, he warned that the Fed would not rule out raising interest rates.

The market initially dropped some 100 points on the Dow, but ended the day only 62 points down. On 4 March, Greenspan told the House Budget Committee that he was not trying to push the market down, but only to explain that the Fed looks at financial markets 'as they are evolving' along with wages and prices of goods and services in developing monetary policies. Republican Congressman Jim Bunning of Kentucky expressed hostility over Greenspan's 'jawboning' the stock market.

On 5 March, Greenspan told a House Banking Committee panel that 'we don't view monetary policy as a tool to ... prick the stock-market bubble'. The Dow Industrial Average rose 93 points. Earlier Greenspan told the National Association of Business Economists that 'You cannot affect the broad level of equity values in this country or anywhere else by jawboning' (Cnnfn.com. 5 March 1997). In his Congressional testimony, Greenspan said that stocks may not be currently overvalued: 'if profit margins continue to rise as analysts on Wall Street expect them to, then the market is properly priced as best we can judge' (Cnnfn.com. 6 March 1997).

On 25 March 1997, the Fed raised the Fed Funds rate by a quarter of a percentage point. From mid March to mid April, the Dow Industrial

Average fell 9.8 percent from its new high of 7085 to a low of 6391. But in late April and early May, the market surged back up, although with notable volatility. On Monday, 12 May, the market closed at another new high of 7293 on the Dow.

THE BULL MARKET CONTINUES

Since the spring of 1997, The Dow Industrial Average has been on a roller-coaster ride, but with each decline a new, higher level has been attained. In July of 1997, the market reached 8000 for the first time. During the third quarter of the year concerns about the Asian financial crises caused naysayers to predict a definitive end to the three-year bull run. On 27 October 1997 the Dow dropped 550 points. After the first 350-point drop, the 30-minute trading halt was activated. When trading resumed, the market fell another 200 points, triggering the one-hour trading halt. With the close of the trading day less than one hour away, the market simply closed early. The decline in North American equity values in the fourth quarter was widely interpreted as the result of negative market psychology – fears of inflation pressures from wage increases, rising interest rates and absolute financial calamity in Asia. Still, the market ended the year with a 23 percent rise in the Dow.

Despite the predictions for a slowdown in the growth rate in the US and lower corporate profits, the Dow continued to rise in 1998, although with continued volatility. It surpassed 9000 on 6 April 1998, but dropped nearly 225 points on 27 April 1998. A number of factors were cited by analysts to explain the continuing bull market, including mega-mergers in the financial services industry and anticipated mergers in the telecommunications, utilities and technology industries, as well as record flows of savings into mutual funds. But the volatility continued. After reaching a new high of 9338 on 17 July, the Dow declined by around 5 percent over the next two weeks. On 4 August 1998, the Dow fell 3.4 percent, closing down 9.1 percent below the 17 July high. Later in August, the Russian government effectively defaulted on its external debt. Although reason suggested that the affect on world markets would be minimal due to Russia's small contribution to world output, the default had cataclysmic consequences on emerging markets. Investors stampeded out of transitioning markets into blue-chip investments. The Federal Reserve System deftly guided the US economy over the rough waters in early 1999 and the Dow began a new surge. Despite lackluster corporate earnings, a negative savings rate in the US and a record trade deficit the Dow surpassed 11,000 before falling back into the mid 10,000s.

Thus the question is: Is the recent performance of the stock market a return to the overvaluation suggested by Greenspan's warning of 'excessive exuberance' or does it reflect rational exuberance by investors?

THE CURRENT STATUS OF SPECULATIVE MARKET THEORIES

In light of these turbulent movements in stock market prices, and the expressions of public concern from the Chairman of the Federal Reserve Board (and others) this would appear to be an appropriate time to consider the nature and status of economic theories of speculative movements in stock prices. This is especially true in view of the increasing dependence upon stock market investments in the retirement plans of a growing number of Americans.

In an article in the *Wall Street Journal*, Wysocki (1996) spoke of the 'esoteric but emerging field of behavioral economics' as challenging the conventional view that investors are rational with their money, so that market prices can become irrational. But there already exists a substantive (albeit relatively small) body of economic literature going back to Thorstein Veblen in 1904, and including John Maynard Keynes and John Kenneth Galbraith in the 1930s and 1950s, respectively, that challenges the conventional view. The primary purpose of this book is to contrast the conventional theory that stock prices reflect what stocks are really worth based on rational expectations of economic fundamentals such as corporate earnings, inflation and interest rates with the dissenting theories advanced by Veblen, Keynes and Galbraith in which the speculative psychology plays a strong if not dominant role. The approach is to trace the development of modern theories of speculative stock markets and to assess the current status of speculative markets theories in light of the 1987 crash and the unusually rapid emergence of a new bull market.

APPENDIX

Eleven Worst Days on Wall Street

[Percentage Loss in Stock Prices in Dow Jones
Industrial Average]

19 October 1987	22.6%
28 October 1929	12.8%
29 October 1929	11.7%
6 November 1929	10.0%
12 August 1932	8.4%
26 October 1987	8.0%
31 July 1933	7.9%
18 October 1937	7.8%
5 October 1932	7.2%
27 October 1997	7.2%
24 September 1931	7.1%
13 October 1989	6.9%

Post-World War II Market Declines

26 May 1946–9 October 1946	23.2%
13 December 1961–26 June 1962	27.1%
9 September 1966–7 October 1966	25.2%
3 December 1968–26 May 1970	35.9%
22 August 1973–5 November 1974	44.4%
21 September 1976–28 February 1976	26.9%
27 April 1981–12 August 1982	24.1%
25 August 1987–19 November 1987	30.5%

1. Introduction: Economists On (and In) the Stock Market

The general public might expect that a book on the subject of what economists have written about the functioning of the stock market, that is, how stock prices are determined, would necessarily constitute a massive volume. In presenting the 1981 Nobel Prize in economics to James Tobin for his contributions in the theory of financial markets, Assar Lindbeck (1992) commented that: 'One of the most common notions among ordinary people concerning economics is that it is mainly about money and finance' (p. 3). The experiences of many academics suggest that most 'ordinary people' think that economics is primarily about the stock market. Students entering introductory courses in economics often expect that the stock market will be a major subject of study. An obvious diminishing of their interest in economics occurs upon learning that little (if any) attention will be given to the stock market. Students with a persistent interest in the stock market are usually guided to courses in finance departments.

The popular impression that the stock market should be of large, if not primary, concern to economists is quite understandable. Economics is usually thought to be about capitalism, and the stock market has long been the popular symbol of capitalism, both to its critics and its proponents. Engels, for example, wrote in 1895 that the stock exchange had become 'the most pre-eminent representative of capitalist production' (Marx 1906, Vol. III, pp. 1045–7).

An ideal of widespread ownership of corporate shares is sometimes advocated as 'people's capitalism'. Certainly, capitalism has long been associated with stock markets in popular fiction. For example, after introducing an embryonic form of industrial capitalism in King Arthur's feudalistic England, Mark Twain's Connecticut Yankee diverted the activities of the Knights of the Round Table from physical combat to attempts to corner the stock market (1949).

In popular imagery, stock markets represent the most exciting aspect of capitalism, creating a virtual Cinderella scenario, when soaring bull markets bring sudden wealth only to subsequently wipe it out during spectacular crashes with the bursting of great speculative bubbles. In the popular mind, the Great Crash of 1929 will probably always be the cause of the Great

1

Depression of the 1930s. Without question, the 1929 crash became one of the defining moments in modern economic and political history, if only because of its great psychological effects and the political responses that resulted in a number of regulatory reforms.

TWO VIEWS OF ECONOMISTS ON THE STOCK MARKET

Against this popular view that economists assign great importance to the stock market is the reality that only a small part of the theoretical economic literature that has evolved since the 1700s has dealt specifically with stock markets. Indeed, the limited attention given to the stock market in principles of economics texts might leave the impression that it has been virtually ignored by economists. But that impression would be incorrect. While the body of economic literature on the functions and functioning of stock markets is relatively small, it does exist and in rather substantive (albeit somewhat scattered) form.

Moreover, this literature is provocative because two distinctly different perspectives are clearly discernible: the rational markets view and the irrational markets view. The former, which constitutes the conventional view, emerged within the neo-classical theory of markets as institutional arrangements which serve the functional purposes of valuation and allocation of scarce resources. To a large degree, the irrational markets view is the speculative markets view (often popularly described as 'the bigger fool theory' and by the expression 'the market is alternately driven by greed and fear'). But it also includes the manipulation of stock prices by organized pools and corporate insiders, which was quite common before the Securities Acts of 1933 and 1934.

The rational markets view has received considerable attention in the recent literature of financial economics. While speculation in stock markets is a frequent subject of comment in financial news media that inevitably casts a shadow of doubt over celebrations of rising stock prices as reflecting real economic gains, relatively little has been done by way of assessing the current status and relevancy of the theories of speculative stock markets which have appeared in the economic literature. The purpose of this book is to examine those theories and to assess whether the various views that have been presented coalesce into a relatively coherent general theory.

Kindleberger (1989) observed that conventional economics has tended to dismiss work dealing with historical episodes of financial irrationality as providing only anecdotal evidence which 'may be taken to amuse, but not to edify' (p. xii). Kindleberger has effectively challenged that view of historical studies. The subject that will be emphasized herein is the theory of speculative markets and not studies of historical episodes. The latter have been used by theorists, some more than others, both as sources of information and as illustrative case studies. But the theories that are examined, while not mathematical in form, deal with general behavioral tendencies.

A review and comparison of prominent speculative theories will demonstrate that John Maynard Keynes presented a general conceptual framework of speculative stock markets that is essentially consistent with an earlier analysis by Thorstein Veblen, and which is illuminated more clearly in the extreme case by John Kenneth Galbraith's model of speculative manias that end in crashes. Further, it will be shown that this Keynesian/Veblenian theory of speculative markets draws support from recent work by Robert Shiller and provides important insights into the performance of the stock market in the 1980s and 1990s.

While the focus is on speculative theories of stock markets, some attention must also be given to the development of the rational markets theory, for several reasons. First, clarity of perception tends to be improved by contrasting a subject with its opposite. Second, and more importantly, most of the economists who contributed to the rational markets view also acknowledged the existence of speculative forces in stock exchange activities and attempted to rationalize speculation. Similarly, except in extreme cases of speculative manias and frenzies, the speculative stock market theories do not rule out all elements of the rational markets view of how stock prices are determined.

At this juncture, brief overviews of the two perspectives would be helpful.

The Rational Markets View

The economic functions of the stock market in the rational markets view are to encourage the accumulation of capital and to allocate existing supplies of capital to their most valuable uses. Maximization of those functions requires that market prices for corporate shares reflect, accurately and fully, the social values of the capital goods, the ownership of which those shares represent. The central theme is on stock prices being formed through a process of market actions based on rational expectations and the role of those prices as requisite to the rational behavior of market participants.

Earlier contributors to the rational markets view, for example Walras, Marshall and Wicksteed cited stock markets as real-world examples of markets with institutional features and functional characteristics that closely approximate the requisite conditions for pure competition. Emphasis was on the establishment of an equilibrium price, with relatively few direct implications for allocating capital resources. Some modern neo-classical economists have continued the practice of citing stock markets as real-world illustrations of competitive markets. Stigler (1966) for example, stated that the conditions for a perfect market 'can be met only in a completely centralized market, which is approximated by a few exchanges such as the New York Stock Exchange' (p. 87; see also Baumol 1965, p. 4). When stock markets are mentioned in principles of economics texts, it is usually as an illustrative example of how supply and demand result in equilibrium prices (see, for example, Teagarthen 1996, pp. 237–8). The central reason to have a stock market is that it serves as a social calculating machine that reports to firms what the market thinks of their future prospects, and so governs the allocation of investment (Barksy and De Long 1989, p. 2).

An important implication quickly evolved from those equilibrium price-formation characterizations of competitive markets: stock markets, like all competitive markets in neo-classical theory, have important social functions. By the early 1900s, stock exchanges were being described in the economic literature as: (1) facilitating and encouraging capital accumulation by channeling short-term savings into long-term investments; and (2) allocating the limited supplies of capital (both real and financial) to the most valued social uses. The prices of corporate shares generated in stock market trading activities became viewed as rational valuations providing both information necessary for rational decisions on the use of capital and incentives to induce firms to make efficient use of capital (for modern summary statements, see Baumol 1965, West and Tinic 1971 and Pratten 1993).

With the optimal functioning of the stock market dependent upon conditions approximating perfect competition, some economists by the early 1900s were commenting on the lack of competition in stock exchanges. This was largely in relation to the then current issue of the need for government regulation of exchanges to control manipulation of prices by insiders and speculation. In the 1920s and early 1930s, several economists, notably Machlup (1940) sought to debunk the claim that stock markets 'absorb' capital and credit. In the post-World War II period, concern continued to be expressed over possible inefficiencies arising from institutional imperfections, in particular the guild-like arrangements of stock exchanges and the role of specialists on the NYSE (see Baumol 1965 and West and Tinic 1971).

Despite those concerns about deviations of the actual stock exchanges from the conditions required for perfect competition, the latest development in the rational markets view of stock markets has been the efficient markets hypothesis which contends that prices of stocks are always rational. While the exact meaning of 'efficiency' remains somewhat controversial, the general implication of the efficient markets hypothesis is that stock markets receive new information about all factors that affect stock prices and adjust stock prices with such speed that market participants are unable to realize above-average trading profits by trading on that information.

In the relatively new field of financial economics, the rational markets approach now takes two forms. The traditional or conventional form, fundamental value analysis, is based on the rational markets theory that developed before World War II. Each stock has an intrinsic value or true economic value which is the expected value (to net out risk) of the present value (discounted value) of future earnings or dividends. At any given time, traders' knowledge of the fundamental economic factors, future corporate earnings, discount rate and risk probability, may be imperfect. Thus the current market price may be above or below the intrinsic value. But information gained through diligent and intelligent research enables informed buyers to identify stocks that are overvalued or undervalued in the market. Arbitrage by the newly informed traders acts to bring market prices to equality with intrinsic values. Hence prices become rational, albeit in a lagged fashion.

In contrast, the efficient markets hypothesis, with its basis in the rational expectations model, maintains that prices always fully reflect all information that is available. Current market prices are interpreted as equilibrium prices, fully reflecting all the information currently available. Any changes in market prices are explained as changes in equilibrium prices in instantaneous responses to changes in information about any and all variables that can influence the value of stocks in the minds of rational investors.

The Speculative Markets View

Among professional traders, financial journalists and the general public, a perception exists that the stock market is influenced by speculative trading – buying stocks only because prices are expected to rise in the near future with the intention of reselling before the prices fall. The belief is also easily accepted among these groups that speculation sometimes takes the form of a true mania, producing great price bubbles that ultimately burst and bring market prices crashing down. Certainly, the historical record lends strong support to such a view.

With perhaps the singular exception of Veblen, those economists who challenged the rational markets view – Keynes, Galbraith and Shiller – generally accepted the idea that the proper social functions of stock markets are those specified in the rational markets view. But they questioned whether stock markets could be relied upon to accomplish those functions, that is, where prices will predictably be rational. A growing number of recent studies have uncovered fascinating anomalies that cast doubt on both the rational expectations and efficient market theories. If prices are not rational, the stock market cannot allocate capital and investment in a socially optimal fashion.

While speculative trading involves buying stocks simply because stock prices are expected to rise in the near future, with the intention of selling quickly to realize capital gains, the nature of the speculative influence over stock prices can take several forms. On the one hand, speculative expectations that stock prices will rise or fall may be a derivative of speculative expectations of increasing or decreasing company earnings. Thus a commercial boom that increases corporate profits may generate speculative expectations of continuing profit increases, which in turn will give rise to a speculative boom in stock prices based on the expectation that stock prices will rise with the capitalization of those rising profits. There is a strong element of this type of speculation in Veblen's analysis of speculative stock markets. In contrast, pure speculation is a psychological phenomenon, with market participants buying stocks based purely upon expectations of the behavior of other market participants. There is an element of this in Veblen's analysis of stock prices, but it is the predominant form of speculation in both Keynes' and Galbraith's works.

In the absence of strong government regulations, speculation of either type may involve manipulative practices. If the speculation in stocks is derived from speculative expectations about corporate profits, those profit expectations may be based on false or incomplete information provided by corporate insiders. In the case of pure speculation, prices of stocks may be deliberately manipulated through phony trading (as well as spreading misinformation) to create the impression of strong forces pushing prices up or down. Manipulation was very common until the Securities and Exchange Commission was established in 1934.

Early economists on speculation

While the development of the rational markets view essentially occurred within neo-classical economics, several earlier economists offered limited comments that suggested the speculative or irrational markets view. Since the market for corporate stocks was very limited in the 1700s and early 1800s, with most of the securities traded being government bonds, classical school economists understandably said little about the stock market. Yet several expressed opinions about the securities markets of the day that suggested a speculative markets view. Hume took a very dim view of social contributions of the trade in 'chequer-notes and India bonds'. He stated that:

> ...what production we owe to Change-alley, or even what consumption, except that of coffee, and pen, ink, and paper, I have not yet learned; nor can one foresee the loss or decay of any one beneficial commerce or

commodity, though that place and all its inhabitants were for ever buried in the ocean. (1955, p. 93, fn)

Although Ricardo made his fortune in the market for government bonds, he mentioned such markets only tangentially in his economic writings, and in such a manner as to raise questions about the rational pricing process:

> In time of war, the stock market is so loaded with the continual loans of government that the price of the stock has not time to settle at its fair level before a new operation of funding takes place, or it is affected by anticipation of political events. In time of peace, on the contrary, the operations of the sinking fund, the unwillingness which a particular class of people feel to divert their funds to any other employment than that to which they have been accustomed, which they think secure, and which their dividends are paid with the utmost regularity, elevates the price of stock, and consequently depresses the rate of interest on these securities below the general market rate. It is observable, too, that for different securities government pays very different rates of interest. (1955, p. 298)

Although Marx had little to say about stock markets per se in the three volumes of *Capital*, he did suggest that stock exchange activities were a form of gambling. In Volume I, he stated that 'the national debt has given rise to joint-stock companies, to dealings in negotiable effects of all kinds, and to agiotage, in a word to stock-exchange gambling and the modern bankocracy' (1906, p. 82). In Volume III, Marx's discussion of credit included a section on the formation of stock companies in which he stated: 'Since property here exists in the form of shares of stock, its movements and transfer become purely a result of gambling at the stock exchange, where the little fish are swallowed by the sharks and the lambs by the wolves' (1906, pp. 520–21).

Neo-classicals and speculation

There is a curious dichotomy between the rational markets view of economists and the great volatility and period instability of stock prices that has persisted throughout the history of stock exchanges. Baumol (1965) wrote that 'one has come to look upon the stock market as the allocator of capital resources par excellence, and aside from some uneasiness about the untoward effects of speculation, one is readily inclined toward the view that the stock market constitutes an allocative mechanism of remarkable efficiency' (p. 4). Speculation was much on the minds of some mainstream economists in the early 1900s, even as the rational markets view was emerging. In 1913, for example, Lavington considered 'The Social Interest in Speculation in the Stock Exchange' in a substantive article in the *Economic Journal*. In 1915, a session of the American Economic

Association meeting addressed stock market speculation, although the focus of the two papers were more on manipulation (Untermeyer 1915; Emery 1915). Several of those who contributed to the rational markets view also expressed concern over speculative excesses. In general, the neo-classical view tended to be that speculation played an important social function and was necessary to capital markets, but with a few concessions made to the popular view that speculation often amounted to a form of gambling.

Even the efficient markets proponents have exhibited a sense of unease about levels of stock prices that seem to defy the label of 'rational'. There has emerged a growing body of literature on 'rational' bubbles that attempts to explain irrational prices within the rational expectations models. The meaning of 'rational' is subject to different interpretations. The rational expectations thesis seems to assert that individuals act rationally because their expectations are fully accurate, that is, they are perfectly prescient. But that has been qualified by an argument that individuals act rationally in utilizing what they think is true information when in fact it is very inaccurate. In the first case, the market outcome has to be rational. But in the second case, the market outcome will not be rational when the 'information' is wrong or incomplete.

ORGANIZATION OF THE BOOK

The institutional structure of the modern stock market is briefly described in the first part of Chapter 2. Since economists writing in different historical periods were observing the institutional structure and character of the stock market in different phases of its development, a substantial part of this chapter is devoted to a historical review of the development of stock exchanges, the volatile movements in stock prices, and the manipulative practices that led to regulations being imposed by Congress in the 1930s. In Chapter 3, the development of the rational markets view is discussed as well as how contributors to the rational markets view attempted to explain the nature and role of speculation in stock markets.

Chapters 4, 5 and 6 focus in chronological order on the three major contributors to the economic literature on speculative stock markets. Chapter 4 examines Veblen's analysis of stock markets that appeared in his theory of modern business enterprise. Chapter 5 examines Keynes' analysis of stock markets within the context of his theory of aggregate demand and the level of aggregate economic activity. Chapter 6 examines Galbraith's analysis of speculative manias and their inevitable crashes.

In Chapter 7, recent developments in the theory of speculative markets are discussed. The topics include the conceptual and empirical work of Shiller on investors' fads and fashions, the attempts by efficient markets proponents to explain the 1987 crash, the models of 'rational' bubbles, and the critiques of the efficient markets hypothesis by Post Keynesians.

Finally, the work concludes with an assessment of the current status of the speculative markets theory in Chapter 8. We argue that the works of Veblen, Keynes, Galbraith and Shiller on speculative markets are sufficiently complementary to form a coherent theory of speculative stock markets. That theory is sufficiently robust to explain degrees of speculative influence on stock prices ranging from mild cases of chronic speculation (Keynes' bubbles of speculation on streams of enterprise) to the relatively rare cases of intense speculative manias that end in great crashes.

ECONOMISTS *IN* THE STOCK MARKET: A DIGRESSION

While the purpose of this book is to investigate the writings of economists *on* the stock market, the experiences of a few major economists as investors/speculators *in* stock markets provide an interesting sidelight. Three prominent economists in three different centuries – Cantillon, Ricardo and Keynes – were successful investors/speculators in financial markets. In his Foreword to the biography of Cantillon by Murphy (1986), Sir John Hicks argued that all three turned their experiences as practical financiers into theoretical models. A fourth major figure in economic thought – Irving Fisher – who was popularly regarded by the public in the 1920s as an expert on the stock market, lost heavily after the market crashed in 1929 and continued to suffer losses until the summer of 1932.

Cantillon

The years 1719–20 saw the first major episodes of speculative bubbles involving stock exchanges. (The earlier great bubble involved tulip bulbs in Holland rather than shares of companies.) In France, John Law's Mississippi Company shares were wildly traded until the bubble burst. In England, the South Sea Company's shares and shares in a number of other companies (some with highly fanciful, even secret, purposes) were wildly traded until that bubble also burst. Remarkably, Cantillon made a fortune in both markets by exiting on a timely basis before prices collapsed. And he realized another fortune speculating on exchange rates during the period when Law was attempting to implement his system. Cantillon also profited from trading in South Sea options in Amsterdam. As a banker, he made large loans to other speculators, but ran into continuing legal difficulties in attempting to collect on those debts.

Murphy (1986) noted that, while Cantillon did not possess 'perfect stock market prescience' as some earlier writers had claimed, 'His stock market speculation was characterized by an uncanny ability to locate himself in Paris, London, and Amsterdam just at the start of each boom' (pp. 187–8). Equally important, he foresaw the false bases of the booms and left the markets early with his gains largely intact.

Ricardo

Several sources, including Hollander (1910), the edited volumes by Sraffa (1951–5) and Weatherall (1976) provide observations on David Ricardo as a stockbroker (or 'jobber') and speculator. His grandfather was a stockbroker in Amsterdam who participated in drawing up new rules for dealing with options on the Amsterdam Bourse in 1739. Ricardo's father also became a stockbroker in Amsterdam and later in London, accumulating a considerable fortune. At the age of 14, Ricardo became a jobber in the London Stock Exchange for his father and by the age of 21 was doing some Stock Exchange business for himself. After marrying against his parents' will, he lost the financial support of his father but was backed by influential friends in the City who had sufficient confidence in his trading ability to set him up as a stockbroker. As a jobber, Ricardo dealt on his own account with brokers and other jobbers, making a market by being always willing to quote prices at which they would deal. Most of the securities traded were government debt, with a few shares of chartered companies such as the Bank of England and the East India Company.

Ricardo was said to possess an extraordinary quickness in perceiving turns of the market and an ability to capitalize on changes in the relative prices of different stocks. His strategy was never to carry his stock transactions to any speculative extent but to sell out on the turn of the market to realize a small percentage on a large sum. Ricardo's 'golden rules' for trading were 'cut short your losses' and 'let your profits run on'. He reportedly said that he made his fortune by observing that people generally exaggerated the importance of events. If there was a reason for a small advance in stock prices, he bought on the expectation that an unrealizable advance would bring profits. When prices were falling, he sold with the expectation that alarm and panic would produce a decline greater than warranted by the circumstances at hand (Ricardo 1955, p. 73).

From 1811 until the end of the war with Napoleon, Ricardo and his partners were successful contractors for every government loan that was negotiated. The last and biggest loan of the war was raised in June 1815, four days before the Battle of Waterloo. Four contractors, including Ricardo, submitted identical bids which the Chancellor of the Exchequer accepted as non-collusive. The market price of the 'stock' (i.e. government bonds) was extremely low, but rose quickly and substantially when news of victory reached the City. Ricardo realized the largest single profit he ever made on this loan. Malthus, who had taken a share of 5000 pounds sterling of the loan, became apprehensive and asked Ricardo to sell his stock at a small profit on opening day.

Keynes

A fairly detailed account of Keynes' investment activities has been provided by Moggridge, who edited Keynes' collected works (see Keynes 1983). As a child in 1905, Keynes made his first purchase of stock out of his 'special fund', the repository of birthday money and various academic prizes. He bought four shares of Marine Insurance Company. His next purchases came in 1910 and, until 1919, his dealings were limited and were usually purchases of additional stocks. In 1913, he netted over five pounds from briefly speculating in US Steel. Keynes became much more active in the financial markets in 1919, beginning his career as a speculator in August of that year. While speculating a little in stocks, his activities were centered on the foreign exchange market. From 1922 onwards, he was a substantial and highly active investor.

While investing on his own account, he was not uniformly successful. During the 1920s, his return on investment was lower than the *Bankers' Magazine* index. After 1929, however, his investments outperformed the market in 21 of 30 years and did so cumulatively by a large margin. He was very active in both the commodity and foreign exchange markets. His portfolio was usually dominated by the securities of a few firms, especially after the late 1920s. Keynes showed a tendency to back his long-term judgement on a substantial scale, when he had the financial resources to do so. He normally carried a substantial portion of his portfolio on borrowed money – frequently more than half. The combination of long-term concentrated holdings, large loans and considerable short-term speculative activity resulted on occasions in substantial decreases in his net worth.

When stock prices collapsed on the London Exchange in September 1929, Keynes had experienced a period of difficulty which had shrunk his assets by some 75 percent over two years, largely due to his commodities speculation. At the end of the year (1929) he sold heavily on a falling market, but still realized substantial capital gains over the year as a whole. When the market recovered during the first months of 1930, Keynes returned as a net buyer on a small scale but became a seller in April.

After 13 October 1930, Keynes' dealing activities virtually ceased. His reasons were indicated in a memo prepared in February 1931 for the Board of the National Mutual. With a great deal of fear psychology being about, prices bore little relationship to 'ultimate values or even to reasonable forecasts of ultimate values', but were determined by indefinite anxieties, chance market conditions and whether some urgent selling came on a market bare of buyers. 'Just as many people were quite willing in the boom, not only to value shares on the basis of a single year's earning, but to assume that increases in earnings would increase geometrically, so now they are ready to estimate capital values on today's earnings and to assume that decreases will continue geometrically.' Stating that such fears were not baseless, Keynes considered the prospects for 1931 to be extremely bad. But there was no reason to panic and join the bears. It was much better and wiser to stand reasonably firm. The situation was quite capable of turning round at any time with extreme suddenness. He advised no sales of securities except for very special reasons. Subsequent price declines would be an increased reason for not selling. If there was a substantial recovery, if the market should turn round violently for political reasons or if Wall Street were to carry to any length one of its usual spring booms, so that buyers were about at decidedly higher prices, then selling should again be considered.

By the end of 1936, Keynes had done very well, with his net assets rising by nearly half a million pounds sterling over the previous three years. His speculations in currencies and commodities had netted him 48,000 pounds over the past 12 months. At the turn of 1937, he was heavily involved in both the New York and London markets, carrying much of his portfolio on credit as his loans came to almost 300,000 pounds. Over the next two years, however, Keynes suffered large losses on commodities and currencies, and his net assets decreased by nearly two-thirds. On an index basis (1922=100). Keynes' net assets peaked in 1936 at 2,350, fell to 794 in 1940, but recovered substantially during the war years to stand at 1,908 in 1945.

Fisher

Irving Fisher's stock market experience has been chronicled in the biographies by his son (Fisher 1956) and Allen (1993). Ever the inventor, Fisher realized commercial success with his visible card-index system that he devised in 1912. He organized his own Index Visible Company to manufacture and promote the system, and by 1929 the firm required a three-store factory and sales offices in New York City. It merged with its chief rival to become Remington Rand, later Sperry Rand. By the time of the 1929 crash, Fisher was heavily in debt because he had borrowed from banks to take advantage of his rights to buy additional Remington Rand stock which accrued to him as an outgrowth of the original merger agreement. He had also subscribed heavily to several young enterprises, hoping that by getting in on the ground floor they might pay off as spectacularly as his Index Visible Company. These ventures turned out to be losers, including one in which the promoter was eventually indicted for misrepresentation of his stock-selling operations.

At the peak of the boom in stocks, Fisher could have liquidated enough of his Remington Rand stock to pay off all his heavy bank loans and still have a net of $8–10 million. Just before the crash, Remington Rand was selling for $50 a share. A year later, it was $28 per share, and ultimately fell to only $1 per share. As his position worsened, when all his collateral was pledged with the banks (including his wife's blue-chip stock) and when the banks were demanding more collateral or reduction of loans, Fisher borrowed a sizeable block of Allied Chemical stock from his sister-in-law. He ultimately had to liquidate that collateral, leaving him with a debt to her of roughly three-quarters of a million dollars. As his position deteriorated, his sister-in-law turned over the handling of their financial relationship to a committee consisting of her lawyer and two nephews. Fisher apparently felt that if he had had a freer rein, the end result might not have been so disastrous.

To make matters worse, the Internal Revenue Service discovered a deficiency of nearly $75,000 in taxes for the boom years of 1927 and 1928, involving sales of Remington Rand stocks to friends with the privilege of subsequent repurchase at a higher price. This device allowed Fisher to improve his cash position without permanently losing the stock, which he was confident would continue to soar in price. He argued that these transactions were loans rather than sales on which capital gains were realized.

With his deteriorating financial position, Fisher was unable to buy back the stock and had to secure releases from the individuals involved to simplify his complicated financial picture. He had to sell his house to Yale, but still received substantial directors' fees from Remington Rand and other corporations. Even so, he had to pay some of the rent to Yale in notes and in the end was obliged to ask Yale to cancel the legal obligations of these unpaid notes. All his remaining assets that had any market value were finally turned over to his sister-in-law in partial payment of the large debt he owed her. The balance was forgiven in her will.

Galbraith and the Market

While Cantillon, Ricardo and Keynes were able to beat the market, only one economist can lay claim to an ability to influence the stock market. In March 1955, when the stock market was rising sharply, Galbraith, with proofs of his newly finished book, *The Great Crash 1929*, in hand, testified before a Congressional committee that the market might be paralleling that of the 1920s. Unknown to him, as he was speaking, stock prices were experiencing a sharp break, falling 1.5 percent. The media suggested that his comments spread a sense of panic to investors, and thus caused the price drop.

While Fisher badly misread the market in both 1929 and in the early 1930s, with damage to both his reputation as an expert on financial markets and his personal fortune, Galbraith has the distinction of having called the crash of 1987. In an article published in the *Atlantic Monthly* in January 1987, Galbraith noted the parallels between the 1920s and 1980s, and cautioned that speculative binges can only end in drastic price adjustments. Virtually on cue, the market experienced the worst one-day crash in history on 19 October 1987.

2. The Stock Market: Structure, Performance and Character

With roots in the bourses of medieval European cities, modern stock markets evolved in conjunction with the evolutionary development of modern business corporations from the joint-stock trading companies organized in the 1500s. In the first section of this chapter, this historical development is traced. In the second section, the institutional structure of modern stock exchanges is highlighted. In the third section, the performance of the stock market in terms of major fluctuations in the level of stock prices, the alternating bull and bear markets and especially the great bubbles that end precipitately in great crashes, is reviewed. The character of the stock market is examined in the fourth section, where special note is made of the various forms of manipulative practice that invariably accompanied stock market speculation prior to the 1930s. In the final section, the evolution of regulations that have been imposed to curb such practices is presented.

THE HISTORICAL DEVELOPMENT OF STOCK MARKETS

The evolution of stock markets has been both a product of and contributor to the emergence and development of the instruments and practices of modern corporate finance. Joint-stock trading companies, the forerunners of the modern corporations, were organized in England and Holland in the 1500s and 1600s to conduct commercial activities in various parts of the world. Tradable shares of those companies were soon being sold in limited quantities on the bourses where commodities and coins were exchanged.

The growth of joint-stock companies was rather slow during the 1700s and early 1800s for both legal and economic reasons. In response to the South Sea Bubble, the British Parliament passed the Bubble Act in 1720 that outlawed joint-stock companies that did not possess a charter from Parliament. Parliamentary charters proved difficult to obtain. The Act was repealed in 1825, and in 1844 Parliament passed an Act which allowed joint-stock companies to gain charters by simple registration. The important feature of limited liability of stockholders was made generally available in 1862.

In America, the granting of corporate charters required special acts of state legislatures until the 1830s. A general incorporation law passed by Connccticut in 1837 was copied by other states. In 1830, Massachusetts passed a general limited liability law, and other states soon followed suit.

When the steam locomotive spawned the transportation revolution, the economic need for corporations was relatively limited. In both Britain and the US, the modern age of corporate enterprise essentially began with the rapid construction of railroads. With the ability to raise large amounts of capital from many small sources, and to spread and limit the risk to individual investors, the corporate form of enterprise became the standard form of organization of railroads in both countries. During the second half of the 19th century, large industrial firms increasingly became incorporated, as did retail firms. In the late 1800s, the holding company, a corporation formed for the purpose of owning stock in other corporations, became the key instrument used by J.P. Morgan and other investment bankers to merge operating companies in existing industries (for example, steel) into huge consolidated entities.

The contrasting comments of Adam Smith and John Stuart Mill on joint-stock companies indicate the extent to which corporate enterprises affected the economic scene in the 19th century. In the *Wealth of Nations*, Smith wrote that the establishment of a joint-stock company was reasonable where the activity involved required greater capital than could be easily collected by a partnership arrangement. However, he thought joint-stock companies would require exclusive privileges to be viable, and suggested that even with such privileges, joint-stock companies could only be successful in those limited economic activities where all the operations could be reduced to a routine. The few cases cited by Smith were banking, insurance, canal construction and operation, and supplying water to large cities (1976, p. 756).

In taking issue with Smith's view, Mill cited several important advantages of the joint-stock principle where large-scale production was involved. The first advantage was the ability to raise large amounts of capital. He cited the need for large staffs of qualified subordinates and what he termed the 'incident of publicity' (1873, pp. 84–5) which in modern terms would be interpreted as supplying information about the internal operations of the firm. While conceding that proprietorships had some advantages, in particular the owners' interest in realizing small profit opportunities, Mill argued that large firms had the advantage of being able to pay for a 'superior class' of directing heads (1873, pp. 86–7).

The great importance of corporation finance by the beginning of the 20th century was repeatedly enunciated in Veblen's writings on the modern business enterprise system. More than any other economist of his time, Veblen emphasized the connection between corporation finance and management of the industrial sector of the economy:

> Through the latter half of the 19th century corporations multiplied and increasingly displaced other forms of business concern, and took over more and more of the control of the industrial system. By this move the conduct and control of industrial production has more and more become a matter of corporation finance. (Veblen 1923, p. 82)

Stock Exchanges

The two dominant stock exchanges – the LSE in Britain and the NYSE in the US – achieved their positions during the 1800s. The LSE evolved during the 1700s from a mercantile market essentially for the purchase and sale of goods into a true stock exchange for the transfer of securities. The beginning of the modern exchange has been dated as 1773, but the LSE received a deed of settlement from Parliament in 1802. At first, daily admission could be gained for a price of sixpence, but the exchange subsequently established a privileged group of securities dealers who ultimately gained a monopoly in the handling of stock transactions. In 1877, a Royal Commission recommended that the exchange should be given the authority to license brokers, thus giving it a legalized monopoly of the stock brokerage business.

By the middle of the 19th century, the LSE had gained undisputed supremacy over Britain's security market. During the first half of the century, several provincial exchanges had developed considerable local importance and took an active part in financing railroads. But a crash in rail stocks and the consolidation of rail lines into national networks created large capital requirements that only the London market could handle.

While not the oldest exchange in the US, the NYSE became the nation's largest stock exchange in the first half of the 1800s. It traces its beginning to an agreement signed by a group of New York City brokers in 1792. By that agreement, the brokers would not buy or sell any kind of public stocks (including bonds) at less than a quarter of one percent commission on the specie values, and would give preferences to each other in their negotiations. Thus two fundamental characteristics of a modern guild or cartel were established: a monopolistic price arrangement for commissions and a pledge to give preference to members. The latter served to discourage members from undermining the cartel by charging lower commissions.

In 1817, the NYSE was organized under a constitution similar to that of the Philadelphia Exchange. The NYSE quickly gained dominance in the US securities markets but a number of regional exchanges in Baltimore,

Boston, Philadelphia, Chicago, San Francisco and Los Angeles continued to operate. Also, the curb-market (so-called because for many years trading actually took place on the street curb in New York City) survived and became the American Stock Exchange in 1952.

An especially important development in recent years has been the growth of the 'over-the-counter market', whose members belong to the National Association of Securities Dealers. In the earlier years, securities of small and little known firms could be purchased or sold literally 'over the counter' in a number of dealers' places of business. But in its modern form, the over-the-counter market is a network of dealers who are tied together electronically through the National Association of Securities Dealers Automated Quotation System (NASDAQ). Dealers quote bid prices, that is, prices at which they will buy stocks and ask prices, that is, prices at which they will sell stocks, with the objective of realizing profits on the spread between the bid and ask prices.

INSTITUTIONAL STRUCTURE OF MODERN STOCK EXCHANGES

In the 20th century, stock exchanges have greatly expanded in size, volume of transactions and speed of operations, but the basic structural form has remained relatively unchanged. The more recent institutional changes have been largely in response to improvements in communications technology, innovative ways of utilizing the exchanges (for example, computerized trading strategies) and government regulations that have been implemented in response to growing public concerns over the fairness of trading arrangements and instability of prices. In this section, we take a brief look at the institutional structure of modern stock exchanges.

Modern incorporated firms are defined as either public or private corporations. 'Public' means that the shares of ownership trade are listed on organized exchanges, for example, the NYSE, or the over-the-counter market (frequently referred to as NASDAQ). 'Private' means that shares can be traded only through privately negotiated transactions between an owner and an interested buyer. As an example, the price of United Parcel Service (UPS) stock is set quarterly by the board of directors. Employees holding UPS stock can sell that stock to the company at the set price. During 1996, UPS purchased over 22 million shares for $615 million (*Wall Street Journal*, 21 August 1997, p. A16). Thus true market prices exist only for the stocks of public corporations.

Corporate shares may be in the form of common stock, endowed with the conventional proprietary rights (including the right to vote for members of the board of directors) or preferred stock, a hybrid instrument with certain features of both common stock (equity) and bonds (contracted debt). Preferred stock represents ownership without the voting privilege, but is entitled to a stated dividend before any dividends are paid on common shares. Payment of that dividend is subordinated, however, to payment of interest and principal on bonds. While both common and preferred stocks of public corporations trade in the stock market, our interest is only with the transactions that establish market prices of the common shares.

The basic operational function of the stock market is to provide an institutional arrangement for transferring ownership of shares that represent partial ownership of public corporations. Because the items traded are existing shares, stock market transactions are referred to as the 'secondary market'. The corporations whose shares are being traded receive no revenues from sales in the stock market. But by increasing the liquidity or marketability of the securities of public corporations, the stock market provides two important indirect functions.

First, an active market for existing stocks increases the ability of public corporations to acquire funds through the issuance of new shares of ownership. Sales of newly issued stocks, referred to as the 'primary market', occur off the stock exchanges through the underwriting services of investment banks. But the fact that, once issued, the securities can be resold in the secondary market makes investors much more willing to purchase them from the underwriting investment bankers.

Second, the market prices of existing shares, which are established by a small percentage of the total existing stocks being traded on a daily basis in the stock markets, provide the value basis for the capitalization or asset valuation of all those corporations whose shares are traded in the stock markets. In an even more indirect fashion, the capitalization of private corporations is based on comparative analyses with public corporations whose stocks are routinely valued in the markets.

The Primary Market

While stock markets are often referred to as the 'capital market' (along with the market for bonds and mortgages), sales of stock result in capital funds being received by the public corporations only when newly issued stocks are sold in the primary market. Those new issues may be either initial public offerings, which are sales of stocks by newly organized public corporations or by private corporations now going public, or secondary offerings, which are new shares sold by a public corporation that already has shares outstanding. In both cases, the issuing corporations will sell the new shares through the intermediary services of investment banks.

Investment banks either underwrite the new issues, that is, contracting to purchase the new stocks from the issuing corporation, or act as brokers making 'best efforts' to find buyers for the new shares. In addition to charging various fees and commissions for such services as preparing the registration statement for the Securities and Exchange Commission, the underwriting investment banks expect to profit by reselling the newly issued stocks at higher prices than they paid the issuing corporations. For initial public offerings, an underwriter sets the price of a stock. That price will reflect consideration of a number of factors, including the highest price at which potential buyers can be expected to take all the shares offered and the lowest price at which issuing corporations will be satisfied. The latter is especially important if the investment banks hope to be able to act as underwriters for those corporate clients on future new issues. The prices of secondary offerings, however, will have to be based on the current market prices of existing shares of the issuing corporations.

The Secondary Market

Prices for stocks traded in the secondary market are determined by market forces of supply (the number of those shares that current owners will be willing to sell at each possible price) and demand (the number of those stocks that investors will be willing to buy at each possible price). Unless corporations issue new stock in the primary market, the existing number of shares places an absolute limit on the quantity that can be supplied, but generally only a small percentage of total existing stocks in any corporation will be traded at any given time. Yet the current valuation of the much larger number of shares not traded will be based upon the prices at which the few actually trade.

Such a valuation is highly tenuous. If owners of very many shares decided to sell at the current market quotations, the increased supply would depress the price, thereby reducing the market value of all the outstanding shares. For that reason, stock market analysts tend to pay particular attention to the volume of trading as well as to the prices that are established.

The Stock Exchanges

Public corporations may list their stocks on an organized exchange, such as the NYSE, or in the over-the-counter market. These exchanges are organized as modern versions of guilds. Only members of an organized exchange or NASDAQ can conduct trades in stocks listed on that exchange. Non-members wishing to buy or sell the listed stocks must secure the services of brokers or dealers who are members. Brokers act as intermediaries, providing the service (for which commissions are charged) of bringing buyers and sellers together. In contrast, dealers 'take positions', buying and selling stocks on their own with the expectation of making profits by the differences between their 'bid' prices and their 'ask' prices. Brokers and dealers may be individuals or incorporated business firms that are referred to as 'brokerage firms' or 'brokerage houses'.

The Role of Market Makers

Because of the guild-like organizational structures of the formal exchanges and the over-the-counter market, two sets of prices are actually involved in stock market transactions: the market prices of the shares traded and the prices of the services of brokers who arrange those trades for their clients. While our interest is with the various theories of how the market prices of shares are determined, it should be recognized that the pricing of brokers' services might influence share prices by raising or lowering the transaction costs of buying or selling.

In the next chapter, the neo-classical economists' reference to stock markets as examples of competitive markets will be examined. But in institutional structure, stock exchanges deviate from competitive markets not only in terms of their guild-like organization but also in the manner in which stock prices are determined at the point of sale. While those prices are generally reflective of supply (the number of existing shares offered for sale at various prices) and demand (the number of shares that are wanted at various prices), they are actually established through the agencies of 'market makers'. These are dealers who stand ready to buy (quote bid prices) and sell (quote 'ask' prices) certain stocks.

On the floor of the NYSE, the 'market making' service is provided by specialists. Each specialist is a member of the exchange who has been granted the right to act as the broker for trades in a particular stock, but is also obligated to act as dealer, buying and selling on his or her own account. In the latter capacity, the specialist is required to make a market – to be ready to buy if the current supply offered exceeds current demand or to sell if the current demand exceeds current supply. The American Stock Exchange also uses the specialist system, but in other exchanges and the over-the-counter market, a number of dealers competitively 'make a market' in the various stocks by quoting bid and ask prices. Since potential traders have the opportunity to shop around to find the most favorable prices, competitive pressures would predictably serve to reduce the spreads between bid and ask prices quoted by the market makers.

Market makers serve the important purpose of keeping the market for listed stocks both liquid and orderly. 'Liquid' means ensuring the opportunity to buy or sell stocks, while 'orderly' means that prices will move up or down in relatively small increments. Some critics have argued that having prices 'made' by monopolist traders, the specialists, represents a non-competitive situation, that is, the spread between the bid and ask prices will be too large (West and Tinic 1971, 149–52). But even if the specialist system were to be replaced by a system of competitive market makers such as exists in the over-the-counter market, the possibility still exists for there to be collusive arrangements among the dealers.

Options and Futures Instruments

While shares of corporate ownership are the instruments traded on stock exchanges, those transactions may be affected by the trading of several types of options and futures contracts based on common stocks. These contracts are often called 'derivative instruments' because their values are derived from the values of the underlying stocks. Options and futures contracts can be used to hedge against losses from adverse price movements. Portfolio managers, for example, could sell futures contracts rather than the stocks being held if a temporary downturn in stock prices was expected. Losses in the market value of the stocks in the portfolio would be partially offset by the gains realized on the sale of the futures contracts. But futures and options can play a major role in speculation by allowing a large amount of stock to be put into play with a relatively small amount of money up front.

Time bargains, options contracts, and puts and calls were actively used in early American securities markets. Time bargains, an institution borrowed from English tradition dating back to at least 1730, have been described as the most popular credit transactions in early American securities markets. These were essentially futures contracts, agreements based on a future transfer of specified securities at an agreed upon price. They were cheap and simple, requiring little cash to initiate and frequently settled on expiration by simply paying the difference between market and contract prices. Although time bargains were not illegal, they had the disadvantage of not being enforceable by law (Werner and Smith 1991, p. 70).

Time bargains were the cornerstone of the early New York securities market, but options contracts similar to time bargains were also used. No cash was put up until the option was exercised. While options contracts were obligations to exercise, puts and calls were not obligated to be exercised (Werner and Smith 1991, p. 69). The more modern form of options to purchase ('calls') or sell stocks ('puts') at specified prices for a specified time appeared later in the 1800s. According to Sobel (1965, p. 114), Russell Sage was responsible for this innovation, which allowed speculators to operate on a limited amount of capital. Margin buying – purchasing stock by borrowing part of the funds needed from brokerage houses – was used prior to 1861. After that, the practice came into its own as speculation became popular among the general public during the Civil War (Sobel 1965, p. 71).

A particularly important modern derivative instrument is the stock index futures contract, a number of which are traded in the commodity markets. In 1982, contracts were offered on the index value of the common stocks making up several major indexes, for example, the S&P 500. The value of the S&P 500 futures contract, for example, is based on the level of the index multiplied by $500. A stock index futures contract can be entered into as a buyer (expecting prices of the underlying stocks to rise) or a seller (expecting the prices of the underlying stocks to fall) by paying a cash margin (usually 5–10 percent). Changes in the market value of the contract are calculated each day and either the buyer or seller must put up additional cash as a maintenance margin. But index futures contracts allow investors/speculators to gain from stock price changes without having actually to purchase the stocks.

Bucket Shops

Bucket shops, which first appeared in the 1800s, were the forerunners of modern derivative instruments whose values are derived from the prices of the underlying stocks. They were publicly condemned as crooked gambling establishments by both social reformers and officials of the stock and commodity exchanges. Bucket shops were only 'pretend' brokerage houses, but allowed people of small means to speculate on movements in stock prices without actually purchasing the stocks, in much the same way that modern stock index futures contracts permit betting on stock price movements without purchasing the underlying stocks (see Raines and Leathers 1994).

Institutional Investors

The rational markets view of stock markets assumes competitive markets. But in addition to the guild-like organizational structures of stock exchanges and the roles of market makers, including the monopolistic positions of specialists on the NYSE, there is also the presence of large institutional investors – pension funds, mutual funds, insurance companies. Their importance as players in the market has increased substantially in recent years. In 1965, individuals directly owned 84 percent of the outstanding corporate shares. By 1980, the percentage was down to 71, and in 1992 it fell below 50 percent (49.7 percent as reported by *Wall Street Journal*, 13 November 1992).

PERFORMANCE: BULLS, BEARS, BUBBLES AND CRASHES

From the beginning of exchanges, stock prices have been extremely volatile. Daily, weekly and monthly fluctuations have always occurred, but the phenomenon that has attracted the most attention is the great bubbles that inevitably burst and end in crashes.

Early Bubbles and Crashes

The first great speculative bubbles in stock prices and their subsequent crashes occurred in 1719–20 in France and England. (As will be noted in Chapter 7, the traditional depiction of these episodes of price surges as 'bubbles' has been recently challenged by some rational markets proponents, such as Garber (1990a and 1990b). The Mississippi Company bubble in France combined speculation in the shares of the company with the issuance of paper money by John Law's bank. Stock could be purchased on the margin, and the bank would lend readily to speculators in the shares. At the peak of the speculative frenzy, the stock was trading at ten times the par value, but even the par value was far above any earnings potential. The combination of stock speculation and paper currency inflation ended in economic disaster as the bubble burst.

The South Sea Bubble in England in 1720 started with speculation in South Sea Company shares but spread to other companies. Not only were people in a frenzy to buy the shares of existing companies, but a number of highly speculative (and in some cases highly fraudulent) new companies were quickly formed in response to the seemingly insatiable demand for shares. The Bank of England, however, did not fan the speculative mania by increasing the money supply, and the bubble soon burst. The resulting distrust of both speculation and joint-stock companies led to the Bubble Act of 1720.

In the US, the general financial crises which occurred in 1837, 1857, 1869, 1873, 1884 and 1893 all included stock market panics. In the case of the 1884 crisis, however, panic spread from the stock market to New York banks (Wilson et al. 1990, p. 90). While the period 1897–1906 witnessed a strong bull market, financial crises which included stock market panics occurred in 1901 and again in 1903. That bull market was particularly important because 'Main Street' had come to 'Wall Street' as the funds of small investors became increasingly important (Sobel 1965, p. 178). The panic of 1903 was referred to as the 'rich man's panic' because the small investors had left the market before prices collapsed, so that only the professional insiders suffered losses. Sobel observed that this 'was the first example of the new power of the small investor, a power which would not be recognized by the usually sensitive Wall Streeters for another generation' (1965, p. 182).

While the panic of 1907 has been depicted by some scholars as exclusively a banking panic (Sobel 1965, p. 188), the stock market was heavily affected. Wilson et al. (1990, p. 91) noted that two stock market crashes actually occurred in 1907 before the main panic and crash in October. From their review of the available literary evidence, they concluded that it was plausible that stock market events led to both banking panics and stock market crashes as opposed to the more traditional argument that bank panics caused stock market crashes (Wilson et al. 1990, p. 92). Whatever sequence of cause and effect hindsight reveals, the general public at the time tended to view the 1907 panic as an artificial crisis deliberately engineered by powerful insiders for the purpose of driving down prices of stocks that they wanted to buy (see White 1909, p. 528). In particular, J.P. Morgan, who was hailed as the hero who saved the hour, was able to purchase a large block of desired stock at a favorable price before the panic ended.

Bull and Bear Markets in the 20th Century

While bubbles and crashes are exciting, the long-term bull and bear market movements are also important. Barsky and De Long (1989, p. 1) found substantial volatility of stock prices in the 20th century, especially over ten year cycles. Since a broad portfolio of stocks represents ownership of a broad share of the economy, and since the productivity of those underlying real assets grew smoothly, it might be presumed that the value of that ownership would also grow smoothly. That was not the case, as the US stock market experienced five major bull and bear markets during the period surveyed. In real-value terms, the market fell by 60 percent over the World War I period 1914–18; rose by 500 percent during the 1920s before crashing in October 1929; dropped by 75 percent in the slide that bottomed out in 1932; rose by 400 percent in the period from the early 1950s to the middle of the 1960s; and dropped by 60 percent during the 1970s (Barksy and De Long 1989, pp. 6–7). Although not included in their study, another bull market emerged in the 1980s that ended with the crash of 1987. In a historically uncharacteristic fashion, yet another one emerged hard on the heels of that crash.

The 1929 and 1987 Crashes

The great bull markets of the 1920s and 1980s both ended in great stock market crashes. During the boom from 1921 to 1929, stock prices quadrupled while industrial production only doubled. In contrast, during the boom period 1896–1907, both stock prices and industrial production doubled (Sobel 1965, p. 228). The Great Crash of 1929 was different from the previous stock market panics not only because it was much bigger and affected a larger portion of the public than earlier crashes, but also because it was not related to a banking crisis. From the spring of 1928 until the autumn of 1929, stock prices surged. As examples, AT&T stock rose from $179 to $335 from March 1928 to September 1929, and Montgomery Ward rose from $132 to $466. It was the era of retail brokerage houses, encouraging and facilitating the entry of small investors into the market, frequently on relatively low margins. But heavy leveraging of stock purchases was a major characteristic of the market in general, as evidenced by the rise in brokers' loans from $6 billion in 1927 to over $9 billion on 1 November 1929.

After reaching a peak in September, the market began to drop. The general opinion of the 'experts', however, was reassuring – the market was simply going through a minor adjustment. It remained fairly stable during most of October, but on Wednesday, 23 October, prices again broke, dropping an average of $18 per share. That drop was accompanied by heavy selling, which continued on 24 October when near panic conditions emerged. A group of bankers contributed $240 billion to buy stocks in an effort to restore confidence. The market temporarily steadied, and held up fairly well on Friday and Saturday. President Hoover assured the country that the production and distribution of goods was on a sound basis.

On Monday, 28 October, prices again fell, and on Tuesday 29 October the Great Crash came, with the 50 leading stocks dropping an average of $50 per share. Irving Fisher's assurance that the market had reached a new permanent high plateau and his later assertion in December 1929 that the crisis had passed proved, of course, to be incorrect. The aftermath of the crash was even more severe than the crash itself. Stock prices declined substantially over the next several years. By summer 1932, the value of stocks listed on the NYSE was approximately 84 percent below their pre-crash high in 1929, and they would not attain that level again until 1954.

During the 1970s, the Dow Industrial Average was on a roller-coaster movement, falling at one time below 600, hitting 1,000 several times, but ending at around 800. The market was relatively flat in the first years of the 1980s, reaching a low of 777 in August 1982. Five years later, in August 1987, the average had soared to 2722, with much of the gain occurring in 1986 and 1897. In January 1987, John Kenneth Galbraith pointed to parallels between the 1920s and 1980s, and advised that another Great Crash was possible. That crash came in October 1987. Between Tuesday 13 October and Monday 19 October, the Dow Industrial Average declined by almost a third. During that period, the value of all outstanding US stocks fell by about one billion dollars. In a single day of trading, Black

Monday, 19 October 1987, stocks in the Dow Industrial Average lost nearly 23 percent of their value, entering the record books as the largest one-day crash in history.

The Brady Commission explanation

Several explanations were offered as the cause of the 1987 crash. Galbraith's speculative markets explanation will be discussed in Chapter 6, and the rational markets explanations will be discussed in Chapter 7. However, one explanation – the 'official' one issued by the Presidential Commission – had little to do with the theory of how stock prices are determined. Rather, the report by the Brady Commission blamed the collapse in stock prices on a failure of the market mechanism associated with new trading strategies by large institutional funds utilizing computerized trading systems and stock index futures contracts.

During the 1980s, powerful computers and stock index futures contracts that traded on the commodity exchanges allowed traders to engage in stock index arbitrage and portfolio insurance. With the actual stocks in an index and the futures contract on that index being virtually perfect substitutes as portfolio assets, the arbitrageurs used powerful computer programs to monitor the spread between the prices of stock index futures contracts and the prices of the underlying stocks in the cash market. If the spread diverged from the normal range, the programs would sell the relatively more expensive asset and replace it with the relatively less expensive one. Portfolio insurance programs were designed to 'dynamically hedge' portfolios of stocks by selling stock index futures contracts when stock prices started to fall.

According to the Brady Commission, the two types of computerized trading combined to create a cascade effect on Monday 19 October 1987. The scenario was as follows. An initial drop in stock prices attributed to fears of rising interest rates, higher trade deficits and possible Congressional action to limit leveraged buyouts caused portfolio insurance programs to sell stock index futures contracts, which caused futures prices to fall. The programs of the index arbitrageurs responded by selling the underlying stocks and buying the futures contracts, which put more downward pressure on the stock prices. In response, the portfolio insurance programs sold more futures, and the cascade effect swelled. General panic selling then set in when the market was unable to cope efficiently with such a huge volume of selling.

While the 1987 crash was larger than the 1929 crash in terms of the percentage drop in stock prices, the post-crash experiences of both the national economy and stock prices were drastically different than that which transpired after the 1929 crash (see Preface).

CHARACTER: MANIPULATION AND SPECULATION

The volatility of stock prices has raised serious questions about the character of the stock market. The next chapter presents the rational markets view that attributes fluctuations in stock prices to fluctuations in the underlying economic factors (or forecasts of factors) that influence corporate earnings. Yet the irrational markets interpretation can draw strong historical support from the well-documented presence of speculation intertwined with manipulation in the markets prior to the new federal regulations imposed in 1933 and 1934.

The character of the stock market was suspect in the early years due to the character of the members of the exchanges. In 1715, popular opinion described the London stock market as 'a complete system of knavery, founded in fraud, born of deceit and nourished by trick, cheat, wheedle, forgeries, falsehoods and all sorts of delusions; covering false news, whispering imaginary terrors, and preying upon those they have elevated or depraved' (quoted in Weiner 1964, p. 177). The LSE still had an unsavory record in the early 1800s, with several of its prominent members becoming involved in scandal and fraud. Similarly, the business reputation of the Tontine Coffee House in New York, where the signers of the Buttonwood Tree agreement met in the 1790s, was low, such that more ethical members would stay only for the stock auctions. Others who hung around the building would attempt to get involved with other deals by betting on a wide range of categories.

As the number of stocks traded and the volume of trades increased on the New York market after 1817, the activity in stocks was largely conducted by speculators, with volume and prices surging in alternate cycles of intense activity and calm (Werner and Smith 1991, p. 69). Inevitably, speculation was inseparable from manipulation. Throughout the 1800s and early 1900s, stock markets were widely viewed as being manipulated to some extent by fraudulent or unethical practices. Ironically, the period in which the traditional form of the rational markets view emerged, from the late 1800s to the 1920s, was the period in which manipulation was particularly active. But the historical record provides numerous examples of individuals and groups manipulating stock prices, going back as early as 1792, when William Duer attempted to manipulate prices upward by buying on time bargains. Duer's strategy was based on an expectation that his buying would push prices upward, allowing him to gain on his 'time bargain' purchases (Werner and Smith 1991, p. 17). Incorporated businesses were thinly capitalized before the Civil War, and with only a small amount of stock outstanding, prices could easily be manipulated by such tactics as 'wash sales' and spreading false information. Although the NYSE before the Civil War officially prohibited 'wash sales', the practice was continued under various disguises for generations (Thomas 1967, p. 58). There were frequent attempts to corner the market in particular stocks, which involved 'bulling' prices upward until all the available stock was controlled. The rising price would entice 'bears' to sell short, borrowing stock and selling it with the expectation of being able to buy it back at a lower price in anticipation of a break in prices. Successful manipulation would mean that the bears would be forced to purchase stocks from those who had cornered the market at a price dictated by the latter. As an example, Jacob Little gained a corner in the Morris Canal and Banking Company stock in 1834, which enabled him to sell stock which he had bought at $10 only a month before at $185 (Sobel 1965, p. 43).

With the expansion in the number of securities traded and the volume of the daily transactions market, the technological innovations in communications and the organization of the large trusts in the late 1800s, the scale of manipulation increased in both the primary and secondary markets. Those who gained control of the boards of directors of railroads and industrial corporations were able to market large amounts of both stocks and bonds at prices that were much higher than those justified by the true market values of the underlying assets. This practice became so frequent that the terms 'over-capitalization' and 'watered stock' entered common parlance. As an illustration, manipulation of the stock of the Eire Railroad allowed the 'Eire Gang' to manipulate prices upward when they wanted to sell their own securities at inflated prices or manipulate prices downward when they wanted to squeeze out other securities holders. Within a period of four years, the Eire Railroad was recapitalized by raising outstanding common stock from $17 million to $78 million, a practice that became a common device in the manipulation of railroad stocks (Werner and Smith 1991, p. 144).

An Illustration of the Manipulative Mentality

Characteristic of the late 1800s is provided by Harriman's reported response to a question as to whether the price of a stock could be boosted from $70 to $80. He responded in the negative, but explained that the price could be bulled up to $150, then sold off at $100 because the public would grab at a stock that was selling at a $50 discount. Harriman and other manipulators also used a strategy of creating a sluggish market for stocks they wanted to acquire, working on the principle that the public would lose interest in the stock and be willing to sell (Thomas 1967, p. 64).

'Bet a Million' Gates, President of American Steel and Wire Company, once sold stock in the company short, then announced in the crowded lobby of the Waldorf Hotel that he was shutting down the steel mills due to poor business conditions. The next morning, he gave credence to that declaration by closing down and dismissing a large number of employees. When the stock fell from the mid $60s to the $30s, he acquired additional stock which he subsequently sold for a profit as the price rebounded, making a profit both on the short sale and on the recovery (Thomas 1967, p. 106).

In the late 1800s, the organization of trusts and holding companies, and the concurrent growing power of large investment banks that organized groups of commercial banks and insurance companies, made increasingly feasible manipulative practices on a much larger scale. Thomas (1967, p. 99) observed that: 'trusts provided powerful stock leverage, control was in the hands of a minority, and the price behavior of the stock was a simple matter of the wishes of the insiders'. Even as trusts were being declared illegal, the holding company was being used widely by large investment bankers to create the power needed to manipulate stock prices extensively. As Edwards (1938) stated:

> The developed stage of security capitalism brought with it the usual evils of overcapitalization of assets, deterioration in the quality of the securities based on these assets, the issuing of fraudulent statements, consequent security price depreciation, intermittent maladjustment between saving and investment with the resultant sharp security price fluctuations and financial panics. (p. 185)

In the 1896 edition of Richard Ely's *Outlines of Economics*, a brief discussion of stock companies included a bitter denunciation of the manipulation of railroad securities by management. Ely asserted that the speculative nature of the management of these corporations had almost destroyed the security of investments in their shares.

> No severer indictment can be brought against the stock gambling of our day than the fact that it has destroyed one of the efficient incentives which society possesses for the general saving of wealth. Who would dare advise a poor widow to invest her savings in railway securities. (Ely 1896, pp. 225–6)

The period from the late 1800s to the beginning of World War I was the era of the great investment bankers, symbolized by J.P. Morgan and associates in his 'money trust', who arranged mergers of or reorganized industrial corporations, frequently issuing new securities at multiples of their asset values. The US Steel Corporation illustrates the practice of over-capitalization. The new holding company was capitalized at $1.4 billion in bonds, common stock and preferred stock, when the assets were valued at only half that amount. That level of capitalization was not justified based on the earnings of the company in the early years but over time expanding profits placed the common stock on a satisfactory earning basis (Edwards 1938, p. 186).

In its commemorative issue on the 100th anniversary of the Dow Jones averages, the *Wall Street Journal* paid special note to the sleaziness of Wall Street in 1896:

> One hundred years ago, only gamblers and manipulators dared venture into the stock market. In the financial district of lower Manhattan, runners, traders, prospectors and speculators peopled an insular hive where clandestine investment pools manipulated share prices with impunity. This was no place for widows and orphans – or any other investors with an aversion to risk. (Kansas 1996, p. R1)

The stock market consequences of the Northern Securities episode illustrate the effects of the competition between Harriman and the Morgan group to control the Northern Pacific railroad company. As the stock price was bid up, traders who had sold the stock short were unable to find shares to buy to cover those positions. Panic selling of their other holdings ensued, resulting in a general collapse of stock prices (Sobel 1965, pp. 164–8). Public suspicion ran high that the panic of 1907 was engineered by Morgan's 'money trust' to enable that group to purchase securities at a favorable price (White 1909).

The Hughes Committee Report

In the wake of the 1907 panic, a Committee was appointed by New York Governor Hughes in 1908 for the purpose of studying the extent and effects of speculation in the securities and commodities exchanges, and to ascertain what changes might be needed in the state's law to deal with speculation. The Committee consisted of a number of businessmen and the economist John Bates Clark. The Committee's recommendations (or lack thereof) are discussed in the section that follows. But it should be noted here that its report divided the patrons of the NYSE into *investors*, who are knowledgeable and pay in full for securities they purchase; *manipulators* with inside connections which enable them to move prices of particular securities up or down; *floor traders*, who are well informed about changes which affect the values of securities, are familiar with trading techniques on the Exchange and have the ability to act in concert with others and thus manipulate values; *outside operators* with capital, experience and knowledge of general conditions of business, who nevertheless tend to lose in the long run, in part due to commissions and in part because gains entice them into larger ventures and thus ruin when bad luck occurs; and *inexperienced persons* who invariably eventually lose (Fetter 1913, pp. 139–40).

The Hughes Committee report stated that: 'It is unquestionable that only a small part of the transactions upon the Exchange is of an investment character; a substantial part may be characterized as virtually gambling' (in Fetter 1913, p. 140). In reviewing the commission's report, White (1909) stated that it was known that 75 percent of the trades on the Stock Exchange are known to be of the gambling type.

On the subject of manipulation by large interests, the committee identified two general types. The first was for the purpose of making a market for new issues of securities. This was said to have certain advantages and was described as non-objectionable if not accompanied by 'matched orders'. The second type of manipulation, however, was designed merely to serve speculative purposes, creating profit opportunities from fluctuations that were planned in advance. The objective was either to create high prices for particular stocks to draw in the public as buyers, allowing the manipulators to unload their holdings or to depress the prices to induce the public to sell. The Committee's report acknowledged that 'There have been instances of gross and unjustifiable manipulation of securities' (Fetter 1913, pp. 141–2).

The Committee's report was highly critical of the curb market's potential for fraud and manipulation, but noted that the NYSE's rule prohibiting its members from becoming members of any other organized exchange kept the curb market from becoming an organized exchange. But that rule was broken by a number of NYSE members. The Committee's report declared that some of the most flagrant cases of abuse in the curb market came from members of the NYSE (in Fetter 1913, pp. 146–7).

Manipulation and the 1920s Bull Market

In the early 1920s, the NYSE instituted several measures, for example, a policing committee to halt stock-rigging practices by members, but ample freedom for stock manipulators was left (Thomas 1967, pp. 142–3). Indeed, during the great bull market of the 1920s, a number of stocks were manipulated by insiders and pools or syndicates that bulled the prices up, then unloaded on gullible buyers. As an example, Billy Durant and his associates manipulated the price of RCA stock, leading to a wild episode in which the stock was being exchanged at the rate of 500,000 shares per day, 100,000 more than was officially available. Durant and crowd pushed the price from 85 to 420, and were able to sell out before prices fell (Thomas 1967, pp. 176–9).

In 1929, massive pools manipulated more than 100 stocks on the NYSE. But the manipulation did not end with the Great Crash of 1929. From June to October 1933, Joe Kennedy's pool manipulated Libby-Owens-Ford stock, first selling short to depress the price and, then creating fictitious market activity to boost the price. The manipulation was very profitable for

Kennedy (Cormier 1962, pp. 2–3) who ironically was appointed by Roosevelt as the first SEC Chairman.

Another form of artificial support of prices was common during the 1920s. Prior to World War I, investment banks generally followed the policy of permitting new issues to find their true market levels, whether above or below the issuing price. The larger investment bankers, for example, the Morgan group, who gained control of corporations, would attempt to see that management followed policies that would create earnings to support the price. In the 1920s, with a large number of new issues hitting the market, syndicates would 'peg' the price for as long as six months. Edwards (1938, p. 234) argued that 'this manipulation of the market created a fictitious price, and gave the appearance of a stable market which deceived no one except the individual investor unacquainted with the technique of security distribution'.

REGULATION OF THE STOCK MARKET

In the 1800s, the stock exchange conducted its operations with little interference from the state or local government. In 1881, legislation proposed in New York to tax security transactions was bitterly opposed by the NYSE and its supporters. Before the early 1900s, participants in stock markets were largely professionals and wealthy individuals, and the general public took more or less an attitude of indifference to losses suffered by members of those groups. But small investors, most of whom would fall in to the Hughes Committee's category of 'inexperienced persons', became more important during the boom period 1896–1907. In the 1920s, many of those purchasing stocks could not qualify as 'investors' as defined by the Hughes Committee, as they possessed neither knowledge nor paid in full for the stocks they were purchasing.

Becoming sufficiently knowledgeable about corporations whose stocks were trading in the exchanges was a difficult task even for market professionals. Throughout the 1920s, the lack of financial information about public corporations, a major departure from the concept of competitive markets, made manipulation by both corporate insiders and outsiders relatively easy. Edwards (1938) observed that in the late 1800s 'Financial statements of this period were unreliable, and the issuing of untrue earning statements was a common practice' (p. 187). Until the early 1930s, relatively little action had been taken by government to correct the situation. In addition, the stock exchanges, organized as modern guilds, continued to enjoy the privilege of self-regulation.

As noted above, the Hughes Committee was given the task of studying the extent and effects of speculation in the securities and commodities exchanges and ascertaining what changes were needed in New York state law to deal with such speculation. Although the Committee's report cited manipulation and speculation, it recommended avoiding any radical changes in the mechanism of the securities exchanges. The exchanges in question were described as 'now so nicely adjusted that the transactions are carried on with the minimum of friction' (Fetter 1913, 139). Further, it argued that any regulatory changes might prove disastrous to the exchanges as well as to the whole country. The only regulation recommended was an affirmation of the guild-like nature of the exchanges namely, self-regulation. The report called for moral suasion on margin buying, and cited the NYSE's prohibition on advertising and exclusion of shady enterprises from its list as being sufficient deterrent to swindling advertisements and circulars that could influence the gullible. A recommendation was also made that exchanges adopt a rule for deciding when a corner exists and to fix a settlement price to relieve innocent people from injury or ruin.

Beginning with Kansas in 1911, a number of states enacted 'blue sky' laws to prohibit the sale of fraudulent securities. That term derived from a statement in a judicial decision that the laws aimed at 'speculative schemes that have no more basis than so many feet of blue sky' (Edwards 1938, p. 384). Blue sky laws fell into two groups, those that were aimed at punishing fraud in the sale of securities without requiring registration of securities, and general blue sky acts that attempted to regulate all but certain exempted securities (Edwards 1938, p. 308).

With the entry of the small investor in the stock market during the 1896–1907 boom, public suspicion that the panic of 1907 was artificially created through manipulation for the profits of J.P. Morgan and his 'money trust' was so strong that Congressional hearings were held. The Pujo Committee recommended that stock exchanges be incorporated, with the issue of securities to the public being regulated by the federal government; that margin requirements be made more stringent; that all forms of stock manipulation be more effectively prohibited; and that companies coming to the public for funds be required to make complete public disclosure of their financial situation (Thomas 1967, p. 123). Before any reform measures could be enacted, however, World War I diverted the public's attention.

The split opinion over whether stock exchanges should be regulated to curb speculation and manipulation was reflected in two papers presented at the December 1914 meeting of the American Economic Association. Both authors were lawyers. Samuel Untermeyer (1915), who had served as legal counsel for the Pujo Committee, argued that some regulation was needed, while Henry Emery (1915) argued against regulation, citing the German regulations that had been rescinded in 1908.

Federal Regulations

In the early 1920s, the NYSE instituted new measures of surveillance, establishing a policing committee to halt stock-rigging practices by its members. But the numerous instances of manipulation by Durant and others indicated the weakness of those measures. After the crash of 1929, the public mood was so strong that Congress finally moved to impose federal regulations. From February to June of 1933, leading financial figures testified before the Senate Banking Committee about practices in the financial sector: 'the tycoons told of unconscionable stock-peddling schemes, reckless banking practices, massive market rigging, and wild pyramiding of utility holding companies' (Cormier 1962, p. 4). Two major pieces of federal legislation ensued as part of the New Deal's emphasis on economic reform.

The Securities Act of 1933, modeled on the British Companies Act of 1844, stressed the principle of full disclosure. It required issuers of new securities to furnish a registration statement to a regulatory body and a digest of the statement (prospectus) to the public 20 days before the stock could be sold.

The Securities Act of 1934 established the Securities and Exchange Commission (SEC) extended the registration requirements to all public stock issues, required securities exchanges to register information about their organizational structures and finance, prohibited various types of manipulative practice (pools and insider trading); authorized the Federal Reserve to set margin requirements, and gave the SEC authority to restrict borrowing by those engaged in the sale of securities. Subsequent legislation extended SEC regulation, including to the over-the-counter market. The SEC depends heavily upon self-regulation by securities exchanges. Its concern is with trading rules designed to ensure fair practice.

In addition, the practice of large commercial banks having investment bank affiliates was widely regarded as both contributing to manipulation and outright fraud with respect to the uninformed public, and to exposing commercial banks to the risks associated with the stock market. Accordingly, the Banking Act of 1933 separated commercial banking and investment banking, and restricted the use of bank credit for the purpose of carrying securities.

The 1964 Securities Acts amendments were in response to scandals in the stock markets arising from unethical behavior and unqualified people in the investment advisory profession. Wall Street had been relatively free of scandals until the bull market of the 1950s began, when 'the manipulators, the broker-thieves, the pool operators; the whole caboodle of stock market swindlers' re-emerged (Cormier 1962, p. 12). The Securities Acts amendments required public reports by widely held companies of substantial size, empowered the SEC to establish minimum standards for character and competence for individuals entering the securities industry, imposed minimum financial requirements on securities firms, and required everyone in the securities industry to belong to an organization with the authority to discipline its own members.

On 13 September 1996 the *Wall Street Journal* reported the following headline: 'Manipulations of Nasdaq-Listed Stocks are Rising, but Investors Keep Buying' (p. C1). The article by Emshwiller focused on the problem of manipulation of prices of stocks that traded in the over-the-counter market during the boom market of the mid 1990s. It pointed out regulators' problems in determining whether price movements are due to 'innocent speculation, fraudulent activity by company officials or illegal manipulations by outside stock traders in which the companies are the victims' (p. C1).

While modern securities markets benefit from more comprehensive regulation than at any time in history, a perception exists that highly intelligent, global speculators (for example, the notorious billionaire currency speculator George Soros) have the technology and financial know-how to affect security prices and profit from the 'inexperienced persons who invariably lose'.

3. Neo-classical Economists on Rational Markets and Speculation

The first part of this chapter traces the development of the rational markets view of stock markets within the neo-classical literature. With 'neo-classical' broadly defined to include Walras, the early writers used the subject of stock markets as case examples in their discussions of competitive market conditions. Subsequently, the focus was expanded to the role of prices in the stock market in allocating resources and providing incentives for the accumulation and employment of capital.

Despite the sporadic appearance of discussions of the stock market in the neo-classical literature, the economic theory underlying the traditional form of the rational markets view had been developed by the early 1900s. In more recent times, the efficient markets form of the rational markets view has emerged in conjunction with the development of rational expectations models in macroeconomics. While the efficient markets view is essentially microeconomic in nature, it remains very weakly developed as economic theory. In addition, the claim that stock markets are efficient has encountered a number of challenges, both as an observed empirical phenomenon and as an analytical concept. Some of those challenges are noted in this chapter, while others are discussed in Chapter 7.

Related events occurred in the field of finance. Attempts in the 1930s to develop portfolio investment strategies based on the traditional rational markets theory of how stock prices are determined became known as 'fundamental value analysis'. (Among the classic works is that of Graham and Dodd (1934) who advised investors to base their decisions on intrinsic value since prices would gravitate to that value (while conceding it to be an elusive concept).) Also important is the dividend discount model developed by Williams (1938) which emphasized earning power as the determinant of intrinsic value. The efficient markets hypothesis has also been associated with portfolio investment strategies that involve 'beating the market' by taking on more risk than the broad market.

Our interest, however, is singularly with the economic theory of how prices are determined, and not with portfolio investment strategies related to those theories. These strategies have been extensively explained and critiqued in the finance literature. On a popular basis, Malkiel's (1990) book, *A Random Walk Down Wall Street*, provides an entertaining explanation of both fundamental value analysis and the portfolio investment strategies related to the efficient markets hypothesis. Bernstein has chronicled the development of the various portfolio investment strategies of the 'new finance' in his 1992 book, *Capital Ideas: The Improbable Origins of Modern Wall Street*.

STOCK MARKETS AS CAPITAL MARKETS

Several problems have prevented the neo-classical theory of stock markets from becoming as well developed as the neo-classical theories of product markets and factor markets. One major problem stems from the frequent identification of the stock market as the 'capital' market, or at least as a significant part of that market. There has been a continuing problem in economic theory of multiple conceptual meanings of the term 'capital'. Not only has this contributed significantly to differences between economists' and non-economists' perceptions of the role and functions of stock exchanges as capital markets, but it has been a thorny issue among economists as well. Machlup (1940), for example, noted that the one word 'capital' was used for three concepts: the produced means of production, the funds made available for the construction of such goods and the funds already invested in such goods (pp. 8–9). He argued that two concepts of capital – real capital and money capital – were adequate for all essential purposes in economic analysis (1940, p. 18) and within that context he described capital markets as having the function of facilitating the exchange of money capital against titles to real capital (1940, pp. 10–11). Others might argue, however, that the problem will be solved only when there is a single concept rather than two.

One consequence is that the relationship between stock market transactions and the accumulation and allocation of real capital (capital goods) often seems more assumed than actually explained in economic theory. The following observation by Machlup (1940) still has substantial validity: 'Studies of the stock market are usually of the nature of more factual descriptions, and refrain from theoretical speculation about underlying relationships between stock-exchange speculation and the capital structure (production structure) of the economy' (p. vii).

In the 1920s an issue arose which points out the confusion between stock markets as capital markets in the microeconomic theory of the neo-classical school and the macroeconomic theory that relates credit, capital and investment in the aggregate setting. As the great bull market in stocks surged, some economists considered the functioning of the stock market within the context of the theory of credit and central banking and attempted to defend stock exchanges from the charge that booming stock markets misallocated or 'absorbed' credit and capital (see Machlup 1940; Balogh 1930).

The Disturbing Presence of Speculation and Manipulation

A second problem encountered by the neo-classical writers is more directly related to their explanations of how stock prices are determined. As the traditional rational markets theory was taking shape in the writings of neo-classical economists, the real-world presence of stock market speculation and manipulation was too obvious to be ignored. Indeed, to a substantial degree, the rational markets argument was developed and presented for the purpose of defending stock exchanges from claims that speculation and manipulation were so rampant that governmental regulation was needed. In the second part of this chapter, we examine attempts by neo-classical economists to reconcile speculation, of a certain kind at least, with the contention that stock markets generate rational prices of shares and thus ensure an optimal accumulation and efficient allocation of capital.

DEVELOPMENT OF THE RATIONAL MARKETS VIEW

> The stock market is among the subjects which have achieved the status of a textbook cliché. Many such volumes have described this institution as a relatively close approximation to a perfect market, indeed, one of the best which is to be found anywhere in our economy. (Baumol 1965, p. 4)

Both the founder of general equilibrium analysis, Leon Walras, and the founder of partial equilibrium analysis, Alfred Marshall, cited stock exchanges as real-world cases of competitive markets that illustrated the mechanical processes by which equilibrium market prices are established. By the early 1900s, neo-classical economists were describing the social functions of stock markets as encouraging capital accumulation by channeling the savings of many individuals to entrepreneurs, and allocating both existing capital and new capital to socially optimal uses by placing values on capital in various alternative employments.

Walras on Stock Markets

Perhaps more than any other neo-classical economist, Walras is associated with the stock market. Kregel (1992, pp. 733–4) has argued that the example that economists usually give of a perfectly competitive Walrasian market is the stock market, and that general equilibrium theory has attempted to generalize the particular form found in the Paris Bourse. In the Walrasian system, equilibrium prices are established through the tatonnement process of an auctioneer calling out prices and an Edgeworth-type recontracting so that no transactions are committed until the market-clearing price is called out (Baumol 1965, pp. 10–11). Walker (1997), however, has pointed out significant differences between Walras's tatonnement model and the manner in which trading actually took place on the Paris Bourse.

In *Elements of Pure Economics* (1874), Walras cited the 'stock market exchange of a large investment centre like Paris or London' as an illustration of 'how competition works in a well-organized market' (p. 84). Securities were described as a special kind of commodity, and although the theory should apply to all cases, Walras (1874, p. 86) wished to consider first the more general cases. After doing so, he returned to the subject of the stock exchange, identifying it as the market for capital goods, as distinct from the market for landed capital and personal capital (1874, p. 311).

Walras's best-known statement about the stock market was with respect to the solution of the equations for capital formation:

> The particular grouping which we have just described actually takes place in the stock exchange, which is the market for new capital goods, where the prices of these goods rise (or fall) through a fall (or rise) in the rate of net income, according as the demand for new capital in terms of the numeraire is greater (or less) than the supply. (1874, p. 289)

The statement contains two significant elements. First, as has often been recognized, the stock exchange illustrates how equilibrium is established between supply and demand in competitive markets. Second, the stock exchange is described as the market for new capital goods, whereas it is generally described as the market for titles of ownership to existing capital goods. Thus Walras seemed to be thinking here of the primary market rather than the stock market proper, which is the secondary market. In a subsequent discussion, Walras identified the stock exchange as the market for capital goods: 'This market for capital goods is, in fact, the same stock exchange we mentioned right at the beginning of our study of pure economics, when we wanted simply to describe the mechanism of free competition in exchange ...'(1874, p. 311). But now he was ready to use his system of equations to 'discuss all the variations in price which take place in the stock exchange' (1874, p. 311). To do so, he offered the following example.

A railroad represents capital (k) and the annual dividend on each share of stock is pk. The price per share in the market (pk_0) will vary in proportion to the past and expected fluctuations in pk. Walras added that 'Frequently these variations in price are purely nominal or, at least, they take place with very little trading in securities' (1874, p. 311). With an indefinite increase in the price of a capital good (*pk*) that price tends increasingly to exceed the ratio of its net income to the current rate of net income, causing demand for this capital good to diminish. Simultaneously, the supply offer of this capital good increases, since the owners could procure a larger income by exchanging a unit of *k* for other capital goods. A similar process occurs in the stock exchange where a rise (or fall) in price brings about a decrease (or increase) in demand and an increase (or decrease) in supply (1874, p. 311).

In this discussion, the trading in the stock exchange appears to involve titles to existing capital rather than new capital goods. But the increase in supply could possibly be interpreted as involving titles to new capital goods (initial public offerings) as well as increased willingness to sell existing shares.

Marshall on Stock Markets

Stock exchanges were mentioned on a number of occasions in Marshall's *Principles of Economics*, primarily as illustrative real-world examples of competitive markets. But stock exchanges were first cited in a discussion in which Marshall was explaining that the concept of 'normal' conditions was not limited to the economic results under free competition but included vital elements that are not a part of competition or even akin to it (1907, p. 35). Two illustrative examples were given which involved the stock exchange.

The first had to do with procedure – the normal arrangement of many transactions rested on the assumption that unwitnessed verbal contracts would be honorably discharged. But the second example related to stock prices: 'the prices of various Stock Exchange securities are affected normally by the patriotic feelings not only of the ordinary purchasers, but of the brokers themselves' (1907, p. 35). This statement is especially interesting because it suggests that stock prices 'normally' are influenced by an irrational factor.

Subsequent discussions described stock markets, in which bonds as well as shares were traded, as illustrative examples of perfectly competitive markets. In discussing the scope and boundaries of markets in Book V, Chapter I, Marshall stated that while the stock market in London is distinctly localized, the 'whole Western World may, in a sense, be regarded as one market for many kinds of stock exchange securities' (1907, p. 325). The conditions for highly organized markets – items traded being in general demand, cognizable and portable – are satisfied in an exceptional way by stock exchange securities (1907, p. 326). Each share or bond of a public company is of exactly the same value as any other share or bond of the same issue (in modern terminology they are 'perfect substitutes') so investors are indifferent as to which share or bond they hold. While securities of small firms may require local knowledge and are not very easily dealt in except on provincial exchanges, the whole of England is one market for the shares and bonds of a large English railway. 'In ordinary times a dealer will sell, say, Midland Railway shares, even if he has not them himself; because he knows they are always coming into the market, and he is sure to be able to buy them' (1907, p. 327).

The most nearly perfectly competitive market is the case of 'international' securities, that is, those of the chief governments and very large public companies such as the Suez Canal and the New York Central Railway. These are in demand in every part of the world and, by means of telegraphic orders, arbitrage keeps prices at almost the same level in all the stock exchanges of the world. News of a rise in the price of shares in one market will cause the price to rise in the other markets. If the price rise is delayed in one market, telegraphic offers to sell in the higher priced market and telegraphic purchases in the other markets will strengthen the tendency for the price to equalize everywhere. Marshall stated that this tendency becomes irresistible unless some markets are in an abnormal condition (1907, p. 327).

Marshall noted that on the stock exchange dealers can generally be sure of being able to sell at a price nearly equal to that which was paid. Consequently, dealers are often willing to buy 'first class' stocks at prices only a fraction lower than the prices at which they offer to sell those stocks. He also recognized the factor of marketability or liquidity. If two securities of the same government are equally good but one belongs to a large issue of bonds and the other to a small issue, so that the first is constantly coming on the market and the latter but seldom, dealers will require a larger margin between their selling and buying prices in the latter case. Marshall stated that 'This illustrates well the great law... that the larger the market for a commodity the smaller generally are the fluctuations in its price, and the lower is the percentage on the turnover which dealers change for doing business in it' (1907, p. 328).

In a footnote comment, Marshall observed that the spread between dealers' bid and ask prices will amount to 5 percent or more for shares of very small and little-known companies. Dealers know that they may have to carry these shares for a long time before finding buyers, and run the risk that prices may fall in the meantime. Dealers also know that if they agree to deliver securities that they do not hold, these securities do not come on the market every day. Thus they may incur much trouble and expense in completing their contracts (1907, pp. 327–8).

Marshall's summary statement has appeared in various economic texts. He stated that 'Stock exchanges then are the pattern on which markets have been, and are being formed for dealing in many kinds of produce which can be easily and exactly described, are portable and in general demand' (1907, p. 328). Ely's statements concerning free competitive markets in the fifth edition of *Outlines of Economics* (Ely et al., 1930) closely echoed Marshall: 'So-called "international securities", such as government bonds, and the stocks and bonds of certain great corporations afford an even better example of goods for which there is a world market and a world price' (p. 174) and the conditions for a free competitive market 'are ideal and are seldom satisfied. They are most nearly approximated on the great stock and produce exchanges' (1930, p. 174).

There is little in Marshall's *Principles*, however, to connect stock exchanges with the functions of capital accumulation and allocation. Indeed, in Appendix E, 'Definitions of Capital', Marshall spoke of capital in connection with the loans in the money market (1907, p. 786) and of the supply of, and demand for, capital (e.g. 1907, p. 790, fn) without ever mentioning stock exchanges as markets for capital.

Wicksteed on Stock Prices

In *The Common Sense of Political Economy*, Wicksteed (1910) explained the establishment of equilibrium prices in stock markets in terms of marginal utility analysis. Issues of ordinary or common shares are claims for a fixed fractional share in a sum of undetermined amount that is dependent upon the success of the corporation and the judgement of the directors. But once issued, the shares will then sell in the market for what they are worth (1910, p. 242) clearly an expression of a rational markets view.

As the 'great popularizer of the marginal utility concept' (H. Marshall 1967, p. 245), Wicksteed explained what stocks are 'worth' in terms of individuals' preferences. Given that market equilibrium prices of shares equal the worth of those shares, Wicksteed explained that those equilibrium prices could change for two reasons. First, the shares have different marginal significance on the preference scales of different investors, which will be reflected in the initial equilibrium prices. But as the positions and circumstances of investors change, the marginal significance of the stocks on their preference scales will change, rising for some and falling for others. The former will want to increase their holding of stocks while the latter will want to sell some of the shares that they are currently holding. Thus demand and supply conditions change as preferences change, and new equilibrium prices are established which reflect those new preferences.

Second, expectations of future earnings may change in ways that are interpreted differently by different individuals. Consequently, some people will decide to buy while others will decide to sell until the marginal significance on the scales of the various investors has been equalized (Wicksteed 1910, pp. 243–5).

Capital Accumulation and Allocation

> The central reason to have a stock market is that it serves as a social calculating machine that reports to firms what the market thinks of their future prospects, and so governs the allocation of investment. (Barksky and De Long 1989, p. 2)

The portrayal of the stock market as an example of perfectly competitive markets establishing equilibrium prices became 'a textbook cliché' (Baumol 1965, p. 4). But by the early 1900s, some economists were explaining the stock market in terms of its functions as a market for capital. Lavington presented a particularly noteworthy analytical exposition in an article that appeared in the *Economic Journal* in 1913.

Lavington described the valuative and allocative functions of stock exchanges as comprising part of the broad complex that forms the market for 'free' capital. The social function of the capital market is to convey capital into the hands of those who are best fitted to use it, that is, to bring capital and business together, thereby lowering the cost of production of business undertakings and increasing the national dividend.

Lavington described the broad capital market as a complex organization consisting of two parts that function as independent elements. The first part encompasses all those institutions and practices which channel savings to users of capital, that is, from pure capitalists to pure entrepreneurs. The second part is an organization – the stock exchange – with the special function of distributing the burden of disutilities of waiting and the bearing of uncertainty among those capitalists who are willing to bear it at the lowest price (1913, p. 37). Its social service in effecting this distribution between different individuals and different times is measured in terms of the reduction of the real costs of supplying the quantity of capital which has been transferred into the hands of the entrepreneur class. Those real costs are the disutilities of risk or uncertainty, pure waiting and financial insecurity, that is, the inability to realize liquid assets from assets being held (1913, pp. 36–7).

As an organization, the function of the stock exchange is to redistribute continuously among capitalists the disutilities involved in the supply of capital outstanding in the hands of entrepreneurs. More specifically, its function is to reduce the amount of two of those disutilities – uncertainty and financial insecurity – by facilitating their rapid redistribution among capitalists in accordance with the changing circumstances of members of that group. By reducing the burden assumed by the capitalist group in the transfer of capital to the entrepreneurs, this redistribution lowers the cost of production of capital. Marketability provided by the stock exchange reduces the cost of financial insecurity in supplying capital, making possible the supply of capital for use over long periods of time, for example in railroads, even though many investors have much shorter time horizons.

Textbook Versions of Rational Markets

By the 1920s, explanations of stock markets as mechanisms that encourage the accumulation of capital and allocate existing capital were appearing in textbooks. For example, in his 1922 text, *Principles of the New Economics*, Lionel Edie stated:

> In one way and another, the market facilities for stocks and bonds supplied by the exchanges are of the greatest importance in the organization of the price system, and are indispensable for a system of economic enterprise in which corporation securities play a primary part. The exchanges make possible a place where the holder of securities can virtually always find an immediate sale for his holdings. The would-be buyer can find offerings of securities to suit every whim or taste, from the ultra-risky to the ultra-safe. People having funds for short periods available for use can place them in remunerative securities for the limited period. The constant bidding and asking of prices between buyers and sellers places a constant valuation upon the securities of any corporation, a valuation which takes fully into account the prospective earning capacity of the corporation. In brief, the services of stock exchanges may be summed up as follows: First, they make it possible for anybody to convert his savings into shares of property which yields income; second, they insure that shares of corporate property will always be marketable, that whenever the holder wants to sell, he may find a buyer; third, they provide a means whereby those who are willing to take the speculative risks of industry may compare their forecasts of industrial and commercial values, and of the future earning power of corporations, and by their competitive and composite judgement adjust property prices to property earning power; they make possible bank credit based on material which can quickly be converted into money; that is based upon collateral security in the form of stocks and bonds. (1922, pp. 392–3)

Similarly, the sixth edition of Ely and Hess's *Outlines of Economics* contained the statement that: 'The principal medium by which capital funds are made available for the purposes which are indicated above is the securities markets where stocks and bonds are sold' (1937, p. 285). Subsequently, the text stated that as long as 'investment bankers and other agencies so direct the stock and bond markets as to maintain an adequate and unrestricted opportunity for the issue, sale, and purchase of honest securities, capital demand and supply will come into equilibrium at the level of maximum average productivity and safety' (1937, pp. 285–6).

The Efficient Markets Hypothesis

The efficient markets hypothesis and the related developments in portfolio investment strategies associated with the work of Nobel Prize recipients Merton Miller, Harry M. Markowitz, William F. Sharpe and others, is the latest development in the neo-classical view of stock markets as representing nearly competitive markets. Cootner (1964, p. 1) stated that 'economists and statisticians alike have brought their research tools to bear on this subject, not primarily to find an easy road to fortune (though who is to say that such a thought did not occur) but to establish the relationship of the securities markets to the ideal constructs of their theories'.

Several statisticians – in particular Bachelier in 1903 (Bernstein 1992, p.18) and Kendall in 1953 (p. 96) – had observed that prices of stocks and commodities appeared to have moved in random fashion, which meant that they were unpredictable. In light of those observations, Paul Samuelson suggested that perhaps the best estimates of intrinsic values are current prices set in the markets. In his 1965 paper, 'Proof That Properly Anticipated Prices Fluctuate Randomly', Samuelson used the concept of 'shadows' to characterize the elusive intrinsic or true values in the sense that future events throw their shadows ahead. People in avid and intelligent pursuit of self-interest could be expected 'to take account of those elements of future events that in a probability sense may be discerned by casting their shadows before them' (1965, p. 785). Since new information that triggers changes in prices arrives in no predictable pattern, prices reflecting those 'shadows' are unpredictable.

In his 1970 *Journal of Finance* article on the efficient markets hypothesis, Fama defined 'efficient markets' as existing when trading systems based on available information fail to produce profits in excess of the market's overall rate of return. Fama reported on three different sets of tests of market efficiency: the weak form in which price behavior contains no information useful for predicting future prices behavior; the semi-strong form in which public information has already been impounded in prices; and the strong form in which all information, including inside information, has been impounded in prices.

In his 1991 *Journal of Finance* article, Fama changed the three categories of market efficiency to return predictability, event studies and private information. 'Return predictability' refers to whether future returns (or prices) can be predicted based on current information. If the market is efficient, future returns will not be predictable. 'Event studies' refer to a particular method of testing whether asset prices reflect efficiently the information being released. If the market is efficient, asset price will quickly reflect the newly released information and trading based on private information will not yield abnormal profits (Fama 1991, pp. 1576–7).

Pratten (1993) noted the relationship between the efficient markets hypothesis and Walrasian markets. The 'same equilibrating processes' are involved in the modern financial markets theory, where models achieve market equilibrium through the Walrasian tatonnement processes. Baumol (1965) pointed out that stock prices are not actually established in that fashion. He asserted that the actual structure of the market was a guild of stockbrokers who relied on monopolistic market makers. Although a number of other empirical studies have challenged the validity of the efficient markets hypothesis, it still stands as the ultimate version of the rational markets view. Markowitz' (1991) work described how an optimizing investor behaves and noted considerations for general equilibrium under the assumption that all investors are optimizers in the microeconomics of capital markets (p. 469).

However, the efficient markets hypothesis does not provide an economic theory of capital markets in the allocative sense. Samuelson (1979, p. 423) cautioned against drawing strong social welfare conclusions from his mathematical proof of randomness in asset prices:

> One should not read too much into the established theorem. It does not prove that actual competitive markets work well. It does not say that speculation is a good thing or that randomness of price changes would be a good thing. It does not prove that anyone who makes money in speculation is ipso facto deserving of the gain or even that he has accomplished something good for society or for anyone but himself. (1965, p. 789)

While a number of empirical studies seemed to confirm the random-walk thesis, Ross (1989, p. 7) commented that 'attempts to formalize the efficient markets hypothesis as a consistent, analytical economic theory have met with less success than the empirical tests of the hypothesis'. In the same vein, Ross described the efficient markets paradigm in the following manner: 'In a sense, like much of economics, it remains a central intuition whose analytical representations seem less compelling than the insight itself' (1989, p. 80).

Despite Samuelson's warning, there are tendencies to claim welfare implications of efficient financial markets (1979). Ross (1989) noted that efficiency in finance has taken on a different meaning from the concept of Pareto efficiency: 'This definition is purposely vague and it is designed more to capture an intuition than to state a formal mathematical result' (p. 2). Yet Ross also argued that while the relationship between efficient capital markets and Pareto efficiency is 'not obvious ... it is not unreasonable to think of efficient financial markets as a requirement for a competitive economy to achieve Pareto efficiency' (1989, p. 2). Ross also stated that 'If the capital market is competitive and efficient then neo-classical reasoning implies that the return that an investor expects to get on an asset will be equal to the opportunity cost of using the funds' (1989, p. 2).

A tendency of efficient markets proponents to confuse informational efficiency and allocative efficiency is exemplified by a statement by Fama:

> This signaling role of prices has an unavoidable implication. If the driving forces in the economy (for example, prospects for capital investment, or for tax changes) produce large shocks to fundamental values, then economic efficiency is served by the immediate adjustment of prices to the new fundamental values. Slow price adjustment benefits some investors, but winners are offset by the losers. More important, slow adjustment of prices to a new equilibrium is socially inefficient: unreliable signals from prices imply less efficient allocation of the economy's real resources. (1989, p. 72)

The analytical weakness of the efficient markets hypothesis highlighted by the 1987 stock market crash will be discussed in Chapter 7. Specifically, we will discuss the attempts by rational markets proponents to explain how such a large change in values of stocks could occur so quickly in the absence of any ascertainable news to indicate a change in information. Certain anomalies have challenged both the concept and the empirical tests of efficient markets, and have now become part of the standard textbook discussion of efficient markets. In particular, if no one can benefit from trading on information, no one will have an incentive to search for information. There are also the 'calendar effects' (January effect, weekend effect) small cap stocks effect, the success of Warren Buffett practicing 'value investing' and Shiller's empirical work (examined in Chapter 7) which suggest that stock prices are too volatile for the prices to be informationally efficient.

THE NEO-CLASSICAL VIEW OF SPECULATION AND MANIPULATION

> Granting that the stock exchange constitutes a reasonably close approximation to a competitive market, it seems all the more reasonable to conjecture that it will serve as a relatively effective allocator of resources. However, a bit more thought can lead us to become somewhat suspicious of this conclusion. (Baumol 1965, p. 6)

> When insiders, or, perhaps, a single celebrated operator, bear or bull a stock, outsiders follow blindly. (Pigou 1913, p. 23)

> An investor is a speculator who has been successful; a speculator is merely an investor who has lost his money. (Samuelson Vol. 4, p. 425)

In his introduction to *The Stock Market Crash – And After* (1930), Fisher presented a concise statement of the rational markets view of stock prices:

> To begin at the beginning: Since every stock price represents a discounted value of the future dividends and earnings of the stock, there are four reasons that may justify a rise in the price level of stocks: (1) Because the earnings are continually plowed-back into business instead of being declared as dividends, this plowing back resulting in an accumulation at compound interest, so to speak; (2) Because the expected earnings will increase on account of technical progress within the industry; (3) Because less risk is believed to attach to those earnings than formerly; (4) Because the 'basis' by which the discounting is made has been lowered. (p. xxii)

Since Fisher was writing in an attempt to rescue the rational markets view from the devastating blow dealt by the 1929 crash, it is not surprising that he asserted: 'When the situation is calmly examined, it is found that all four of these causes were at work, tending to raise the prices on the stock market during the years preceding the panic of 1929' (p. xxii).

Fisher was not the first rational markets economist to wrestle with this problem. From Walras and Marshall and afterward, contributors to the rational markets view have found it impossible to ignore speculation and its frequent companion, manipulation, as factors contributing to stock market fluctuations. In fact, a substantial part of the rational markets argument was developed in discussions of speculation and manipulation which sought to defend the stock exchanges from criticism and demands for government regulation. This task was especially pressing as speculation was widely viewed as a form of gambling. While none attempted to defend manipulation, all of the rational markets economists argued that some forms of speculation were not only essential to well-functioning stock exchanges but were beneficial to society in terms of allocating capital resources over time.

Walras on Speculation

Walras addressed the role of speculators in explaining why there are markets for existing capital goods. Two aspects of speculation were mentioned. First, the net income from new capital goods is not known to the same extent as the net income from existing capital goods. Consequently, putting savings into new capital goods involves greater risk. The more prudent and circumspect savers choose to buy existing capital goods, while those who sell existing capital goods then invest the proceeds of those sales in new capital goods. Walras stated that applied economics studies the role of these speculators whose business it is to classify capital.

In addition, the price of capital goods varies not only by reason of past changes but also of expected changes either in gross income or in rates of depreciation and insurance. Those expectations differ among individuals. Hence some people will sell capital goods which they fear, correctly or incorrectly, may be subject to a decrease in net income and use the proceeds to buy other capital goods which they hope, correctly or incorrectly, will experience an increase in net income. Walras stated that only in the case of capital goods proper are the gross incomes, depreciation rates and premium rates of insurance all subject to change. Since this makes their prices quite variable, they are constantly being bought and sold for speculation.

Walras argued that once the decision has been made on the basis of the expected rate of net income to exchange capital goods, both new and old, the exchange then takes place in conformity with the mechanism of free competition and the law of offer and demand (1874, pp. 310–11). Manipulation of market prices is not indicated in the Walrasian system.

Bagehot on Speculation

Although Bagehot is not usually classified as a neo-classical economist, he was 'an orthodox economist' (Moore 1996, p. 245). His recognition of speculation in the British stock market is therefore of some relevance. In *Economic Studies* (1880), Bagehot wrote that a great speculative fund existed in England that was always ready to go anywhere that promised high profits. When profits in many trades suddenly become greater than usual, the stock exchange becomes 'instantly animated', with the market booming for all kinds of securities. Ordinary businessmen who experience above-average profits in their own small lines of business, which they know well, begin to think they know enough about business in general to properly assess all risks and could do well in the London market, where in fact, most invariably lose (1880, pp. 46–7).

In an Appendix comment, Bagehot also qualified several textual discussions of price being formed in competitive markets by supply and demand as being less than realistic. He noted that the assumption that sellers own what they sell is not always true, as illustrated by the stock exchanges where short sales are common. Moreover, where a few dealers hold securities in small quantities, short sellers can get caught in corners. The seller's price thus depends on his expectations about what the buyer will pay and what he will have to pay, and the risk involved in covering his short sale. Bagehot also cited the case where the buyer does not possess the money, which is another common situation on the Stock Exchange. Then the buyer must have expectations about not being able to borrow the money on profitable terms, and the risk of being able to do so (1880, pp. 210–11).

Bagehot described these as 'legitimate' transactions. In contrast, it was understood in 'time bargains', which were very common on the Stock Exchange, that there was no intent to consummate the transactions. Rather, that type of contract would be settled at some point simply by paying the difference. If the price rises, the buyer pays the difference, and if it falls, the seller pays the difference. Bagehot stated: 'The bargain is, in fact, a bet disguised as a sale' (1880, pp. 211–12).

Bagehot then discussed bulls as speculators who buy and bears as speculators who sell. The 'common outside public' tend always to be bulls, while the 'inside or professional operators' are bears who live on the 'folly of the outside world' (1880, p. 212). 'Time bargains' are often influenced by preceding bargains. People will rush to buy when prices are rising, betting they will rise more. Not as many people, but still many, will be eager to sell when prices are sinking. Many of these speculators have good reason for their positions. Bagehot commented that attempts to rig the stock market are more successful than in other lines of business: 'A league of knowing speculators, which can make the market rise a little, will be sure to be imitated by a crowd of unknowing ones, and will be able to make money at their cost' (1880, p. 212).

Marshall on Speculation

We noted earlier that Marshall's first discussion of the stock exchange included the comment that 'the prices of various Stock Exchange securities are affected "normally" by the patriotic feelings not only of the ordinary purchasers, but of the brokers themselves' (1907, p. 35). On the subject of speculation in general, for example dealings in corn 'futures', Marshall stated that many of the largest fortunes are made by speculation rather than by truly constructive work. He described much of this speculation as being associated with anti-social strategy and even with evil manipulation of the sources from which ordinary investors derive their guidance. But Marshall was very cautious in recommending any reforms. He warned that a remedy is not easy and may never be perfect, and that hasty attempts to control speculation by simple regulations had invariably proved either futile or mischievous. Marshall saw this as being one of those matters in which the rapidly increasing force of economic studies may be expected to render great service to the world in the course of the 20th century (1907, p. 719).

Indirect references to stock market speculation that smacked of outright manipulation by insiders appeared several times in *Principles*. In reference to the management of joint-stock companies, Marshall stated: 'When powerful joint-stock companies are working in harmony, and are not directly or indirectly involved in speculative ventures on the stock exchange, or in campaigns for the crushing or for the compulsory fusion of rivals, they generally look forward to a distant future, and pursue a far-seeing if a sluggish policy' (1907, p. 604). Even more obliquely, Marshall also commented that when the law of increasing returns results in large stocks of capital being combined together into modern trusts, 'then began that careful "grading" of goods for sale in distant markets, which has already led to national and international speculative combinations in produce and stock-exchanges' (1907, p. 672). In that passage, Marshall described such combinations as 'the source of some of the gravest practical problems with which the coming generation will have to deal'. Marshall also made reference to over-capitalization and stock-watering as occurring when the temporary increases in profits lead to new issues of shares which are eagerly absorbed by the public. Such cases, he noted, were common in America (1907, p. 417, fn).

But Marshall also presented a positive view of speculation. In a footnote, he declared that it has been well observed that a speculator who is not manipulating prices by false intelligence or any other means, correctly anticipates the future and makes his gains by shrewd purchases and sales on the stock exchange or produce markets, and generally renders a public service by pushing forward production where it is wanted and repressing it where it is not (1907, p. 432, fn).

Fisher on Speculation

In *Elementary Principles of Economics*, Fisher (1912) discussed speculation immediately after discussing arbitrage. He insisted that his purpose was not to determine whether speculation was good or bad, a discussion of which belongs to 'applied economics', but rather to show that speculation, so far as it is good, tends to equalize prices in time. Most of the references were to commodity market speculation, but speculation in the stock market seemed to be implied.

Fisher's defense of speculation rested on the equalization of prices between different periods of time which results in a large saving in the stocks which need to be carried and mitigates impending price rises or declines (1912, p. 341). This equalization of price is largely accomplished by a special class called speculators by withdrawing ('bulls') or adding ('bears') to present supply (1912, p. 338).

But while Fisher's stated purpose was only to consider the benefits of 'good' speculation, he nevertheless also discussed 'harmful' speculation that occurs when speculators guess wrongly and aggravate price inequality (1912, p. 342). Because the interests of the speculator and the public are fortunately identical to a large extent, 'there is a premium put on wise and beneficial speculation and a penalty on unwise and injurious speculation' (1912, pp. 342–3).

But Fisher admitted that despite such penalties, much speculation was of the latter nature because many engaging in speculation lack both 'adequate equipment' and 'independent judgement as to the causes making for a rise or a fall in prices' (1912, p. 343). Given the more limited access of the public to commodity exchanges, Fisher's subsequent comments on the evils of speculation, quoted immediately below, would seem to relate to stock market speculation:

> During recent years the general public have been beguiled into the folly of entering the speculative market, but the public have no special knowledge of market conditions, and their participation in speculation is almost as apt to aggravate as to alleviate the inequalities in prices. In such cases speculation becomes mere gambling. In fact, it is worse than gambling, for evils are more extensive, being shared by the consumers and producers and all who are affected by the price fluctuations thus caused. Such evils of speculation are especially grave when, as usually happens, the general public speculate in a mass, i.e., all in the same direction. Like sheep, they tend to follow the same leader, and the great bulk of their mistakes are apt to be in the same direction. (1912, pp. 343–4)

While the 'chief evils of speculation are largely the work of the unprofessional speculators, just as the chief evils of reckless automobile driving are due to untrained chauffeurs', Fisher conceded that the professional speculator may sometimes 'rig the market' and manipulate prices. In such cases, the professional speculator 'is apt to be a mischief-maker' (1912, p. 344)

Wicksteed on Speculative Stock Markets

Earlier we noted that Wicksteed stated that in the secondary market stocks will sell at equilibrium prices which are equal to their worth. But Wicksteed also stated that stock markets provide the example for all that needs to be said on the subject of purely speculative or gambling markets (1910, p. 238). 'The great law of the market' holds for stock exchanges 'subject only to secondary disturbances from the fringe of speculative and gambling transactions that twines around it' (1910, p. 248). After explaining changes in equilibrium stock prices in terms of differences in marginal preferences change, Wicksteed observed that the fluctuations in stock prices 'may become the subject of a purely speculative transaction', with people buying only because the price is expected to rise with the intention of quickly reselling before payment has to be made on settlement day (1910, pp. 245–6).

Wicksteed seemed to think, however, that most of the losses arising from speculation were attributable to the commissions paid on the frequent transactions (1910, p. 246). Moreover, with the exception of 'corners', Wicksteed seemed to downplay the significance of speculative transactions:

> ... so long as there is any real market at all, that is to say, so long as there is any commodity or privilege which is actually being bought or sold, the quantity of that commodity that exists, and the communal scale of preferences, determine its marginal significance, and therefore its price, at any moment. Speculative purchasers and holders count just as much as others do if they actually purchase and hold, but, as their ultimate purpose is to sell, they are speculating on the prices at which they will be able to unload. That is to say, they speculate on the conditions of the market as they withdraw from it; and these conditions depend of course, ultimately, on the values attached to the stock by the genuine purchasers who mean to hold. The speculators who do not buy at all, but merely bet, can only affect the market in an indirect and transitory manner. (1910, pp. 447–8)

But Wicksteed stated that if 'speculation results in the establishment of a "corner" or monopoly, it may produce a disastrous disorganization, and the gambling is always ruinous collectively to those who engage in it and profitable only to the agents' (1910, p. 248). Wicksteed chose not to discuss transactions in options, which he described as merely another form of betting on the rise or fall of stocks (1910, p. 247), a rather popular view in the early 1900s (see Raines and Leathers 1994).

White on Speculation

In a *Journal of Political Economy* article on the Hughes Committee report, White (1909) presented what appears to be the typical argument. Speculation has two redeeming features: it provides insurance and it exerts a steadying effect on prices. White argued against regulation of stock markets in part because regulators could not tell the difference between speculation and investment. Those who bought with the intention of holding may decide to sell to realize capital gains if the price rises (1909, pp. 532–3).

White briefly addressed the 'evils' of speculation, which he described as being 'moral, private, and personal' (1909, p. 533), properly defined as the gambling spirit which is part of human nature. While stock exchanges facilitate gambling, they should not be regulated on that basis. There are different kinds and degrees of speculation, some of which may be 'tainted' with gambling, but it is too difficult to separate 'speculation' and 'overspeculation' (1909, p. 533). Still, White endorsed the legal ruling which defined as legitimate trading in contracts that are legally enforceable, that is, something can actually be delivered and paid for, and as gambling the mere betting on rise or fall in quotations, as in the case of bucket-shop operations (1909, p. 233).

White's argument with respect to the danger of speculators spoiling the markets rested in part on his claim that the public is protected because there are so many speculators with different opinions and they have so little information that their activities basically balance out (1909, p. 533). Commenting on stock price manipulation by speculators, White at one point commented that at any given time the 'state of opinion' may be manipulated, but he subsequently declared that the popular opinion that speculators could make the market rise or fall was completely wrong (1909, p. 533).

Lavington on Speculation

One of the most analytical discussions in the earlier neo-classical literature was Lavington's 1913 *Economic Journal* article that used marginal analysis to consider the social implications of stock market speculation. The social contributions of speculators are reductions in two disutilities: uncertainty and financial insecurity. The direct product is an increased utility in the form of increased exchangeability of securities by reducing financial insecurity (the imperfect availability of invested resources). In addition, there is a secondary indirect product in a reduction in the amount of uncertainty for investors in general. That reduction occurs as prices of securities more closely approximate their investment values as financial insecurity is reduced. The total efficiency gain comes from a reduction in the deterrents to the supply of capital, which results in a lower supply price of capital and thus a reduction in the cost of business undertakings.

These contributions to society, however, are dependent upon competition. Efficiency requires that buyers and sellers have equal information. But the intelligence acquired by speculators not only reduces their costs of bearing 'uncertainty' but also provides them with superior information which enables them to transfer wealth from others to themselves. This advantage can only be destroyed by sufficient competition to reduce the price of their services to the costs of producing those services. If competitive conditions do not hold, the private gain to the speculator exceeds his social contribution, and he tends to invest in intelligence beyond the margin at which its social value is equal to its cost. The visible result is an unduly large transfer of wealth to the speculator, which results in a net social waste.

In applying his analysis to the real-world situation, Lavington argued that estimating the efficiency gains provided by speculators requires considering the extent to which competition exists and estimating the indirect effects of the speculators' operations. Prominent indirect effects include some that are not measurable, for example the instability that speculative practice induces in living, which destroys the relation between 'conduct and consequence' which is the basis for rational action, and the speculators' influence on the price of securities. Lavington conceded that conditions in stock exchanges are more conducive to allowing speculators to manipulate stock prices because of the relatively small numbers of individual issues. In addition, speculators' activities may have an exceptionally large influence because the income from securities is often less definite and certain than that from produce, and the securities are held in vast quantities by a public that is very imperfectly informed and therefore highly susceptible to suggestion. The public demand curve for securities may thus be influenced by price fluctuations.

However, Lavington argued that on balance in the real exchanges that include speculators of every shade of skill and experience, and with trust companies that direct large funds with a judgement that is far superior to that attained by the investing public, it is impossible to doubt that in particular cases prices may be distorted, but on the whole the influence of speculators upon prices yields a considerable net advantage to society. In addition, Lavington argued that competition in the stock exchange appears to be sufficient to ensure a considerable net social gain from the direct service of speculators in reducing uncertainty.

Untermeyer and Emery on Speculation and Regulation

Two lengthy papers on stock market speculation and the question of the need for public regulation were presented at the December 1914 meeting of the American Economics Association and published in the *American Economic Review* in 1915. Both authors were lawyers rather than economists, so neither added any theoretical treatment. But their arguments clearly presented the popular view that speculation demanded regulation on the one hand and the rational markets view that speculation played a fundamentally beneficial role on the other.

Untermeyer, who had been the legal counsel for the Pujo Committee, favored regulation, citing the guild-like organization of the NYSE, its monopolistic control over the telegraphic delivery of price quotations as an essential input to brokerage businesses, and its failure to curb manipulation. Indeed, the paper dealt primarily with the problem of manipulation as exposed by the Pujo Committee. Untermeyer stated that he was concerned only with speculation that was accompanied by manipulation or short selling: 'Manipulation is the great curse of the Exchange', and 'Manipulation is dishonest speculation' (1915, p. 46).

The other author, Emery, staunchly defended the stock exchange against regulation, citing what had become the standard neo-classical argument in favor of speculation. Stock exchanges arise as a result of speculation

(1915, p. 73) and speculation cannot be curbed without damaging the machinery by which stock exchanges carry out their important social functions. Manipulation is greatly exaggerated (1915, p. 82). In a statement suggestive of the future efficient markets hypothesis proponents, Emery asserted that stock prices 'represent with absolute exactness what we all think now' whether or not they reflect actual future income streams (1915, p. 78). He also emphasized that it is impossible for regulators to separate investment and speculation, and if speculation at times dominates over investment that only indicates that people have switched from being in an investment mood to being in a speculative mood (1915, p. 79). Emery concluded with an argument that public interference with the machinery of the stock exchange is injurious to that machinery and that the professional insiders of the exchange know best how to make that machinery function best.

Stigler on Speculators and Efficient Stock Markets

We can close this brief survey of the neo-classical view on speculation by turning to one of the leading neo-classical economists of modern times. Stigler (1964) argued that 'efficient capital markets are the major protection of investors' (p. 124) but gave the classical defense of the speculators (albeit in the form of the specialists on the NYSE) in explaining the properties of efficient markets. Efficient markets allow buyers and sellers to deal with one another, but the textbook assumption of stationary conditions of supply and demand must be abandoned. Efficient stock markets must have resilience, the ability to absorb market bid or ask orders without an appreciable fluctuation in price (1964, p. 127). In efficient markets: (1) a transaction takes place if a bid equals or exceeds the lowest asking price; (2) higher bids are filled first, then lower bids; and (3) prices fluctuate only within the limits of the speculator's cost (under competition) of providing a market (1964, p. 129).

The role of the speculator is to 'iron out unnecessary wrinkles in the price chart' (1964, p. 130). In appraising the performance of the market under changing conditions, the criterion of efficiency in a stationary market – that price should be constant over time – must be abandoned. Instead, the performance of the two functions of the speculator must be judged. First, how efficiently does he perform his function of facilitating transactions by carrying inventories and making bid and ask prices? How effectively does he solve the problem of ascertaining the 'true' market price? Second, how efficiently does he predict changes in equilibrium prices, or, in other words, how closely does he keep bid and ask prices to levels that in retrospect were correct? (1964, p. 133).

4. Stock Markets in Veblen's Theory of Business Enterprise

Thorstein Veblen, a critic of both neo-classical economics and the pecuniary values of the business enterprise system, was one of the first major economists to give serious analytical attention to the nature and consequences of modern financial practices, instruments and markets in an economy dominated by large corporations. His analysis of corporate finance, which included references to the stock market, constituted an important element in his theory of the business enterprise system.

Themes presented in Veblen's 1900 essay 'Industrial and Pecuniary Employments', and in his 1903 essay 'The Use of Loan Credit in Modern Business' (see Dorfman 1934, p. 216) were incorporated in *The Theory of Business Enterprise*, published in 1904. The discussions of the stock market and stock prices in that book provide the basis for this chapter. The nature of business capital was subsequently discussed in two essays that were published in 1908 in *The Quarterly Journal of Economics*. Corporate finance was also discussed in several later books, especially *Absentee Ownership* (1923). But except for the suggestion in the latter that the Federal Reserve system, working in conjunction with the large financial institutions, would be able to prevent the financial crises of the past, Veblen did not present anything substantially new about the stock market in any of those works. Moreover, the crash of 1929 and the bank failures of the early 1930s showed that Veblen was wrong in his assessment of the Federal Reserve's ability to stabilize the financial markets. Instead, Veblen's earlier analysis of financial practices and financial crises in *The Theory of Business Enterprise* was quite compatible with the events of the 1920s and 1930s.

THE HISTORICAL SETTING

Veblen's perspective was undoubtedly shaped in part by observations on both corporate financial practices and the operations of the stock market in that historical period. As we noted in Chapter 2, the period 1896–1907 saw a bull market that attracted a growing number of smaller investors. But the

manipulation of stock prices by corporate insiders and professional traders
was a common practice. In his research, Veblen was able to draw upon
new sources of information about corporate finance and the role of the large
investment bankers. Dorfman (1934, p. 223) noted that 'Authoritative
evidence as to the nature of corporation finance was scarcely available
when Veblen was writing *The Theory of the Leisure Class*, but now such
data were at hand in the nineteen volumes of the Report of the Industrial
Commission'.

While this was a boom period overall, the stock market experienced a
panic in 1901 and the 'rich man's' panic of 1903. Dorfman described the
1901 episode as a wave of speculation resulting from the promotion of the
US Steel Corporation by the Morgan interests, and the 1907 panic as wiping
out the 'poor man':

> The promotion of the corporation occasioned an outburst of speculation
> during April 1901 which was something rarely paralleled in the history of
> speculative manias. Old and experienced capitalists, as well as younger men
> asserted publicly that the old traditions of finance no longer held, and that a
> new order of things must be reckoned with. The outside public, meantime,
> seemed to lose all restraint. The New York Stock Exchange was forced to
> declare a one-day holiday to give its members a rest. Newspapers were full
> of stories of hotel waiters and dressmakers who had won fortunes on the
> market. But the 'poor man' was wiped out in 1901. The stock market was
> almost wrecked by the battle for control of the Northern Pacific, between
> Morgan and Hill on the one hand and the Harriman and Standard Oil
> interests on the other. (Dorfman 1934, pp. 205–6)

As Dorfman's description indicates, the market was heavily subjected to
both speculation and manipulation, which Veblen dealt with in *The Theory
of Business Enterprise*. But Veblen's analysis of stock markets was
complex and sophisticated, such that it included the traditional rational
markets view (fundamental value analysis), suggestions of the efficient
markets view, and both types of speculative markets – speculation in stocks
that derives from commercial speculation and pure price speculation driven
by mob psychology.

To put Veblen's analysis of stock markets into proper perspective, we
begin with his analysis of the nature of business capital.

THE NATURE OF BUSINESS CAPITAL

Veblen did not accept the neo-classical claim that competitive stock
markets allocate capital to the most socially beneficial uses for the same
reason that he did not accept the neo-classical view of the allocative

efficiency of competitive product markets. Neo-classical welfare axioms in general confused the process of making money with the process of making goods. Neo-classical economic theory failed to recognize that pecuniary values generated in market activities do not reflect real social welfare that is served by the production of serviceable (as opposed to vendible) goods. Competitive markets allocate economic resources, including real capital goods, to producing outputs that will maximize the pecuniary profits of businessmen, with the consumers' demands being based on emulation and conspicuous display rather than utility maximization and therefore easily influenced by advertising. What the market recognizes and responds to are pecuniary values, and it is the strategy of large businessmen to maximize their pecuniary profits.

Yet Veblen did not regard neo-classical theory as being totally irrelevant in analyses of the institutions and activities of business enterprises. On the contrary, he recognized that an understanding of the former is requisite to an understanding of the modern economy, given that: 'The business man, especially the business man of wide and authoritative discretion, has become the controlling force in industry, because, through the mechanism of investments and markets, he controls the plants and processes' (1904, p. 2). Accordingly, economists must recognize that: 'A theory of the modern economic situation must be primarily a theory of business traffic, with its motives, aims, methods, and effects' (1904, p. 4). Such a theory requires an understanding of the pecuniary value system because 'The motive of business is pecuniary gain, the method is essentially purchase and sale. The aim and usual outcome is an accumulation of wealth' (1904, p. 20). With industry being carried on by means of business investment (1904, p. 186) and since 'invested wealth is capital' (1908, p. 352), understanding the nature of business capital is a requisite component of a theory of business traffic.

Within this constrained setting, neo-classical economics provides a theory of pecuniary phenomena – prices and valuation of assets – generated by the market activities of agents motivated by pecuniary gains from buying and selling. The most readily noted examples of Veblen's use of neo-classical theory to explain pecuniary phenomena include his observations that monopolistic firms restrict production to establish profit-maximizing prices (1904, pp. 258, 262), his observation that in competitive markets reductions in costs due to new machine technology will result in lower market prices (1904, p. 230) and that excise taxes (including tariffs) have the effect of raising prices and reducing the quantity (1904, p. 256). But his analysis of price formation in markets for corporate securities represents the purest case in which independent and dependent variables are all of a pecuniary nature; one set of pecuniary values (prices of securities) explained in terms of related sets of expected pecuniary values (future earnings or future prices of the same securities). Indeed, Veblen's discussion of markets for corporate securities as functional elements in his theory of business capital provides an especially clear example of his scorning neo-classical welfare theory but accepting standard market theory to explain the pecuniary valuation of business assets.

Because industry is carried on by means of business investment (1904, p. 186) and 'invested wealth is capital' (1908, p. 352), understanding the nature of business capital is requisite to a theory of business traffic. In his essay on industrial and pecuniary employments, Veblen distinguished between industrial capital and pecuniary capital:

> Wealth turned to account in the way of investment or business management may or may not, in consequence, be turned to account, materially, for industrial effect. Wealth, values, so employed for pecuniary ends is capital in the business sense of the word. Wealth, material means of industry, physically employed for industrial ends is capital in the industrial sense. Theory, therefore, would require that care be taken to distinguish between capital as a pecuniary category, and capital as an industrial category, if the term capital is retained to cover the two concepts. (1900, p. 308)

In *The Theory of Business Enterprise* (1904), Veblen criticized the neo-classical concept of capital for confusing the older concept of capital as productive goods and the modern business concept of capital as pecuniary assets. As a matter of habit, economists continue to speak of capital as a stock of material goods required in industrial production – equipment, raw materials and means of subsistence (1904, pp. 133–4) But the concept of capital changed as competitive proprietary business gave way to the dominance of large corporations whose securities trade in financial markets. The concept of capital must now be understood within the context of the pecuniary logic and institutions of modern business enterprise:

> As a business proposition, 'capital' means a fund of money values ... this fund of money values (taken as an aggregate) bears a remote and fluctuating relation to the industrial equipment and other items which may (perhaps properly) be included under the old-fashioned concept of industrial capital. (1904, pp. 135–6)

In the evolutionary development of the concept of capital as the 'pecuniary magnitude of the business community's invested wealth' (1904, p. 131), capital was first viewed as 'the capitalized (aggregated) cost of industrial equipment, etc.' (1904, p. 136). That view 'had its significance for economic theory a hundred years ago' (1904, p.136) but was 'no longer of particular use for a theoretical handling of the facts' (1904, p. 137). In the late 19th century, rates of profit or earnings on invested wealth took 'the central and dominant place in the economic system' (1904, p. 89) and an 'orderly increase' of wealth through gains from investment became a 'normal phenomenon' in the 'common-sense view' of businessmen (1904, pp. 86–7). Accordingly, the basis of capitalization gradually shifted from the cost of material equipment to the earning capacity of the corporation as a going concern (1904, pp. 136–7) Capital is 'invested wealth' (1908, p. 352) and business investments 'are made for profit, and industrial plants and processes are capitalized on the basis of their profit-yielding capacity' (1904, p. 85).

Capital as business assets falls into two categories: tangible and intangible (1908, pp. 352–3). The former are claims of ownership of the material means of production ('invested wealth yielding an income' (1908, p. 357, fn3)) while the latter represent an owner's right to claim the income derived from the firm's immaterial wealth, largely in the form of goodwill and monopoly position (1908, pp. 362–3, 1904, pp. 138–40) Both are items of capitalized wealth and represent expected 'income streams' (including anticipated capital gains) sufficiently definite in character to be estimated in set percentage terms per time unit (1908, p. 373).

A large part of Veblen's discussion of capital centered on the 'strategic use of credit' (1904, p. 121) as a competitive necessity in business and the increasingly ambiguous relationship between capital and credit, for example, 'aggregate nominal capital' was 'capital plus loans', while effective capitalization was based on the putative earning-capacity (1904, p. 107). Financial innovations in the form of new corporate securities, especially the preferred stock, added 'another increment of confusion to the relation between modern capital and credit' (1904, p. 119; see also Raines and Leathers 1992). Rutherford (1980, p. 116) has observed that the reasons are not clear as to why Veblen argued that common stock tended to represent the firm's capitalized goodwill while the tangible assets (the material equipment) will be covered by credit instruments (1904, p. 116, p. 147, fn). But as we will note in the next section, the linking of common stock with goodwill plays a role in his explanation of fluctuations in stock prices.

The social welfare implications of the nature of modern capital are significantly negative. For example, in the earlier phase of the evolutionary development of the modern business enterprise system, capitalization was based on 'ordinary profits'. But under the pervasive influence of corporation finance, even the concept of 'ordinary profits' changed in the last decade of the 19th century. The market competition that determined a uniform rate of profits gave way to strategic moves by and for the interest of the larger businessmen. The 'prospective profit-yielding capacity of any given business move' became 'the ultimate conditioning force in the conduct and aims of business' (Veblen, 1904, p. 90). Any differential advantage that gives rise to an income may be capitalized (1908, p. 362): 'Whatever ownership touches, and whatever affords ground for pecuniary discretion, may be turned to account for pecuniary gain and may therefore be comprised in the aggregate of pecuniary capital' (1900, p. 311). Thus the capitalized incomes created by using the monopoly powers of large business to retard production to keep prices higher become pecuniary assets for the owners but represent welfare losses for society.

As a second example, Veblen argued that in the long run, the efficiency of the machine process results in lowered costs of production of capital goods. As long as markets remain competitive, the lower costs result in increased supplies of outputs, which cause product prices to fall. In turn, the falling product prices reduce earning capacity, which results in lower capitalization (1904, pp. 229–30). Thus a gain for society in the form of decreasing costs of production will be viewed by owners of business capital as imposing a hardship (1904, pp. 230–31).

THE FUNCTIONING OF STOCK MARKETS

The prices of corporate securities quoted on organized exchanges are the basis for the valuation of business assets. As a consequence, 'the precise magnitude of the business community's invested wealth ... depends from hour to hour on the quotations of the stock exchange' (1904, p. 131). These fluctuations in the aggregate 'invested wealth' are potentially important due to their influence on production and investment decisions of the businessmen who control industry. As the major case in point, abrupt decreases in capitalization that occur during the financial crises which follow periods of 'speculative inflation' result in severe curtailment of industrial production and investments (1904, p. 191; see also p. 210). But while the functioning of stock markets constitutes an integral part of Veblen's capital theory, a clear and consistent explanation of how stock prices are determined is never fully developed in his exposition which tended to emphasize the role of credit. In a curious way, versions of both the rational and irrational markets views of stock prices seem to be suggested in *The Theory of Business Enterprise*.

Critical examinations of Veblen's views on corporation finance (e.g., Dirlam 1958; Arrow 1986) have given relatively little attention to the functioning of stock markets. At a time when leading neo-classical writers were still writing about stock exchanges as real-world examples of equilibrium prices being established under conditions resembling perfect competition, Veblen was emphasizing the role of stock markets in the valuation of corporate capital. The standardization of corporation properties (both tangible and intangible) into 'merchantable form' and subdivided into numerous 'convenient imaginary shares' (1904, p. 155) greatly facilitated the traffic in vendible capital. With active trading in the financial markets, the effective capitalization 'is given by the quotations of the company's securities' (1904, p. 138). Perhaps Veblen's clearest statement on the subject appears in a footnote comment:

> In effect, the adjustment of capitalization to earning capacity is taken care of by the market quotations of stock and other securities; and no other method of adjustment is of any avail, because capitalization is a question of value, and market quotations are the last resort in questions of value. (1904, p. 118, fn)

With the 'effective capitalization' taking place in the stock markets, such that the 'precise pecuniary magnitude of the business community's invested wealth . . . depends from hour to hour on the quotations of the stock exchange' (1904, p. 131) and with those quotations fluctuating frequently and often substantially, how did Veblen explain the determination of stock prices? As we will now note, Veblen's sporadic comments relating to stock prices in *The Theory of Business Enterprise* suggested both forms of the rational markets view as well as both types of speculative markets, with and apparently without manipulation by insiders.

A Traditional Rational Markets View

Veblen's base-line explanation of prices of corporate securities in terms of a running commentary seems to be a version of fundamental value analysis, which holds that prices will ultimately be established at levels equal to the discounted value of future earnings (the 'intrinsic values'). In the short term, market prices may deviate from their intrinsic values, thus creating windows of opportunity for research to identify underpriced and overpriced stocks. The consequent buying and selling activities of market participants who become informed through research ultimately move prices to levels equal to the intrinsic values.

A fundamental value view seems to be rather strongly indicated by Veblen's repeated statements that the value of any given block of capital turns on its earning capacity (e.g. 1904, p. 152; see also p. 137). The following is a particularly clear statement: 'the purchase price of a given fractional interest in the corporation as a going concern fluctuates so as to equate it with the capitalized value of its putative earning-capacity, computed at current rates of discount and allowing for risk' (1904, p. 118, fn). In addition, his argument that the common stock tends to represent the capitalized value of goodwill also tends to support a fundamental value analysis interpretation. A firm's 'good-will is the nucleus of capitalization in modern corporation finance' (1904, p. 117) and if that goodwill experiences a large and rapid change, 'it is the quotation of the common stock that measures and registers the advantage which thereby accrues to the concern' (1904, p. 147).

But for a fundamental value analysis interpretation to be credible, divergences between current market prices and prices based on actual earning-capacities must tend to be eliminated over time by market forces. In several statements, Veblen indicated that current prices based on putative or presumptive earning-capacities may differ appreciably from the actual earnings capacity (1904, p. 155) In some of his comments, this discrepancy appears to correspond to situations of incomplete information that in fundamental value analysis is ultimately eliminated through research by market players. (But as we will note later, Veblen also attributed such discrepancies to manipulation of prices by insiders.) For example, Veblen stated that:

> . . . putative earning-capacity is the outcome of many surmises with respect to prospective earnings and the like; and these surmises will vary from one man to the next, since they proceed on an imperfect, largely conjectural, knowledge of present earning-capacity and on the still more imperfectly known future course of the goods market and of corporate policy. Hence sales of securities are frequent, both because outsiders vary in their estimates and forecasts, and because the information of the outsiders does not coincide with that of the insiders. (1904, pp. 155–6)

The requisite tendency for divergences between market prices and actual earning-capacities to be eliminated over time by market forces is suggested in several of Veblen's comments. He explicitly states that market quotations of corporate securities will 'roughly adjust the current effective capitalization to the run of facts, whatever the nominal capitalization may be' (1904, p. 116). In this context, the 'run of facts' would seem to be actual earning-capacities.

A tendency for discrepancies between 'actual and imputed earning-capacity' (1904, p. 155) to be eliminated is also implied in Veblen's discussions of situations which more strongly suggest two other explanations of stock prices, namely manipulated markets and speculative markets. (Both are examined in detail below. At this point we only want to note the support for a fundamental value analysis interpretation.) Corporate insiders could profit by knowing that actual earnings-capacity differed from the expectations of earnings-capacity by outside investors (1904, pp. 155–8). But for inside traders to be able to profit from trading on such knowledge, market prices must tend to move towards levels that reflect actual earning-capacities. In addition, Veblen explained that after rising above actual earnings-capacity during periods of 'speculative prosperity', stock prices fall to levels that equate with actual earnings-capacity (1904, pp. 192–3).

A Random-walk Efficient Markets View

An efficient markets view is suggested by several of Veblen's discussions of stock prices. One particular statement in *The Theory of Business Enterprise* suggests the random-walk version of the efficient markets hypothesis. Efficient markets proponents claim that information is impounded so quickly in stock prices that extraordinary trading profits cannot be consistently realized by trading on information. In a risk-adjusted setting, traders can 'beat the market' only through luck. Three different forms or degrees of market efficiency are identified based on the amount of information involved. In the weak-form or random-walk version, prices of stock cannot be predicted based on historical or current price data. Because information changes on a random basis, stock prices follow a similarly random pattern. In the semi-strong form, above-average gains cannot be realized by trading on public information. In the strong form, it is impossible to beat the market by trading on any information, including insider information.

The following passage in *The Theory of Business Enterprise* (1904) includes a statement that seems to declare the random nature of stock price movements:

> ...the earning-capacity which in this way affords ground for the valuation of marketable capital (or for the market capitalization of the securities bought and sold) is not its past or actual earning-capacity, but its presumptive future earning-capacity; so that the fluctuations in the capital market – the varying market capitalization of securities – turn about imagined future events. The forecast in the case may be more or less sagacious, but, however sagacious, it retains the character of a forecast based on other grounds besides the computation of past results. (1904, pp. 153–4)

At first glance, this passage might perhaps be interpreted as meaning that stock prices move chaotically rather than to new equilibrium levels as specified in the efficient markets hypothesis. According to the hypothesis, current prices are always equilibrium prices and price adjustments are instantaneous movements to new equilibrium levels consistent with the new information. But, as we noted above, the establishment of equilibrium prices is clearly suggested in Veblen's statement that 'the purchase price of a given fractional interest in the corporation as a going concern fluctuates so as to equate it with the capitalized value of its putative earning-capacity, computed at current rates of discount and allowing for risk' (1904, p. 118, fn) On that basis, the price 'pulsations' described by Veblen (1904, p. 168) would appear to be random movements in equilibrium prices which cannot be predicted based on historical data.

On a more general basis, Veblen's consistent indication that stock prices equate with the capitalized value of putative earning-capacities suggests an efficient markets view of current prices as always being equilibrium prices. This has implications that support several Post Keynesian criticisms of the efficient markets hypothesis with respect to the meaning of 'information'. Attempts to place the efficient markets hypothesis within the framework of rational expectations have led to the assertion that all information is rational, that is, expectations about earning-capacity are rational, so that market prices are always rational.   But Post Keynesian analyses by Andersen (1983/84) and Glickman (1994) have revealed that markets may be informationally efficient without information being rational.   Veblen seems to present a case example with his statement that current prices reflect 'putative' earning-capacities. But given the dictionary definition of 'putative' as 'commonly accepted or supposed', this only means that stock markets efficiently process as 'information' all expectations and perceptions of market participants that may influence their buying and selling of stocks. Thus the market is informationally efficient, but without the presumption that 'information' means knowledge about the actual earning-capacity. (This point will be discussed further in Chapter 7.)

Irrational Markets: Manipulated Prices

If Veblen seems to have presented the random-walk version of the efficient markets hypothesis, he definitely rejected the strong form version that asserts that even insider information cannot lead to above-average trading profits. In *The Theory of Business Enterprise*, Veblen emphasized that stock prices could be, and extensively were, manipulated by insiders. The 'putative' earning-capacity of a given block of capital as perceived by outside investors often differs appreciably from the actual earning-capacity which is known by its managers. It is often in the interest of the corporate management that a discrepancy between actual and imputed earning-capacity should arise:

> The community's interest demands that there should be a favorable difference between the material cost and the material serviceability of the output; the corporation's interest demands a favorable pecuniary difference between expenses and receipts, cost and sales price of the output; the corporation directorate's interest is that there should be a discrepancy, favorable for purchase or sale as the case may be, between the actual and the putative earning-capacity of the corporation's capital. (1904, p. 158)

Armed with inside information and often giving out false or partial information (1904, p. 156) or deliberately mismanaging the corporation to create lower market valuations, corporate insiders (including the great investment bankers putting together mergers and pursuing take-over schemes) were able to profit by selling out their stocks (or by selling short) when they knew the putative earning-capacity exceeded the actual earning-capacity or by buying stock (1904, p. 155) when the reverse occurred.

> The ready vendibility of corporate capital has in great measure dissociated the business interest of the directorate from that of the corporation whose affairs they direct and whose business policy they dictate, and has led them to centre their endeavors upon the discrepancy between the actual and the putative earning-capacity rather than upon the permanent efficiency of the concern. (1904, p. 159)

Veblen indicated that manipulation was a highly ubiquitous practice because it was so rewarding for the corporation managers:

> The aim and substantial significance of the 'manipulations' of vendible capital here spoken of is an ever recurring recapitalization of the properties involved, whereby the effective capitalization of the corporations whose securities are the subject of the traffic is increased and decreased from time to time. The fluctuations, or pulsations, of this effective capitalization are shown by the market quotations of the securities ... It is out of these variations in capitalization that the gains of the traffic arise, and it is also through the means of these variations of capitalization that the business men engaged in this higher finance are enabled to control the fortunes of the corporations and to effect their strategic work of coalition and reorganization of business enterprises. Hence this traffic in vendible capital is the pivotal and dominant factor in the modern situation of business and industry. (1904, p. 168)

Yet as strongly as Veblen emphasized the manipulation of stock prices by insiders on pages 155–68 in the chapter on 'Modern Business Capital', his other discussions of stock prices, including those relating to 'speculative prosperity' or 'speculative inflation', seem to deal with stock markets that are largely free of such manipulation. (See Dirlam 1958, pp. 204–8, for a contrasting analysis of Veblen's views on manipulated markets and those of the reformers who pushed for the type of securities markets legislation that was implemented under the New Deal.)

Irrational Markets: Speculation

But Veblen also presented the speculative markets view. To explain the nature of the speculative stock markets in his analysis, it must be shown that Veblen emphasized the role of credit expansion in periods of 'speculative prosperity', but he explicitly stated that the 'speculative inflation' and the subsequent financial crises are neither caused by nor limited to expansions of credit.

> The manner in which the capitalization of collateral, and thereby the discrepancy between the putative and actual earning-capacity of capital, is increased by loan credit during a period of prosperity has been indicated in some detail in Chapter V above. But it may serve to enforce the view there taken, if it can be shown on similar lines that a period of prosperity will bring on a like discrepancy between putative and actual earning-capacity, and therefore between putative and eventual capitalization of collateral, even independently of the expansion effected by loan credit. (1904, pp. 193–4)

Veblen's discussions of speculative stock prices are complicated because two different types of speculative market are involved in Veblen's analysis. In the most explicitly discussed case, stock prices become irrationally high due to speculative expectations about earning-capacities. In the other case, which is less explicitly discussed, stock prices become irrationally high due to speculative expectations about stock prices, with no consideration of earning-capacities. This, of course, is the case of pure stock market speculation with all the implications of irrational psychological factors influencing market participants.

The first case is extensively discussed in *The Theory of Business Enterprise* in terms of a general period of 'speculative prosperity' that involves a 'speculative inflation in industrial investments' (1904, p. 247) and an 'inflation in capitalization' (1904, pp. 243–4). Veblen described such episodes as following a particular pattern of changes in pecuniary values. A period of 'speculative advance' or 'speculative inflation' emerges from a period of business prosperity that is initiated by 'some traceable favorable disturbance of the course of business' (1904, p. 194) In the typical case, prices begin to rise in one industry or sector due to increased demand. As long as prices rise faster than costs, actual earning-capacities increase in that particular industry. Under modern conditions, the transmission of the effects of the 'favorable disturbance' of business throughout the economy occurs very quickly. Expectations of increases in earning-capacities permeate throughout the economy and quickly result in increased capitalization of corporate assets. Hence stock prices rise based on what turns out to be speculative expectations about corporate earnings.

Speculative markets of this nature are not necessarily inconsistent with Veblen's indication that stock prices always reflect putative earning-capacities. During periods of 'speculative inflation' those putative values become highly over-optimistic. Nor are speculative markets of this nature inconsistent with insider manipulation, as expectations about rising commercial profits may rest on fraudulent or incomplete information deliberately released by the insiders.

The second case of speculative markets is pure stock market speculation. The absence of any serious consideration of the earning-capacities of the corporations whose securities are being traded distinguishes pure speculative markets from fundamental value analysis. Veblen never explicitly associated periods of 'inflationary prosperity' with pure stock market speculation. Indeed, that phenomenon was mentioned in only a few brief passages in *The Theory of Business Enterprise*, in one of which he described it as 'the mere buying and selling of stocks by outsiders for a rise or decline' (1904, p. 165; see also pp. 122–3). Moreover, several of his comments even seem to preclude any significant role of pure speculation.

In his discussion of manipulation of stock prices, Veblen observed that the 'elusive and flexuous character of the elements of wealth engaged' and 'the absence of an ascertainable ordinary rate of earnings' led economists to describe traffic in vendible capital as 'speculative business' (1904, pp. 164–5). But trading in stocks based on expectations of price changes was 'a typical form of speculative business' only for outsiders. The term 'speculative' was inadequate in the case of insiders, for whom 'traffic in vendible capital' was so secure that the bulk of the great fortunes was acquired in that manner (1904, p. 167) At one point, Veblen also seems to rule out, or at least to downplay, the 'gambling element' by drawing a distinction between speculation of a gambling nature and modern 'speculative inflation': 'The great episodes of speculation and collapse that occurred during earlier modern times were not of the nature of speculative inflation affecting the entire business community occupied with industry. They are rather of the nature of commercial speculation verging on gambling' (1904, p. 246).

In continuing that discussion in a footnote, Veblen added that:

> So impressive a fact has the gambling character of early periods of inflation and crises been that it led economists to look for gambling as a matter of course in later phenomena that have been classed as inflation and crises, even when no gambling element has been obviously present. It has been felt that gambling must presumptively be present whenever there is inflation or crises, because the showing of history runs that way. (1904, p. 246, fn)

While Veblen spoke of speculation repeatedly in terms of over-capitalization (which means 'overcapitalization as compared to earning-capacity, for there is nothing else pertinent to compare it with' (1904, p. 118, fn)) he never explicitly stated that it occurs in the stock market. Rather, his discussions of the over-capitalization during 'speculative inflations' were in terms of the collateralized value of corporate assets, primarily for loan purposes but also on an implicit basis as contract collateral (1904, pp. 197–8).

Yet certain elements of the psychological features of pure stock market speculation are most definitely indicated. In *The Theory of Business Enterprise*, Veblen stated that both 'business depression and exaltation are, at least in their first incidence, of the nature of psychological fact, just as price movements are a psychological phenomenon' (1904, p. 186) The relevance of that statement to stock market speculation becomes more apparent in light of related comments in his earlier essay on industrial and pecuniary employment. There, Veblen commented that pecuniary capital 'is a matter of market values' and subsequently noted the psychological basis of market values and, hence, of pecuniary capital:

> Market values being a psychological outcome, it follows that pecuniary capital, an aggregate of market values, may vary in magnitude with a freedom which gives the whole an air of caprice – such as psychological phenomena, particularly the psychological phenomena of crowds, frequently present, and such as becomes strikingly noticeable in times of panic or of speculative inflation. (1900, pp. 310–11)

In a somewhat similar vein, Veblen also commented in *The Theory of Business Enterprise* that stock prices are affected by the 'tone of the market' (1904, p. 148) and that

> The market fluctuations in the amount of capital proceed on variations of confidence on the part of the investors, on current belief as to the probable policy or tactics of the business men in control, on forecasts as to the seasons and the tactics of the guild of politicians, and on the indeterminable, largely instinctive, shifting movements of public sentiment and apprehension. So that under modern conditions the magnitude of the business capital and its mutations from day to day are in great measure a question of folk psychology rather than of material fact. (1904, pp. 148–9)

On that basis, a pure speculative markets view is implicit in Veblen's discussion of periods of 'speculative inflation'. While stock market inflations are essentially the product of the psychology of commercial booms and are enhanced (but not caused) by credit inflation (1904, p. 109), something along the lines of a speculative mania is suggested in a continued rise in stock prices for some time after the prospects of increased earning-capacities have disappeared. Veblen noted that prosperity is substantially a 'psychological phenomenon' (1904, p. 195) with prices rising throughout the economy because prosperity becomes a habitual fact (1904, p. 194). The business expansion is only partly in response to actual increases in demand. To a larger degree, it is in response to 'a lively anticipation of advanced demand' which 'pushes up prices in remoter lines of industry' (1904, p. 195). That anticipation proves largely false as a combination of rising costs and weakening demand eliminates opportunities for higher earning-capacities.

But the false prosperity may continue for a time for two reasons. One is the existence of numerous contracts that must be filled, which supports demand for outputs in those industries. The other reason is directly relevant to the suggestion of a speculative mania, namely that the psychological effects of prosperity produce a 'habit of buoyancy, or speculative recklessness, which grows up in any business community under such circumstances' (1904, p. 196).

Thus there is a strong implication that pure stock market speculation does occur during a 'speculative inflation'. But if that happens, stock prices no longer equate to putative earning-capacities as Veblen so consistently indicated, but rather to expectations of continued rising prices which fits the definition of 'bubbles'.

The Stock Market and Financial Crises

The end consequences of periods of speculative inflation are financial crises that involve drastic liquidations. Critical analyses of Veblen's theory of financial crises (e.g. Brockie 1958, Scott 1996) have given little, if any, attention to the fundamental role played by the stock market. In his examination of the place of corporation finance in Veblen's economics, Dirlam commented in a footnote that Veblen 'places primary emphasis on the consequences of the eventual discovery by the business community that the putative earning capacity on which the inflationary credit was based is inconsistent with actual earnings' (1958, p. 201). But Dirlam said nothing about the role of the stock market in recognizing and revealing that information.

What happens to stock prices before and during financial crises is left incompletely explained. As we noted above, Veblen explicitly indicated that during the period of 'buoyancy, or speculative recklessness' stock prices become irrational, that is, prices based on speculative expectations exceed levels consistent with actual earning-capacities. But as we will now note, he also indicated that the over-capitalization is brought to an end by rational action in the stock market. At some point, stock markets evidently perceive that share prices are out of line with actual earning-capacities and adjust prices to reflect actual earning-capacities. But exactly when and how the stock market goes from speculative pricing to rational pricing based on information about actual earning-capacities is not clear. On the one hand, plummeting stock prices seem to be implied in Veblen's discussion of financial crises. On the other hand, his explanation of how crises begin indicates that stock prices are at rational levels when the liquidations commence, which raises the questions of how stock prices become rational and what happens to stock prices during the great liquidations.

Veblen did not speak explicitly about a stock market crash in his analysis of the crisis that ends a period of speculative inflation. Instead, he emphasized the role of credit and debt, and focused in particular on the valuation of the properties that have been pledged as collateral (1904, p. 193). Nevertheless, a drastic drop in stock prices is implied in Veblen's depiction of the mass liquidation that brings about abrupt decreases in capitalization. The discrepancy between the accepted capitalization at inflated levels and the actual earning-capacities 'is not felt until the climax, when a widespread realization of the discrepancy brings on an abrupt readjustment, in the crisis which follows inflation' (1904, p. 244).

The scenario of liquidation was described as follows. Firms have large contracted payments as well as large contracted loans. To meet the former, they call the latter:

> The initial move in the sequence of liquidation may be the calling in of a call loan, or a call for additional collateral on a call loan. At some point, earlier or later, in the sequence of liabilities the demand falls upon the holder of a loan on collateral which is, in the apprehension of his creditor, insufficient to secure ready liquidation, either by a shifting of the loan or by a sale of the collateral. The collateral is commonly a block of securities representing capitalized wealth, and the apprehension of the creditor may be formulated as a doubt of the conservative character of the effective capitalization on which it rests. (1904, p. 192)

This precipitates a wave of calls on debtors, and in Veblen's words 'the sequence of liquidations thereby gets under way, with the effect, notorious through unbroken experience, that the collateral all along the line declines in the market' (1904, p. 193)

Veblen's statement that a crisis 'has as a sequel, both severe and lasting, a shrinkage of capitalization throughout the field affected by it' (1904, p. 191) also suggests that stock prices fall rather drastically during the crisis. That interpretation gains support from his subsequent comment that 'The shrinkage incident to a crisis is chiefly a pecuniary, not a material, shrinkage; it takes place primarily in the intangible items of wealth, secondarily in the price rating of the tangible items' (1904, p. 191). The primary shrinkage of the capitalized value of intangible assets certainly suggests falling prices of stocks in view of Veblen's assertion that common stock represents the intangible assets.

While this suggests that stock prices adjust abruptly to rational levels, Veblen also seems to indicate that the stock market becomes rationally efficient before the actual crises begins, which provides the information that initiates creditors' actions that precipitate the great liquidation of business assets. In Veblen's words: 'there is an apprehension that the property represented by the collateral is overcapitalized, as tested by current quotations, or by the apprehended future quotations, of the securities in question' (1904, p. 192). Thus

> The immediate occasion for such a crisis . . . is that there arises a practical discrepancy between the earlier effective capitalization on which the collateral has been accepted by the creditors, and the subsequent effective capitalization of the same collateral shown by the quotations and sales of the securities on the market. (1904, p. 193)

The impression that stock prices reach 'rational' levels before the great liquidations and do not substantially decline during the liquidations gains support from Veblen's discussion of the differences between the crises of the late 19th century (and early 20th century) and the crises of the early 19th century. During the latter, capitalized values typically fell below levels consistent with actual earning-capacities (1904, p. 248). After the psychological shock of the abrupt collapse in capitalized values had worn off, the under-capitalization encouraged business expansion that led to recovery and the beginning of a new period of speculative prosperity. But by the end of the 19th century, under-capitalization no longer tended to occur after a crisis. In explaining the tendency for chronic depression in the absence of 'wasteful expenditures' due to a persistent decline of profits (1904, pp. 251–2). Veblen stated that 'the cost of production of productive goods has since then persistently outstripped such readjustment of capitalization as from time to time has been made' (1904, p. 254). After a crisis has reduced capitalized values,

> The persistent efficiency and facile balance of processes in the modern machine industry has over-taken the decline in capitalization without allowing time for recovery and subsequent boom. The cheapening of capital goods has overtaken the lowered capitalization of investments before the shock-effect of the liquidation has worn off. (1904, pp. 254–5)

The absence of under-capitalization as an aftermath of modern financial crises suggests an 'efficient' markets view of current quotations in the stock markets, that is, prices reflect actual earning-capacity. The speed of the stock market in doing so is suggested in Veblen's comment:

When a speculative movement has been set up by extraneous stimuli, during this late period, the inherent and relatively rapid decline of earning-capacity on the part of older investment has brought the speculative inflation to book before it has reached such dimensions as would bring on a violent crisis. (1904, p. 254)

An additional element of confusion about the level of stock prices at the precipitation of a crisis is created by Veblen's inclusion of the term 'apprehended future quotations' (1904, p. 192) along with 'current quotations' of stock prices as revealing the over-capitalization of assets. 'Apprehended future quotations' could mean that current quotations are recognized as being irrationally high and consequently future stock prices are expected to fall to rational levels. Such an interpretation would give support to the interpretation that stock prices fall drastically during crises to shrink capitalization down to levels consistent with actual earning-capacities. But there is the unanswered question of how lower stock prices are apprehended by creditors who start the liquidation by demanding repayment of call loans. If, as Veblen consistently argued, current market prices reflect putative or presumptive earning-capacities, why have stock prices not already adjusted? That is, how can 'apprehended future quotations' be different from current prices if stock markets are informationally efficient? On the other hand, if the market is not informationally efficient, who correctly forecasts the lower future stock prices?

CONCLUDING STATEMENT

In some respects, Veblen's different explanations of stock prices may represent little more than a curious degree of inconsistency in his analysis of business capital. As Walker (1977, p. 85) has observed inconsistency of positions in other aspects of Veblen's work, it would not be at all surprising that inconsistencies appear in his discussions of stock prices. But given the role of stock markets in providing the information that triggers the financial crises that end periods of speculative inflation, the absence of a complete and consistent explanation of how stock prices are determined is particularly noteworthy.

5. Keynes on Speculative Stock Markets

The purpose of this chapter is to develop a systematic and comprehensive statement of J.M. Keynes' views on the psychological and institutional factors that explain his theory of the highly speculative nature of the US stock exchange. Through an exegesis of Keynes' writings in *A Treatise on Money* (1930) and *The General Theory of Employment, Interest and Money* (1936) real-world episodes of stock exchange booms and busts are explained by the elements of spontaneous optimism, irrational expectations and trading manias inherent in speculative psychology.

Keynes made speculative stock markets an influential factor in *The General Theory of Employment, Interest and Money* through the impact of stock prices on the level of new investment and on the level of consumption. Keynes' comments on the speculative nature of stock markets have been widely cited, quoted and paraphrased. According to Merton Miller (1991), Keynes has become 'the patron saint of the bubble theorists' (p. 103). However, Keynes actually developed a broad analytical framework in which key elements lead to speculative tendencies that can range in intensity and force from relatively mild chronic speculation to bursts of speculative mania.

TWO ANALYSES OF STOCK PRICES

Between Volume I of *A Treatise on Money,* 'The Pure Theory of Money', and *The General Theory of Employment, Interest and Money,* Keynes presented two analyses of the determination of stock prices and why those prices are important to the performance of the aggregate economy. The relevant analysis is that presented in *The General Theory,* but a summary of the analysis presented earlier in *Treatise* is included in this chapter for two reasons. First, it is important to show how Keynes' thinking about financial markets and stock prices changed during a relatively brief period of time. Second, certain parts of Keynes' discussions of stock prices in Volume II of

Treatise, 'The Applied Theory of Money', clearly anticipated his later analysis.

ORGANIZATION OF THE CHAPTER

In the first part of this chapter, the economic relevance in Keynes' analyses of pricing of corporate shares in the secondary market is examined. The traditional functions of capital development and allocation of capital resources are delineated. However, Keynes was primarily interested in the effects of stock prices on the aggregate level of economic activity – the stability of the overall level of prices in *Treatise* and the level of employment in *The General Theory*.

Given that stock prices have some influence on the aggregate economy's performance, we examine in the second and third parts of the chapter, respectively, Keynes' analyses of the functioning of modern stock markets as presented in *Treatise* and in *The General Theory*. In both books, Keynes concluded that the process by which stock prices are determined could not be relied upon to generate prices that will contribute to desired performance of the aggregate economy. In *The General Theory*, he also argued that stock markets are unlikely to allocate capital resources to optimal social use.

In the fourth part of the chapter, we examine the economic consequences of speculative markets in Keynes' analysis, with attention to both chronic and manic episodes of speculation. In the fifth part, we examine what Keynes seemed to think would be the appropriate policy actions to control stock market speculation.

THE ECONOMIC IMPORTANCE OF STOCK PRICES

In *The General Theory*, Keynes commented that the stock market as an institution is supposed to have the proper social purpose of capital development and directing new investment into the most profitable channels in terms of future yields (1936, p. 159). But in the analyses of aggregate economic activity presented in *Treatise* and *The General Theory*, stock prices merited attention because of their indirect influence on the instability of the aggregate economy. In *Treatise*, Keynes' discussions of prices of securities were in terms of how they affected overall price stability through their influence on the level of new investment. In *The General Theory*, Keynes was primarily concerned with explaining how aggregate demand influenced the level of employment. Stock prices were an important factor in the theory of aggregate demand through their influence on the levels of both investment and consumption.

Stock Prices and Investment

In the aggregate analyses of both *Treatise* and *The General Theory*, Keynes emphasized the importance of the level of new investment. But the explanations of how stock prices affected the level of new investment in Volume I of *Treatise* and in *The General Theory* were somewhat different, with Volume II providing something of a transition. In Volume I of *Treatise*, prices of new investment goods were influenced by stock prices. When stock prices are rising, price levels of new investment tend to rise, which stimulates investment (1971a, p. 226). Keynes 'was disposed to sympathize' with the argument that the speculative booms of the 19th century provided an artificial stimulus to investment, making possible much of the economic progress over that period (1971a, p. 246).

The influence of stock prices on prices of new investment goods, however, was not deterministic. In Volume II of *Treatise*, Keynes observed that stock prices may rise without any significant increase in prices of new investment goods, as was illustrated by the small effect the 1929 market boom in the US had on the prices of new fixed capital (1971b, p. 222). Even so, Keynes argued that the decreasing levels of stock prices that began with the market crash of 1929 did cause a disinvestment in working capital and promoted profit deflation by discouraging investment (1971b, p. 176).

In Volume II of *Treatise*, Keynes noted that rising stock prices have the same effects on the ability of companies to raise capital as a decrease in the interest rate. The very high stock prices in the late 1920s, at a time when short-term interest rates were also high, 'offered joint stock enterprises an exceptionally cheap method of financing themselves ... it was cheaper than at any previous time to finance new investment by the issue of common stock. By the spring of 1929 this was becoming the predominant method of finance' (1971b, pp. 174–5).

In *The General Theory*, Keynes explained the influence of rising stock prices on the level of new investment within the theoretical framework of investment as a function of the marginal efficiency of capital and the current interest rate. With interest rates held constant, a rising marginal efficiency of capital stimulates investment in the same way that a lower interest rate stimulates investment if the marginal efficiency of capital is held constant. In a footnote, Keynes remarked that whereas he had stated in Volume II of *Treatise* that high stock prices had the same effect as low interest rates, an increase in marginal efficiency of capital would have the same effect on new investment as lower interest rates (1936, p. 151, fn).

In a more descriptive passage, Keynes noted that the daily revaluations of the Stock Exchange, which primarily facilitate transfers of ownership of old investments, inevitably exert a decisive influence on the rate of current investment. Entrepreneurs will have little reason to develop new enterprises if values based on current quoted prices on the stock exchanges will allow them to purchase existing enterprises at lower cost. Similarly, entrepreneurs have an inducement to spend extravagant sums on new projects which can be floated off on the Stock Exchange at an immediate profit (1936, p. 151).

Stock Prices and Consumption

In addition to affecting investment, stock prices also affect consumption through the psychological 'paper wealth' effect. In Volume II of *Treatise*, Keynes suggested 'a generalization of permanent value' (1971b, p. 217). On an aggregate basis, a nation is no richer if the market value of stocks increases because people choose to value their prospects over a payback period of 20 years rather than 10 years. But individuals holding those stocks will tend to feel richer and, consequently, will be inclined to increase spending and reduce saving. Conversely, when stock prices fall, the 'psychological poverty' encourages individuals holding stocks to reduce consumption and increase saving (1971b, pp. 176–7).

The wealth effect on consumption was restated in *The General Theory* in terms of the effect on the marginal propensity to consume. Keynes commented that the propensity to spend of those who are actively interested in their stock investments, especially if those investments are being carried with borrowed funds, is perhaps more influenced by changes in the value of their investments than by changes in their incomes. Indeed, for a 'stockminded' public such as in the United States, a rising stock market may be an almost essential condition for a satisfactory propensity to consume. On the downside, a decreasing marginal propensity to consume due to falling stock prices tends to aggravate a decline in the marginal efficiency of capital when stock prices collapse (1936, p. 319).

The 'Right' Level of Stock Prices

In *The General Theory*, Keynes expressed little confidence in the stock market's ability to establish prices that would accomplish either the allocative function or the stabilization function. With respect to the allocative function, Keynes declared that 'There is no clear evidence from experience that the investment policy which is socially advantageous coincides with that which is most profitable' (1936, p. 157). More pointedly, he commented that: 'The measure of success attained by Wall

Street, regarded as an institution of which the proper social purpose is to direct new investment into the most profitable channels in terms of future yield, cannot be claimed as one of the outstanding triumphs of *laissez-faire* capitalism' (1936, p. 159). Nor were stock prices likely to contribute to a stable marginal efficiency of capital function. To explain his assertion, an explanation of Keynes' view of how stock prices are determined is necessary.

DETERMINATION OF STOCK PRICES IN *TREATISE*

As the introduction to this chapter noted, Keynes presented two explanations of how stock prices are determined. The first, which pertained to securities in general, that is, to bonds as well as stocks, is found in Volume I of *Treatise*, within the theoretical framework of money and price stability that Keynes was then attempting to develop. That explanation, couched in terms of the public's preferences for saving deposits relative to securities at current prices, reappeared in *The General Theory* only in relation to bond prices in the discussion of liquidity preference.

The second explanation, which was Keynes' major explanation, pertained explicitly to stock prices and emphasized the influence of 'mob psychology' on the behavior of uninformed investors in modern investment markets. There is perhaps some hint of this in the generalized explanation of security prices in the references to 'bullish' and 'speculative sentiment' in Volume I of *Treatise*. Irrational behavior of investors was explicitly described in the second volume of *Treatise*, and was subsequently analyzed more fully in Chapter 12 of *The General Theory*. Additional clarification was presented in Keynes' 1937 *Quarterly Journal of Economics* article, 'The General Theory of Employment' (1973a, pp. 109–23).

Stock Prices and Preferences for Savings Deposits

Keynes' purpose in *Treatise* was to explain the process by which the overall price level is determined and the method of transition from one equilibrium level to another (1971a, p. 120). He proposed to depart from the traditional approach which ignored the purposes for which money is employed, and to start instead with the aggregate flow of earnings or money income, divided into: (1) those parts generated by the production of consumption goods and of investment goods, respectively; and (2) the parts spent on consumption goods and on savings, respectively (1971a, p. 121).

Within that framework, an analysis of overall price stability requires explaining prices of consumer goods, which in equilibrium will equal the cost of production, and prices of investment goods, which are determined by a different set of circumstances. Equilibrium requires that the output measured in the cost of production, divided between consumption goods and investment goods, be equal to expenditure divided between current consumption and savings. When that happens, consumption goods prices will equal their cost of production. Price stability requires that efficiency earnings, that is, the cost of production, be constant and that the cost of new investment be equal to the volume of current savings. But if the two divisions are not equal, that is, if new investment is not equal to savings, then prices of consumption goods will not be stable (1971a, pp. 122–3).

Subsequently, the analysis focused on the role of money. Keynes divided the total quantity of money into income deposits, business deposits and savings deposits, and identified the uses of money as the 'industrial circulation' and the 'financial circulation'. 'Industry' referred to the business of production and those attendant activities that bring goods ultimately to consumers, while 'finance' referred to the business of holding and exchanging existing titles to wealth, including stock exchange transactions and speculation, as well as conveying current savings to entrepreneurs (1971a, p. 217).

While Keynes' purpose was to explain the factors that determine the volume of the two different circulations, it is what he said about stock prices that is relevant here. Prices of securities were first considered in relation to the price level of new investment goods. The saving decision requires not only choosing between consumption and the ownership of wealth, but also the subsequent decision of whether to hold wealth through 'hoarding', that is, holding bank deposits, or 'investing' by holding securities. Securities represent the existing stock of non-liquid wealth, and consist of loan capital (bonds) and real capital (shares) (1971a, p. 222). Saving and investment decisions relate entirely to current economic activity, but deciding whether to hold wealth in the form of bank deposits or securities relates to both the current incremental increase in wealth and the existing stock of capital (securities). While the incremental increase is only a minor element of the total stock of capital, the prices of both existing and new securities affect the prices of new investment goods.

In the long run, the value of securities depends entirely on the value of consumption goods:

> It depends on the expectation as to the value of the amount of liquid consumption goods which the securities will, directly or indirectly, yield, modified by reference to the risk and uncertainty of this expectation, and multiplied by the number of years' purchase corresponding to the current rate of interest for capital of the duration in question; and where the goods represented by the securities are capable of being reproduced, the anticipated value of the consumption goods yielded by the capital goods will

be influenced by the cost of production of the capital goods in question, since this affects the prospective supply of such goods. (1971a, p. 228)

But in the short run, prices of securities depend on neither the cost of production nor the prices of new fixed capital. Rather, the critical factor is the 'opinion' or 'sentiment' of individuals in developing their preferences for holding wealth in savings deposits or in securities (1971a, p. 228). An increase in preferences for savings deposits accompanied by a decrease in preference for securities means that the preference for deposits has increased in relation to the current prices of securities. But the reduced preference for securities at these prices is a variable that depends upon expectations about the rate of interest on savings deposits and the future return on securities, which depends on both the prices of securities and the interest rate on savings deposits. If prices of securities fall sufficiently, wealth-holders can be tempted back into them. Security prices stabilize when a level is reached at which the public is satisfied with the current level of savings deposits.

As long as the change involves the public increasing (or decreasing) the preference for savings deposits and decreasing (or increasing) the preference for securities, changes in prices of securities can be explained simply as portfolio switching. Securities are sold and prices fall, or securities are bought and prices rise. But Keynes introduced the factor of 'borrowed funds'. Those who prefer to save rather than hold securities may loan their savings deposits, either through the bank or directly, to those who prefer to hold securities purchased with borrowed funds. The former are bears who expect prices of securities to fall, while the latter are bulls who expect prices to rise. In the Preface to the Japanese edition of *Treatise*, Keynes explained that by 'bearishness' he meant the 'propensity to hoard' (1971a, p. xxv).

Price stability occurs when public sentiment is neither bearish nor bullish. If it is 'bearish', prices will fall, and if it is 'bullish', prices will rise. Equilibrium is established as the 'average of opinion' changes with prices of securities. At equilibrium, the factors of production are fully employed, the public is neither bearish nor bullish of securities and is maintaining a level of savings deposits consistent with the normal proportion of its wealth, and the volume of saving is equal to both the cost and to the value (that is, the value of securities) of new investments (1971a, p. 132). However, if the volume of saving becomes unequal to the cost of new investment, or if public disposition toward securities takes a bearish or a bullish turn, prices of securities will start changing (1971a, p. 132). Moreover, two different opinions can develop, with bulls expecting prices to rise and bears expecting prices to fall. The latter will increase their preferences for savings deposits, while the former will increase their preferences for stocks carried on borrowed funds, supplied in part by the bears. An abnormal rise in the savings deposits that is accompanied by a rise of security prices probably indicates a bullish sentiment that is not being sufficiently offset by the rise in security prices; this appeared to be the case on a large scale in the US during 1928 and 1929. Thus Keynes added that it was correct to pay attention to the increases and decreases in brokers' loans, since an increase meant that the rise of security prices had gone still further beyond the point at which it would be just enough to offset the bullishness of average sentiment, in the sense that it had led to an increase in the bear position (1971a, pp. 224–5).

The Role of Money and Credit

A major part of this discussion involved the role of the banking system, which goes beyond simply channeling the savings deposits of bears to loans to bulls and, in particular, considered what a central bank should do with respect to the money supply in response to rising security prices.

The actual level of security prices is a function of the degree of bullishness of opinion and the behavior of the banking system (1971a, p. 128). Falling security prices can be prevented if banks satisfy an increased bearishness of the public by creating savings deposits by purchasing securities from those who prefer to hold more deposits and fewer securities. Overall price stability requires that the cost of new investment should be equal to the volume of current savings, and the latter is 'that price level at which the desire of the public to hold savings deposits is equal to the saving deposits which the banking system is willing and able to create' (1971a, p. 129). Once the volume of savings deposits created by the banking system is established, 'the price level of investment goods (whether new or old) is solely determined by the disposition towards 'hoarding money' (1971a, pp. 129–30). Subsequently, Keynes stated that 'a change in the disposition of the public towards securities other than savings deposits, uncompensated by action on the part of the banking system, will be a most potent factor affecting the rate of investment relative to saving and a cause of disturbance, therefore, to the purchasing power of money' (1971a, p. 130).

Earlier Keynes had explained that a rise in security prices brought on by bullish speculation is likely to stimulate rises in the price level of new investment, which increases the attractiveness of investment. But there are also monetary effects that come into play. If there is a consensus of bullish opinion, with savings deposits falling, the supply of money for industrial purposes is increased which allows for increased investment. Changes in the financial situation can create price instability by altering the quantity of money available for industrial circulation and altering the attractiveness of investment.

How, then, should the central bank react to rising prices of securities? Since price instability will occur unless the first effect is balanced by a change in the total money supply and the latter by a change in the terms of lending, the central bank faces a dilemma. Increasing the money supply to ensure that the financial circulation does not take from the industrial circulation will encourage the bull market, with every probability of rising prices of new investment leading to over-investment in the future. But not increasing the money supply may reduce the industrial circulation, causing the rate of interest to rise which will result in deflationary tendencies (1971a, p. 227).

Keynes argued that to stabilize the overall price level, both finance and industry should have all the money they want to stabilize prices, but at an interest rate at which the rate of new investment relative to saving exactly balances the effect of bullish sentiment (1971a, p. 227). In the short run, the value of securities is a function of opinion or sentiment, and prices of securities can increase without increasing the supply of money for the finance purpose due to the high velocity of circulation in that sector and the institutional means for transactions in securities.

> If everyone agrees that securities are worth more, and if everyone is a 'bull'
> in the sense of preferring securities at a rising price to increasing his savings
> deposits, there is no limit to the rise in the price of securities and no
> effective check arises from a shortage of money. (1971a, p. 229)

Accordingly, Keynes argued that monetary authorities should not be concerned with the level of prices of securities but should be concerned if prices of existing securities threaten to encourage new investment to exceed savings. The main criterion for interference in the markets should be the probable effects on the prospective equilibrium between savings and new investment (1971a, p. 230).

Speculative Stock Markets in *Treatise*

Even before publication of *The General Theory*, the major thrust of Keynes' discussions of stock prices was on the influence of mass psychology on investors' behavior within the institutional arrangements provided by modern stock markets. In Volume I of *Treatise*, Keynes stated that 'opinion has a dominating influence' (1971a, p. 229) on security prices and identified four possible types of speculative markets for securities: (1) a bull market with a consensus of opinion, that is, security prices rising but insufficiently so that savings deposits are falling; (2) a bull market with a division of opinion, that is, security prices are rising but insufficiently so that saving deposits are rising; (3) a bear market with a division of opinion, that is, security prices are falling more than sufficiently so saving deposits are falling; and (4) a bear market with a consensus of opinion, that is, security prices are falling insufficiently so that saving deposits are rising (1971a, p. 226).

Keynes said nothing of substance in Volume I about the psychological and institutional nature of speculative markets. There are only hints of psychological factors in the dependency of stock prices in the short run on 'opinion' or 'sentiment', that changes as the prices of securities change, and in the comment that the volume of financial circulation of money, that is, the transactions within 'a circle of financiers, speculators and investors', depends in part on 'the state of speculative sentiment' (1971a, p. 42).

Investor Psychology in 'The Applied Theory of Money'

More descriptive comments about irrational behavioral tendencies of investors in Volume II of *Treatise* laid the foundation for the expanded discussion of speculative psychology in *The General Theory*. In noting the extent to which expectations about the near future influences portfolio investment decisions, Keynes commented that 'part of the explanation which we are seeking is to be found in a psychological phenomenon which appears even more strikingly in the current market valuation of common shares' (1971b, p. 322). To rational outside observers, the degree to which the value of a company's shares tends to be sensitive to short-period fluctuations in its known or anticipated profits would seem absurd. As a cited case example, a railroad company's shares were highly sensitive to weekly traffic returns which are known to be influenced by necessarily transient factors such as good or bad harvests, a strike in the district served by the railroad, or even an international exhibition (1971b, p. 322). Consequently, prices of those shares fluctuate far in excess of any possible changes in profits due to the events in question.

Although Keynes acknowledged the extremity of such cases, he asserted that those who closely follow stock prices will have observed that market valuations exhibit a strong bias toward the assumption that conditions and results characteristic of the present and the recent past, and even more so those which are expected to be characteristic of the near future, will be lasting and permanent. The ignorance of even the best-informed investors about the more remote future is much greater than their knowledge. Inevitably, they will be influenced by the small amount that is known for certain (or almost certain) because that limited knowledge is the main source of any clue about future trends (1971b, p. 323).

If even the best-informed are incompletely informed, the vast majority of people buying and selling securities make their decisions without possessing even the rudiments of the knowledge required for a valid judgement. In such a state of ignorance, they are the prey of hopes and fears that are easily aroused, and just as easily dispelled, by transient events. Keynes remarked that this is one of the odd characteristics of the capitalist system that must not be overlooked when dealing with the real world (1971b, p. 323).

Keynes offered a further reason why the best informed may often profit by anticipating 'mob psychology rather than the real trend of events, and to ape unreason proleptically' (1971b, p. 323). The market valuation of stocks is determined not by expectations of the purchase price of all outstanding shares but rather by the small fringe of those shares that are actually being traded. Most of those involved in that trading are professional financiers or speculators who do not intend to hold the shares long enough for the developments in the more remote future to have any effects. Since their intent is to resell the shares to the mob within a short period, their expectations of the trend in mob psychology, formed largely by their past experiences, will naturally have a substantial influence on their actions. As long as the mob can be relied upon to act in a certain way, whether rational or not, the better-informed professionals will profit by acting in the same way a bit sooner (1971b, pp. 323–4).

In addition, Keynes introduced the factor of human nature. Most people are too timid, greedy, impatient or nervous about their investments to take long views or to place even as much reliance in the dubieties of the long period as might be reasonable. Since fluctuations in the market values of investments can easily wipe out the results of much honest effort, the apparent certainties of the short period, no matter how deceptive they may be suspected to be, are invariably much more attractive (1971b, p. 324).

DETERMINATION OF STOCK PRICES IN *THE GENERAL THEORY*

In *The General Theory*, Keynes stated that capital resources would be allocated to their most profitable uses if investments were made based on their prospective yields over the long term. But he argued that for several reasons, stock prices tend to be influenced by short-term expectations. Defining enterprise as 'the activity of forecasting the prospective yield of assets over their whole life' and speculation as 'the activity of forecasting the psychology of the market' (1936, p. 158), Keynes explained why the latter would often, but not always, tend to predominate.

The analysis of speculative behavior in stock markets in Chapter 12 of *The General Theory*, 'The State of Long-Term Expectation', involves three major factors: human nature, the problem of intractable uncertainty and the institutional features of modern markets for corporate securities. The first two combine to create a speculative psychology on the part of market participants. Since the third only facilitates the influence of the first two on the behavior of those who buy and sell stocks, we will begin with a brief examination of this.

Institutional Features

Keynes argued that speculative tendencies 'are a scarcely avoidable outcome of our having successfully organized "liquid" investment markets' (1936, p. 159). While the motive force is the speculative psychology that influences investors' behavior, several institutional features relating to modern investment markets are important.

First, the separation of ownership and management of modern corporations means that most owners of corporate shares have no personal involvement with the management and no special knowledge of the real or prospective circumstances of those enterprises. Keynes argued that the element of real knowledge in the valuation of investments by those who either already own them or are contemplating purchasing them has seriously declined. As a result, day-to-day fluctuations in profits of existing investments of an ephemeral and non-significant character tend to have an excessive, often even an absurd, influence on the market. He cited as examples the rise of prices of icehouse stocks in the summer in the US, and the aforementioned example of railroad stocks in Britain (1936, pp. 153–4).

Second, by providing opportunities to sell shares of ownership quickly, organized investment markets made 'liquid' for individuals investments which are fixed for the community, and which in earlier days would have been fixed for individuals as well. Prior to the emergence of modern exchanges, decisions to invest in private business depended on a supply of people who chose to be in business as a way of life, with no precise calculation of prospective profit and with investment decisions being largely irrevocable. But modern stock markets revalue many investments every day, and those revaluations give a frequent opportunity to the individual (but not to the community as a whole) to revise his or her commitments. Keynes likened the ability to quickly sell one's investments in the stock market, and just as quickly buy them back, to a situation in which a farmer could move his capital out of and back into the farming business whenever he chose within a very short period (1936, p. 151).

A third institutional feature, which may be much more important today than in Keynes' time, was the pressure on institutional investment managers to take short-run views. Perhaps based on his own experiences, Keynes somewhat bitterly stated that:

... it is the long-term investor, he who most promotes the public interest, who will in practice come in for most criticism, wherever investment funds are managed by committees or boards or banks. For it is the essence of his behavior that he should be eccentric, unconventional and rash in the eyes of average opinion. If he is successful, that will only confirm the general belief in his rashness; and if in the short run, he is unsuccessful, which is very likely, he will not receive much mercy. Worldly wisdom teaches that it is better for reputation to fail conventionally than to succeed unconventionally. (1936, pp. 157–8).

In a footnote, Keynes commented that the practice of institutional investors to calculate capital gains as well as income from their investment portfolios further contributed to a heavy interest in short-term price changes (1936, p. 157, fn).

Human Nature

In Volume II of *Treatise*, Keynes described most people as being too timid, greedy, impatient or nervous about their investments to take long views. In *The General Theory*, he commented further, explaining why those buying stocks typically take a short-run view: 'life is not long enough – human nature desires quick results, there is a peculiar zest in making money quickly, and remoter gains are discounted by the average man at a very high rate' (1936, p. 157). In addition, he spoke of a 'gambling instinct', which many do not have, and to which those possessing it must pay 'the appropriate toll', presumably in losses (1936, p. 157).

There is also the element of 'animal spirits', defined as 'a spontaneous urge to action rather than inaction', which results in 'spontaneous optimism' (1936, p. 161). This merits special note because it is sometimes interpreted as part of Keynes' discussion of the speculative psychology of stock market participants. That interpretation, at least on an explicit basis, is not correct. Keynes stated that 'Even apart from the instability due to speculation, there is the instability due to the characteristic of human nature that a large proportion of our positive activities depend on spontaneous optimism rather than on a mathematical expectation' (1936, p. 161).

Moreover, the discussion of animal spirits was actually in terms of the effects of spontaneous optimism on the undertaking of new businesses or 'enterprise'. Keynes argued that if entrepreneurs in the real world made their decisions based on exact mathematical calculations of expected profits and losses, few new enterprises would be started. Individual initiatives to undertake new ventures will be adequate only when 'reasonable calculation' of outcomes is supplemented and supported by the animal spirits producing hopes of future benefits sufficient to suppress fears of losses (1936, p. 162).

But while Keynes did not explicitly relate 'animal spirits' to the behavior of those buying stocks, he did state as a general proposition that positive activities depend more on spontaneous optimism than on mathematical expectation, 'whether moral or hedonistic or economic' (1936, p. 161). Thus there is ample reason to expect that same element of 'spontaneous optimism' to play an important role in influencing the decisions to purchase shares of stocks.

The Problem of Uncertainty

We now come to what is perhaps the core element in Keynes' explanation of why decisions to buy or sell stocks rest on short-term expectations, and why those expectations conventionally rest on 'what average opinion expects the average opinion to be' (1936, p. 156). That element is the problem of uncertainty and how individual investors attempt to cope with that problem.

In *The General Theory*, Keynes explained that the marginal efficiency of capital depends on the relation between the supply price of a capital asset and its prospective yield. The latter is determined 'not by the "best" opinion' but rather 'by the market valuation as determined by mass psychology' (1936, p. 170). Expectations of prospective yields depend on partly existing facts which can be assumed to be known more or less for certain, but also on future events which can only be forecasted with varying degrees of confidence. Keynes referred to the state of psychological expectation which covers the latter as the 'state of long-term expectation' (1936, pp. 147–9).

A critical factor introduced in *The General Theory* that was missing from the anticipatory discussion in Volume II of *Treatise* was the 'state of confidence' as a major determinant of the marginal efficiency of capital. Keynes asserted that economists had not carefully analyzed this determinant. Long-term expectations depend not just on the most probable forecast, but also on the confidence which investors attach to the forecast (1936, pp. 148–9). In forming expectations, facts about the existing situation exert a disproportionate influence. Investors cannot reasonably assign significant weight to matters that are very uncertain, and will be guided instead on facts which are known with some degree of confidence, even if they are not particularly relevant to long-run yields. In the 1937 *Quarterly Journal of Economics* article, Keynes explained that uncertainty meant that no probability could be assigned to it: 'We simply do not know' (1973b, pp. 113–14).

The Nature of Speculative Psychology

The two elements of human nature and intractable uncertainty combine to produce a speculative psychology, which involves 'conventions'. Keynes acknowledged that conclusions about the state of confidence in forecasts must mainly depend upon the actual observations of markets and business psychology. Thus he stated that 'This is the reason why the ensuing discussion is on a different level of abstraction from most of this book' (1936, p. 149). But a generalized fact is the extreme precariousness of the basis of knowledge on which estimates of prospective yield must be made.

In effect, investors have tacitly agreed to rely on a convention or practical rule: to assume that the existing market valuation (however arrived at) is uniquely correct in relation to existing knowledge of facts which influence yields of investment and that the market valuation will change only in proportion to changes in that knowledge (1936, pp. 152–3). Keynes elaborated further in his 1937 *Quarterly Journal of Economics* article. The 'convention' that investors fall back on has three important principles: (1) the prospect of future changes, which cannot be known, is largely ignored by assuming the present provides a 'more serviceable guide to the future' than historical experience indicates; (2) current prices are assumed to reflect the existing state of opinion which correctly sums up future prospects; and (3) each investor attempts to conform with the behavior of the average behavior of market participants. Thus 'The psychology of a society of individuals each of whom is endeavouring to copy the others leads to what we may strictly call a conventional judgement' (1973a, p. 114).

Even though these valuations are not uniquely correct, there will be a considerable measure of continuity and stability so long as investors can rely on the maintenance of the convention. With organized stock markets providing 'liquidity', each investor feels that the only risk that he faces is of a genuine change in the news over the near future. Since his own judgement is shaped by the convention, he does not think the likelihood of such a change is very great, and if it does appear imminent, he will have time to revise judgement and change investments before very much happens. Thus the investment seems reasonably 'safe' for the individual investor in the short run and hence over a succession of short periods, without any concern about the long run (1936, pp. 152–3).

The Behavior of Professionals

In conventional market theory, competition between expert professionals possessing both judgement and knowledge would be expected to correct the vagaries of the ignorant individual left to him or herself. But Keynes argued that the energies and skills of professionals in the stock market are mainly employed in attempting to foresee changes in the conventional basis of valuation a short time ahead of the general public (1936, p. 154). Professionals 'are concerned, not with what an investment is really worth to a man who buys it "for keeps", but with what the market will value it at, under the influence of mass psychology, three months or a year hence' (1936, pp. 154–5). This is the inevitable result of an investment market organized along the lines described above: 'For it is not sensible to pay 25 for an investment of which you believe the prospective yield to justify a value of 30, if you also believe that the market will value it at 20 three months hence' (1936, p. 155). Thus the professional investor is forced to be concerned with anticipating impending changes of the kind which experience has shown exert the most influence on the mass psychology of the market.

In one of his better-known passages, Keynes laid much of the blame on the 'liquidity' provided by modern stock markets:

> This is the inevitable result of investment markets organized with a view to so-called 'liquidity'. Of the maxims of orthodox finance none, surely, is more anti-social than the fetish of liquidity, the doctrine that it is a positive virtue on the part of investment institutions to concentrate their resources upon the holding of 'liquid' securities. It forgets that there is no such thing as liquidity of investment for the community as a whole. The social object of skilled investment should be to defeat the dark forces of time and ignorance which envelop our future. The actual, private object of the most skilled investment today is to 'beat the gun', as the Americans so well express it, to outwit the crowd, and to pass the bad or depreciating, half-crown to the other fellow. (1936, p. 155)

Describing this as a game similar to Snap, Old Maid or Musical Chairs, which professionals in the stock market can play even when trading among themselves, Keynes noted that it does not require any faith in the long-term validity of the conventional basis of valuation. It only requires not acting too quickly or too slowly. Keynes then changed the metaphor to the then popular newspaper competitions which involved picking the prettiest face out of a hundred photographs, with the winner choosing the face which comes closest to the average preferences of all the competitors as a whole. Strategically, each individual attempts to pick not the face that he finds the prettiest but the one he thinks will most likely appeal to the other competitors, each of whom is attempting to follow the same strategy. The result is that intelligence becomes devoted 'to anticipating what average opinion expects the average opinion to be' (1936, pp. 155–6).

Keynes acknowledged that there are some serious-minded individuals in the market who continue to purchase investments on the best genuine long-term expectations they can form. But he cited several factors which work against the predominance of such individuals in modern investment markets. One of these is an element of human nature that we noted above, namely, the tendency to want quick results, the desire to make money quickly. For those lacking the gambling instinct, long-term investment is very boring. Another factor is also one that we noted above, namely, that institutional investment managers are under pressure to concentrate on short-run gains (1936, p. 157).

Two other factors also come into play. First, investment based on genuine long-term expectation is so difficult as to be scarcely practicable. Investors who attempt it have to work harder, assume greater risks and suffer more disastrous mistakes than those who simply try to guess better than the crowd how the crowd will behave. Less intelligence is required simply to 'beat the gun' than to defeat the forces of time and ignorance of the future. Second, an investor who proposes to ignore short-term market fluctuations will need greater resources for safety and will be unable to operate on as large a scale, or not at all, on borrowed funds (1936, p. 157).

CONSEQUENCES OF STOCK MARKET SPECULATION

Because of the famous following passage, Keynes is often interpreted as a 'bubble' theorist who saw all stock markets as simply gambling casinos:

> Speculators may do no harm as bubbles on a steady stream of enterprise. But the position is serious when enterprise becomes the bubble on a whirlpool of speculation. When the capital development of a country becomes the by-product of the activities of a casino, the job is likely to be ill-done. (1936, p. 159)

Thus Keynes' theory of speculation in stock markets was very broad. It allowed for both episodes of relatively mild chronic speculation (bubbles on a steady stream of enterprise) and instances in which the forces of speculation become so strong as to create speculative manias (whirlpools of speculation upon which float bubbles of enterprise).

Chronic Speculation

Keynes' comments on the LSE and Wall Street are illustrative of differing degrees of the influence of speculation on stock prices. Keynes thought the influence of speculation was much greater in the New York market: 'The measure of success attained by Wall Street, regarded as an institution of which the proper social purpose is to direct new investment into the most profitable channels in terms of future yields, cannot be claimed as one of the outstanding triumphs of *laissez-faire* capitalism' (1936, p. 159). The differences between the extent to which speculation influenced the London and New York markets were due to both psychological and institutional reasons. With respect to the former, Keynes suggested that 'Americans are apt to be unduly interested in discovering what average opinion believes average opinion to be; and this national weakness finds its nemesis in the stock market' (1936, p. 159). Americans are by nature speculators, buying only in hopes that changes will produce short-run capital gains.   In contrast, many Englishmen still purchased stocks for income. A similar argument had been made earlier. In a 1932 lecture on the world's economic crisis and the way of escape, Keynes commented that while common stock values were notoriously volatile in America, it was only an extreme example of the general case 'owing to the psychology of its people' (1981, pp. 51–2).

But while Americans were more prone than Englishmen to be speculators in the stock market, the predominance of speculation in Wall Street was not entirely due to differences in 'national character'. In *The General Theory*, Keynes noted several institutional factors that kept the LSE inaccessible and very expensive to the average Englishman: the jobber's 'turn', high brokerage charges and a heavy transfer tax payable to the Exchequer (1936, pp. 159–60).

Keynes indicated that speculation may occur in a mild chronic form by his cautionary statement at the end of Chapter 12 that it should not be concluded that everything depends on waves of irrational psychology. On the contrary, the state of long-term expectation is often steady and, even when it is not, the other factors exert their compensating effects.   In discussing both speculative psychology and 'animal spirits', Keynes was reminding his readers that: (1) human decisions affecting the future cannot depend on strict mathematical expectation, since the basis for making such calculation simply does not exist; and (2) that an innate urge to activity is what 'makes the wheels go round'. Keynes described this decision-making process as one in which our 'rational selves' choose 'between the alternatives as best as we are able, calculating where we can, but often falling back for our motive on whim or sentiment or change' (1936, p. 163).

Keynes also mentioned several important factors which tend to mitigate the effects of our ignorance of the future. While he was referring more directly to new investment rather than to stock market investments, one cited case seems to be quite relevant to the relationship between stock prices and prospective yields. Keynes stated that for many individual investments, the prospective yield is legitimately dependent upon short-term yields due to both the operation of compound interest and the likelihood of obsolescence with the passage of time (1936, pp. 163–4).

In addition, Keynes stated that after giving full consideration of the influence of short-period changes in the state of long-term expectations, changes in the rate of interest will still have a substantial, though not decisive, influence on the rate of investment in 'normal circumstances' (1936, p. 164). Clearly, this suggests that any speculation that exists in the stock market exerts a relatively mild influence on stock prices, such that their short-term fluctuations do not cause much fluctuation in the marginal efficiency of capital.

Something along these lines seemed to be suggested earlier in Volume II of *Treatise*. After describing the psychological 'half-unreasonable' characteristics of the market, Keynes argued that depending upon these characteristics is not as precarious as it might seem. Indeed, it was a case of a 'homeopathic cure'. These characteristics are the source of many of the troubles which monetary management seeks to remedy. If investors were capable of taking longer views, fluctuations in the natural rate of interest, that is, the rate which equates the level of new investment with the level of savings, would be milder since the real prospects do not suffer such large and quick changes as the spirit of enterprise. Since the willingness to invest is stimulated and depressed by immediate prospects, depending on short-term influences for countering a violent and perhaps unreasoning change in sentiment is not unreasonable (1971b, pp. 322-4).

In the last paragraph of Chapter 12 of *The General Theory*, Keynes stated that 'it seems likely that the fluctuations in the market estimate of the marginal efficiency of different types of capital, calculated on the principles I have described above, will be too great to be offset by any practicable changes in the rate of interest' (1936, p. 164). This clearly indicates that Keynes thought stock market prices would be so strongly influenced by short-term expectations, which rest on precarious foundations, that stock price fluctuations would lead to changes in the marginal efficiency of capital that could not be offset by changes in the interest rate. Does this mean that he was a 'bubble theorist'?

Speculative Manias, Bubbles and Crashes

Despite Keynes' oft-quoted comment about enterprise becoming a bubble on a whirlpool of speculation, and the historical fact of the Great Crash of 1929, his comments on the more acute cases of speculative bubbles that end in equally spectacular crashes were actually rather brief and sporadic, both in reference to real-world events (particularly the 1929 crash) and in his more theoretical discussions. While it seems reasonable to assume that the spontaneous optimism of 'animal spirits' could contribute to speculative binges, Keynes did not explicitly make that connection. Rather, as we noted earlier, 'animal spirits' were linked to enterprise. Yet the psychology of speculative manias can easily be viewed as an extreme manifestation of the elements of human nature described by Keynes. In particular, people want quick results, experience a peculiar zest in making money quickly and discount distant gains at very high rates (1936, pp. 156–7).

Moreover, it does not require much of a stretch to conclude that 'animal spirits' could easily produce the manic optimism that is characteristic of stock market bubbles. Keynes further described the nature of unstable stock prices with his statement that as a result of animal spirits, slumps and depressions, fluctuations will tend to be exaggerated and prosperity will tend to be 'excessively dependent on a political and social atmosphere which is congenial to the average business man' (1936, p. 162). Fears aroused by political developments were capable of upsetting 'the delicate balance of spontaneous optimism' which rests on the 'nerves and hysteria and even the digestions and reactions to the weather' of those who invest (1936, p. 162). Again, while Keynes was speaking of entrepreneurs, the same pattern would seem easily to apply to stock market investors.

Several passages in both *Treatise* and *The General Theory* suggest that Keynes' theory of speculative stock markets can easily accommodate extreme cases such as the 1929 crash. In 'The Applied Theory of Money', Keynes stated that because the 'vast majority' of investors in corporate stocks 'do not possess even the rudiments of what is required for a valid judgement', they 'are the prey of hopes and fears easily aroused by transient events and as easily dispelled' (1971b, p. 323). He expanded upon that subject in *The General Theory*:

> A conventional valuation which is established as the outcome of the mass psychology of a large number of ignorant individuals is liable to change violently as the result of a sudden fluctuation of opinion due to factors which do not really make much difference to the prospective yield; since there will be no strong roots of conviction to hold it steady. In abnormal times in particular, when the hypothesis of an indefinite continuance of the existing state of affairs is less plausible than usual even though there are no express grounds to anticipate a definite change, the market will be subject to waves of optimistic and pessimistic sentiment, which are unreasoning and yet in a sense legitimate where no solid basis exists for a reasonable calculation. (1936, p. 154)

In his discussion of the trade cycle in *The General Theory*, Keynes described the onset of the 'crisis' in terms of a sudden collapse in the marginal efficiency of capital which is based on precarious expectations of the future yield on new capital goods:

> It is of the nature of organized investment markets, under the influence of purchasers largely ignorant of what they are buying and of speculators who

are more concerned with forecasting the next shift of market sentiment than with a reasonable estimate of the future yield of capital-assets, that, when disillusion falls upon an over-optimistic and over-bought market, it should fall with sudden and even catastrophic force. (1936, pp. 315–16)

This was repeated in his 1937 *Quarterly Journal of Economics* article as Keynes elaborated on the conventional rules that guide rational investors in the face of great ignorance of future events.   After listing the three important principles – the assumption that the present is more revealing than past experience would suggest; the assumption that the existing state of opinion reflected in current prices is based on a correct view of future prospects; and a strategy of attempting to conform with the behavior of average opinion – Keynes stated that such a flimsy foundation is subject to sudden and violent swings:

> The practice of calmness and immobility, of certainty and security, suddenly breaks down. New fears and hopes will, without warning, take charge of human conduct. The forces of disillusion may suddenly impose a new conventional basis of valuation. All these petty, polite techniques, made for a well-paneled board room and a nicely regulated market, are liable to collapse. At all times the vague panic fears and equally vague and unreasoned hopes are not really lulled, and lie but a little way below the surface. (1973b, pp. 114–15)

In *Treatise*, Keynes commented that the 1929 crash was only one contributing factor to the slump of 1930, but

> ... it greatly aggravated matters, especially in the United States, by causing a disinvestment in working capital. Moreover, it also promoted the development of profit deflation in two other ways – by discouraging investment and by encouraging saving. The pessimism and the atmosphere of disappointment which the stock-market collapse engendered reduced enterprise and lowered the natural rate of interest; whilst the 'psychological' poverty which the collapse of money values brought with it probably increased saving. (1971a, p. 176)

Stock Market Credit and Speculation

The role of debt in speculative markets was not stressed in *The General Theory*, but operating on borrowed funds seemed to be a normal practice in Keynes' discussion of security prices in *Treatise*. Where a divergence of opinion developed, those of a bearish sentiment loan, either through the intermediation of banks or more directly through broker loans, to those of a bullish sentiment who prefer to carry securities on borrowed funds.

The use of debt for speculation was indicated in Keynes' comment on professional financiers as 'speculators':

> The value of a security is determined, not by the terms on which one could expect to purchase the whole block of the outstanding interest, but by the small fringe which is the subject of actual dealing: ... Now this fringe is largely dealt in by professional financiers – speculators you may call them – who have no intention of holding the securities long enough for the influence of distant events to have its effect; their object is to re-sell to the mob after a few weeks or at most a few months. It is natural, therefore, that they should be influenced by the cost of borrowing ... (1971b, pp. 323–4)

At the same time that Keynes was discussing the division of the money supply between the industrial circulation and the financial circulation and the lending of savings of bears to the bulls who prefer to carry securities on borrowed funds, and was arguing that the monetary authorities should keep the terms of lending and the total money supply at sufficient levels to satisfy financial circulation while providing the optimum amount for industrial circulation, Machlup (1940) was defending the stock market from the charge that speculative stock markets 'absorb' credit and capital, and Fisher (1930) was arguing that the excessive increases in stock prices in 1929 (above the justifiably high plateau of prices based on expected future earnings) was due to the influence of too easy credit.

There is a hint of that issue in Keynes' comment with respect to the dual function of the banking system – the direction of the supply of resources for working capital through loans to producers and the industrial circulation and the direction of the supply of resources through the investments (presumably bonds) it purchases directly and the loans made to the stock exchange and to people carrying stock on borrowed funds, and of the supply of money needed for the financial circulation to satisfy the bullishness of the financial sentiment so as to prevent its reacting on the value and volume of investment. Keynes remarked that 'respectable bankers' in London, though perhaps not in New York, would like to avoid the second function because they view financial business as not being self-liquidating and savoring of speculation (1971b, pp. 310–11).

Keynes expressed doubt about that view, noting that financial loans are more liquid than industrial loans and probably lead to fewer defaults. On the issue of lending to speculators, he commented that banks do have to be more on the lookout against ill-informed and reckless borrowers in making financial loans, but other types of loans should also sometimes be encouraged and sometimes be discouraged (1971b, pp. 311–12).

Speculating with borrowed funds was briefly mentioned several times in *The General Theory*. At one point, Keynes cited two facets of the state of confidence. There is the speculator's confidence in himself, but he does not have unlimited command over money at the market rate of interest. The second facet is the state of confidence of the lending institutions toward those seeking to borrow, sometimes described as the state of credit. A collapse in stock prices may be due to a weakening of either the speculative confidence or lenders' confidence, but a recovery requires an increase in both (1936, p. 158), which suggests that debt is a necessary but not sufficient condition for a speculative rise in prices.

The contribution of borrowed funds to a speculative market was also indicated by Keynes' inclusion as one of the factors that discourages long-term investment strategies the necessity for the investor to operate less on borrowed funds (1936, p. 157). In conjunction with that observation, it may be noted that Keynes' own personal investments were usually highly leveraged (see Keynes 1983, p. 12). Still, in a 1928 paper which utilized the type of analysis he was developing in *Treatise*, Keynes argued that 'the importance of call money to the stock market, except over short periods, is overestimated' (1973b, p. 58).

CONTROLLING SPECULATIVE MARKETS

Keynes was rather limited in his suggestions for controlling speculation. In *The General Theory*, he stated that no maxim of orthodox finance is more anti-social than the 'fetish of liquidity', and that 'The spectacle of modern investment markets has sometimes moved me towards the conclusion that to make the purchase of an investment permanent and indissoluble, like marriage, except by death or other grave cause, might be a useful remedy for our contemporary evils' (1936, p. 160).

On a more practical basis, the resemblance of stock exchanges to casinos led Keynes to comment that it is usually agreed that casinos should be regulated in the public interest, making them inaccessible and expensive. Certain institutional factors had kept the speculative forces more at bay in the LSE: the high jobber's 'turn', high brokerage charges and the heavy transfer tax combined to reduce the liquidity of the market (1936, pp. 159–60). Keynes suggested that a 'substantial Government transfer tax' on transactions in the New York market might serve to reduce the extent of speculative trading. This would force the investor to direct his mind to the long-term prospects only.

But as Keynes' critics, such as Merton Miller, are prone to note, he remarked that a little consideration reveals a dilemma, namely, that while the liquidity of investment sometimes impedes the course of new investment it often also facilitates it. The thought that his commitment is liquid tends to calm the nerves of the individual investor and makes him more willing to accept the risk. If individual purchases of investments were illiquid, new investment would likely be severely impeded as long as the individual had alternative ways of holding his savings. As long as individuals can employ their wealth by either holding or lending money, they will not be very interested in purchasing actual assets unless they know that those assets can quickly be sold in organized investment markets (1936, p. 160).

Federal Reserve Policies

Keynes was critical of the actions taken by the Federal Reserve before and after the 1929 crash. In a paper written in September 1928, he argued that the Federal Reserve had misinterpreted the rise in stock prices as a sign of inflation (1973b, pp. 57–8). He argued against the Federal Reserve using a tight money policy to curb the rise in stock prices, stating that except over short periods, the importance of call money to the stock market was over-estimated: 'What really matters to the stock market is how the ordinary investor is feeling about the business outlook' (1973b, p. 58). Tight money would not curb stock prices on its own, but it could cause a depression that in turn would depress stock prices. Past experiences suggested that stock prices were destined to go to levels above any reasonable criterion, even with 'good trade as a permanency,' and 'will, in due course, boil over of themselves' (1973b, p.58). Keynes suggested that

> The way to keep a head of steam on stock price and to prevent them from boiling over is to fasten down a lid on the saucepan at present. It may be that it is call money reasonable in quantity and price, with A (a bear) frightened into repurchasing, perhaps against his better judgement, and nothing more to go for, which will preclude the ultimate decline. (1973b, pp. 58–9)

In Volume II of *Treatise*, Keynes wrote that in 1929 'genuine' borrowers, those borrowing for purposes of actual new investment, had been squeezed out of the market by a combination of the Federal Reserve's tight money policy and the increasing presence of 'artificial' borrowers, a group which included speculative borrowers who were borrowing short term to participate in the stock market (1971b, pp. 341–42).

On 25 October 1929, the day after the first round of selling in the New York market, Keynes sent a cable to the *New York Evening Post* that presented a 'British View of the Wall Street Slump' (1981, pp. 1–3). He expressed relief over what appeared to be the removal of 'an incumbus which has been lying heavily on the business life of the whole world outside America' (1981, p. 1) and took a rather optimistic view. While British markets had had problems with some speculative stocks, 'first-class British securities are stronger in the market now than they have been for some time and there is in authoritative circles a new spirit of hopefulness about the future' (1981, pp. 1–2). Interest rates had been driven so high world-wide by the 'extraordinary speculation in Wall Street' that new enterprise outside America had been depressed and commodity prices were falling (1981, p. 2). Keynes described this as being due 'to a wholly artificial cause' which if it had lasted another six months would have produced 'a real disaster' (1981, p. 2). The Wall Street crash raised the prospect of falling interest rates which would result in a world-wide recovery of enterprise.

Keynes conceded that he might be 'a bad prophet' but was certain that he was 'reflecting the instinctive reaction of English financial opinion as to the immediate situation' (1981, p. 2). He predicted that the London market would not suffer any serious direct consequence from 'the Wall Street slump' except for some 'Anglo-American securities' (1981, p. 2). The longer run was less certain, but Keynes had no doubts about the stimulative effects of lower interest rates, once they arrived: 'The world always underestimates the influence of dear money as a depressing influence and of cheap money as a reviving one' because of the lag between cause and effect (1981, p. 3).

After the 1929 crash, Keynes continued to be critical of the Federal Reserve's pre-crash attempt to curb stock market speculation:

> The high market rate of interest which, prior to the collapse, the Federal Reserve System, in their effort to control the enthusiasm of the speculative crowd, caused to be enforced in the United States – and, as a result of sympathetic self-protective action, in the rest of the world – played an essential part in bringing about the rapid collapse. For this punitive rate of interest could not be prevented from having repercussion on the rate of new investment both in the United States and throughout the world, and was bound, therefore, to preclude an era of falling prices and business losses everywhere. (1971b, p. 176)

If liquidity is necessary to make individuals willing to hold investments rather than liquid assets, and if monetary policy cannot curb inflation, what can be done? One of Keynes' more frequently cited comments appeared in his discussion of the trade cycle:

> Thus with markets organized and influenced as they are at present, the market estimation of the marginal efficiency of capital may suffer such enormously wide fluctuations that it cannot be sufficiently offset by corresponding fluctuations in the interest rate. Moreover, the corresponding movements in the stock-market may, as we have seen above, depress the marginal propensity to consume just when it is most needed. In conditions of *laissez faire* the avoidance of wide fluctuations in employment may,

therefore, prove impossible without a far-reaching change in the psychology of investment markets such as there is no reason to expect. I conclude that the duty of ordering the current volume of investment cannot be safely left in private hands. (1936, p. 320)

CONCLUDING STATEMENT

In Volume II of *A Treatise On Money*, Keynes' comments about irrational behavioral tendencies laid the foundation for the expanded discussions of speculative psychology in *The General Theory*. He argued in the latter work that stock prices are most influenced by a small fringe of speculating traders who profit by anticipating mob psychology rather than focusing on real-world events. Further, he defined speculation as the activity of forecasting the psychology of the market and explained that such activity dominated the determination of stock prices in the short run. He attributed this to the conventions of human nature that desire quick results, are predisposed to spontaneous action and are inherently optimistic. The result is, according to Keynes, that the preponderance of intellectual energy in stock market activity is devoted to anticipating what average opinion expects the average opinion to be (1936, pp. 155–6).

6. Galbraith's Model of Speculative Stock Markets

While Merton Miller (1991) has referred to Keynes as the 'patron saint' of bubble theorists, that title might more fittingly be given to John Kenneth Galbraith, whose institutionalist-historical analyses have focused squarely on great stock market booms and crashes. Galbraith's book, *The Great Crash 1929*, published first in 1955, has become a classic which serves as a financial history complement to Fredrick Lewis Allen's (1931) classic account of the social history of the 'roaring twenties' in *Only Yesterday*. White (1990, p. 67) has stated that 'Galbraith's classic book still provides the most commonly accepted explanation of the 1929 boom and crash'. *The Great Crash 1929* was reissued in 1988 without textual changes, but in a new Introduction entitled '1929 and the Crash of '87', Galbraith provided a post-crash analysis of the Reagan bull market and its collapse in October 1987. Galbraith's comment on why the book has stayed in print since 1955 is as follows: 'At any moment when it might otherwise be dropping out of sight, some new euphoric episode and the aftermath have restored it to relevance' (1994, p. xii).

Galbraith also has the distinction of being the only economist blamed for a drop in the market. In 1955, the publication of *The Great Crash 1929* coincided with the stock market's recent recovery of the pre-1929 crash high after a period of some 25 years. With the market on a bull run, Galbraith was asked to give expert testimony on the state of the stock market before the Senate Banking Committee. While he was speaking to the committee, stock prices began falling. The news media immediately reported the downturn as the market's reaction to Galbraith's comments on speculative markets before the Senate Committee, proclaiming that 'Egghead Scrambles Stockmarket'.

Although that incident was indicative only of the media's susceptibility to false impressions of cause and effect, Galbraith's reputation as the leading authority on the nature and pattern of speculative markets was enhanced by a display of prophetic powers in predicting with astonishing accuracy the 1987 crash. In an article in the January 1987 issue of the *Atlantic Monthly*, entitled 'The 1929 Parallel', Galbraith described striking similarities between the bull markets of the 1980s and those of the 1920s, and warned that such speculative binges inevitably come to crashing ends. When the largest one-day drop in stock prices in history occurred in October of that year, few, if any, journalists, credited Galbraith for bringing on the crash.

The stock market played a large role in Galbraith's novel, *A Tenured Professor*. In the story, a young Harvard economics professor develops a highly successful model for predicting stock prices, not based on 'rational behavior, rational responses, rational expectations', but on 'irrational expectations' (1990, p. 10).

It should be noted, however, that Galbraith's concern with speculative bubbles and stock market crashes stands virtually isolated from his broader institutional theory of modern corporate capitalism presented in varying stages in *American Capitalism* (1952) and *The Affluent Society* (1958) and developed fully in *The New Industrial State* (1971). The stock market merits little attention in the general Galbraithian theory because the large corporations administered by the informal collective entity of the various specialists within the organization (the 'technostructure') have achieved considerable autonomy from both the financial markets and stockholders. With respect to the supply of capital, Galbraith stated that 'No form of market uncertainty is so serious as that involving the terms and conditions on which capital is obtained' (1971, p. 38). But the large corporations have reduced that uncertainty by securing sources of capital from their own earnings, thereby escaping 'the risks of the market' (1971, p. 38). However, no attempt is made to reconcile Galbraith's work on speculative stock markets and his general theory of corporate enterprise since that work stands solidly on its own.

AN INSTITUTIONALIST MODEL OF SPECULATIVE MARKETS

In Chapter 1 we noted Kindleberger's response to the conventional theorists who have tended to dismiss the literature on speculative markets as merely anecdotal. No doubt that charge would be leveled particularly at Galbraith's work because of the style in which his analytical examination of speculative markets has been presented. In *The Great Crash 1929*, Galbraith was highly critical of the conventional theory of stock markets and especially of speculative bubbles and their consequences. The book is largely a historical account, often humorous, of developments and events prior to, during and after the great bull market of the 1920s, which ended in what was, until the 1987 crash, the worst stock market collapse in history. As such, it added substantially to the history of the 'roaring twenties' documented in Allen's *Only Yesterday*. But somewhat loosely woven into the historical narrative is an institutionalist model of speculative bubbles which Galbraith briefly summarized in his 1987 article in the *Atlantic Monthly* and again in his new Introduction to the 1988 edition of *The Great Crash 1929*. That model is much more than anecdotal in the sense that Galbraith emphasizes certain constants which emerge as controlling circumstances.

At the very core is a psychological factor in the form of a pervasive mood of financial euphoria, which manifests itself in a social personality trait that leads to an eagerness on the part of a large number of people to speculate on stocks. When this personality trait achieves the status of what Galbraith terms a 'controlling circumstance', stock market speculation becomes central to the culture despite the fact that it is not characterized by massiveness of participation (1988, p. 78). Given the presence of the speculative mood as a motive force, certain institutional factors contribute by facilitating the speculative stock market transactions. Of particular importance are arrangements that allow speculators to operate heavily on borrowed funds, resulting in highly leveraged markets. Finally, certain actions and, equally important, inactions, on the part of public officials contribute to the intensity and prolongation of speculative binges, which make the inevitable crashes that much larger when the bubbles burst.

Galbraith's institutionalist model was developed in *The Great Crash 1929* with specific references to one particular historical episode – the great bull market of the 1920s and its spectacular crash. But as shown by Galbraith's prediction of the 1987 crash and his post-crash analysis in the Introduction to the 1988 edition of *The Great Crash 1929*, the model is of a general form which makes it applicable to any case situation in which the requisite factors happen to combine. As Galbraith stated: 'It can be said with some assurance that in economic, social, and political matters, if the controlling circumstances are the same or similar, then so will be at least some of the consequences' (1988, p. xi).

With the events leading up to the 1987 crash paralleling those of the 1920s in a number of ways, the consequences would predictably be similar:

> ... financial history was subject to the same controlling circumstances. In consequence, what happened in 1987 was more or less predictable, and anyone familiar with the 1929 experience (and with other past cycles of financial euphoria and not infrequent insanity) was under a strong compulsion to predict it. (1988, p. xii)

In a footnote, however, Galbraith referred to his own prediction in the *Atlantic Monthly* article, but modestly counseled that 'all economists should be duly cautious in citing their valid predictions' (1988, p. xii).

ORGANIZATION OF THE CHAPTER

Our tasks in the next two sections of this chapter are to examine Galbraith's institutionalist model of speculative stock markets in terms of the psychology of speculative manias and the contributing institutional factors. In the final section, we examine Galbraith's views on the consequences of speculative manias which inevitably end in crashes, and on policies and actions by the appropriate officials to control speculative manias. The implications of the stock market's strong recovery from the 1987 crash and the new bull market that continue to run in 1999 for Galbraith's analysis of speculative stock markets will be considered in Chapter 8.

THE PSYCHOLOGY OF SPECULATIVE MANIAS

The key theme of Galbraith's model is that the driving force behind all speculative manias is mass psychology of speculative euphoria. What Galbraith termed the 'dynamics of speculation' (1987, p. 62) begin with people initially buying stocks based on their perceptions, which may or may not be accurate, that underlying circumstances justify expectations of rising stock prices in line with the going rates of return on investment. Such perceived circumstances may include improving economic conditions, a weakening of inflation, a tax structure that is more favorable to business profits and capital ownership, the empowerment of a pro-business government, growing corporate profits and large dividends, and declining interest rates. Typically, the price rises dissipate as expectations turn pessimistic. But on occasion, the powerful motive force of speculative psychology emerges and exerts its influence over the mentality of market participants. On this 'indispensable element of substance' that justifies some increase in stock prices, a 'world of speculative make-believe' is built (1988, p. 3) as a classic speculative bubble develops.

Galbraith rejected the argument that people will always speculate if only they can get the money (1988, p. 11) and the long-accepted explanation that easy credit in 1929 impelled people to borrow money to speculate on stocks (1988, p. 169). While a speculative bubble rests on a highly leveraged market, as we note in the next section, speculation does not start simply because of easy money. In fact, the cost of borrowing was relatively high in 1928 and 1929: 'Far more important than rate of interest and the supply of credit is the mood. Speculation on a large scale requires a pervasive sense of confidence and optimism and a conviction that ordinary people were meant to be rich' (1988, p. 169).

This may be the normal mind-set for a few, those who perennially expect to find the philosopher's stone or the pot of gold at the end of the rainbow.

But it runs counter to the habitual frame of mind that has been conditioned by life's harsh and frequently disappointing experiences in most people. As Galbraith expressed it, 'When people are cautious, questioning, misanthropic, suspicious, or mean, they are immune to speculative enthusiasms' (1988, p. 170). How does a large number of people who are ordinarily endowed with a healthy sense of skepticism come to accept a view that they would normally scorn as being foolishly irrational and unrealistic?

Galbraith does not pretend to identify the source of the speculative psychology. Rather, he states flatly that 'We do not know why a great speculative orgy occurred in 1928 and 1929' (1988, p. 169). But once such a speculative mania emerges, the psychological characteristics and behavioral pattern of development are quite clear.

Any long-continued increase in stock prices brings about a change in the perception of the participants in the market that can best be described as a mood change that results in a mentality warp. The psychological elements that spawn and sustain a classic speculative bubble manifest themselves in a particular personality trait that is marked by the convergence of an inordinate desire to get rich quickly with a minimum of physical effort (1988, p. 3) and a newly gained conviction that ordinary middle-class people are intended for 'quick, effortless enrichment' (1988, pp. 4–5).

Galbraith stressed that the speculative mood originates from internal rather than external sources. There are no evil seductive spin-masters engaging in mass hypnosis or casting spells to cause large numbers of people temporarily to lose their financial sanity. On the contrary, when the speculative mood seizes them, people do not need to be persuaded to believe but rather only seek an excuse to believe (1988, p. 3). It is still necessary to reassure those who require some tie, however tenuous, to reality. But while the process of assurance achieves the status of a profession, with many 'official optimists' (1988, p. 70) explaining (for fees or to encourage commissions on frequent trades) why there are perfectly good reasons for rising stock prices, people are not seeking to be persuaded of the reality of things but only to find excuses for escaping into the new world of fantasy (1988, pp. 11–12).

Nor is 'easy money' the factor that induces the speculative mood. While Galbraith assigned a prominent role to debt as an institutional contributor to a speculative bubble, such that speculative markets invariably are highly leveraged, the proposition that people will always speculate if only they can get the money to finance it is invalid (1988, p. 11). There have been numerous periods of easy credit without speculation appearing. Moreover, the cost of borrowed funds was relatively high in 1929 (1988, p. 169). In the absence of the speculative mood of euphoric optimism, low interest rates and easy lending terms simply do not create speculative binges. But when such a mood exists, high interest rates will not contain the demand for borrowed funds to be used for speculative buying.

A related aspect of the influence of the speculative mood is a change in people's attitude towards savings. Galbraith argued that as a requisite to a speculative bubble, saving must be plentiful. While speculation is substantially encouraged by use of borrowed funds, it must be nourished in part by those who participate. If savings are growing rapidly, people will place a lower marginal value on their accumulation and will be willing to risk some of it against the prospect of a greatly enhanced return. Speculation, therefore, is most likely to break out after a substantial period of prosperity rather than in the early phases of a recovery from depression (1988, pp. 169–70).

A curious aspect of the speculative mood is an element of faith, an extraordinary willingness to trust in the good intentions and even the benevolence of others. Political, social and business leaders typically regarded with cynicism and distrust suddenly become individuals possessing great wisdom, integrity, vision, financial creativity and strength of both fortune and character. Those most closely associated with the financial markets and institutions are particularly celebrated as modern white knights, since it is through their agency that ordinary people will reap new riches. These remarkably talented and knowledgeable men and women understand how to make the market build their fortunes effortlessly and in the process of so doing happily allow the masses of ordinary people to share in the gains by participating in the rising markets (1988, pp. 79–80)

As the boom develops, the 'big men' loom more and more omnipotent in the perceptions of the speculative minds (1988, pp. 12–13). In the late summer of 1929 'The conviction that the market had become the personal instrument of mysterious but omnipotent men was never stronger' (1988, p. 79). In humorous ridicule of conventional theory, Galbraith explained that this builds on the ritual that is thought to be of great value in influencing the course of the business cycle. By prominent public figures affirming solemnly that prosperity will continue, it is believed that one can help ensure that prosperity will in fact continue (1988, p. 16). Even Wall Street professionals become susceptible to the belief in the power and benevolence of well-positioned insiders. Galbraith noted that the lore of the competitive market portrays the market as the most impersonal of markets, that is, as resembling a perfectly competitive market. The prophets and defenders of the Stock Exchange guard no doctrine more jealously. But even the most devout Wall Streeter allows himself or herself on occasion to believe that more personal forces have a hand in their destiny–that there are somewhere around the 'big men' who put stocks up and put them down (1988, pp. 12–13).

As the speculative bubble develops, people increasingly buy stock only because prices are expected to keep rising (1988, p. 18). At some point, the euphoric mood intensifies and the pure speculative instinct becomes a controlling circumstance. A state of extreme financial delusion now exists. In this fantasy world, individuals and institutions of presumed financial acumen and self-identified genius will confidently ride the market up, secure in the conviction that their special genius will allow them to time the market perfectly so as to sell out just before the end comes (1988, p. xiii).

As the tendency to look beyond the simple fact that market prices are increasing to the reasons on which those market values depend greatly diminishes (1988, p. 4), people exhibit a growing reluctance to concede that the end has come (1988, p. 6). A 'compelling vested interest in euphoria' buoys the bubble along (1987, p. 62). Galbraith noted that before both the 1929 and 1987 crashes

> Those who dissented or doubted were held not to be abreast of the mood of the times; they did not appreciate the new world of Calvin Coolidge and Herbert Hoover or, in these last years, that of the innovative and indominable Ronald Reagan. The vested interest in euphoria leads men and women, individuals and institutions, to believe that all will be better, that they are meant to be richer, and to dismiss as intellectually deficient what is in conflict with that conviction. (1988, pp. xii–xiii)

Yet while the speculative mood is a controlling circumstance, its grip on people appears to be actually rather light, as indicated in Galbraith's statement:

> In 1929, a robust denunciation of speculators and speculation by someone in high authority and a warning that the market was too high would almost certainly have broken the spell. It would have brought some people back from the world of make-believe. Those who were planning to stay in the market as long as possible but still get out (or go short) in time would have got out or gone short. Their occupational nervousness could readily have been translated into an acute desire to sell. Once the selling started, some more vigorously voiced pessimism could easily have kept it going. (1988, p. 32)

The Immunizing Effect of Crashes

As we will discuss in more detail in the final section, speculative manias inevitably end in crashes which occur as the mood of fantastic optimism and confidence turns suddenly to one of panic. But with respect to the mood that induces financial insanity, Galbraith stated that:

... a speculative outbreak has a greater or less immunizing effect. The
ensuing collapse automatically destroys the very mood speculation requires.
It follows that an outbreak of speculation provides a reasonable assurance
that another outbreak will not immediately occur. With time and the
dimming of memory, the immunity wears off. A recurrence becomes
possible. Nothing could have induced Americans to launch a speculative
adventure in the stock market in 1935. By 1955 the chances were very
much better. (1988, p. 171)

The immunizing effect of the crash of the Florida real estate bubble in the
1920s was inconsequential, with the speculative urge finding much more
fertile ground in the stock market. The immunizing effect of the 1929 crash
was much longer lasting, with the market not recovering the pre-1929 crash
high for almost 25 years. But by the 1980s it had apparently completely
disappeared, providing prophetic credence to the observation that Galbraith
made in 1955:

Yet, in some respects the chance for recurrence of a speculative orgy
remains good. No one can doubt that the American people remain
susceptible to the speculative mood – to the conviction that enterprise can be
attended with unlimited rewards in which they, individually, were meant to
share. (1988, p. 189)

Such a recurrence did come in the 1980s, with a new speculative mood
emerging with features similar to that of the 1920s. As in the 1920s, there
were the beliefs that economic matters would only get better and that every
participant was meant to get richer.

Scapegoating

A related aspect of the group behavioral tendencies associated with the
psychological mood shift that drives a speculative bubble is the need to
seek someone or something to blame, to find a scapegoat. Frequently, those
individuals who were given credit for the good times, who received the
greatest adulation when the market was soaring, are subsequently blamed
for its collapse. Galbraith maintains that there is a tendency of capitalism
'to single out for the most ostentatious punishment those on whom it once
seemed to lavish its greatest gifts' (1987, p. 65). Those trusted on the way
up are subsequently blamed for the market's fall. Financial genius before
the fall is the oldest rule of Wall Street (1987, p. 66). Since the
consequence is one of averaging out in that regard, little concern needs to
be spent on those heroes who become the scapegoats. More importantly,
this reflects an unwillingness on the part of the public to concede the true
nature of a speculative binge as an exercise in financial irrationality.

The irrational tendency to assign scapegoats does not mean that certain institutional factors cannot be identified as contributors to the duration and intensity of speculation. On the contrary, while Galbraith offered no explanation for the emergence of that mood – 'We do not know why a great speculative orgy occurred in 1928 and 1929' (1988, p. 169) – he provided a detailed analysis of the institutional developments in the market that provided the great opportunities for the speculative mood to maximize its influence over market participants.

CONTRIBUTING INSTITUTIONAL FACTORS

The ability of the speculative mood to produce a sizeable speculative bubble depends in large part on the existence of institutional arrangements that facilitate speculative buying. Galbraith cited several institutional factors that contributed to speculative manic buying in both the 1920s and the 1980s. These were developments in corporate finance which made speculative trading much easier and with greater leverage per dollar of participants' own money, and tax policies which substantially increased the disposable income of the affluent.

Leveraged Markets

With typical humorous ridicule, Galbraith commented that corporate finance is assumed to lend itself wonderfully to change and development. Both speculation and the underlying euphoria are nourished by whatever is the latest and, it is believed, quite remarkable innovation (1988, p. xiv). In the Introduction to the 1988 edition of *The Great Crash 1929*, Galbraith cited as one of the controlling circumstances in the 1980s which paralleled the 1920s 'the present commitment to seemingly imaginative, currently lucrative, and eventually disastrous innovations in financial structures' which has the consequence of an immensely leveraged market, a structure resting on a mountain of debt (1988, p. xiv). In the speculative bubbles of both 1929 and 1987, 'the core of action was leverage' (1988, p. xv).

At some point in the growth of a speculative boom, an increase in market price becomes the only aspect of property ownership of any relevance. Since the only reward to ownership is the increase in values, speculators crave innovative arrangements that would separate the right to increased value from the other aspects of property ownership. The genius of capitalism is that a real demand does not go long unsatisfied: 'In all great speculative orgies devices have appeared to enable the speculator to concentrate on his business' (1988, p. 18).

Such innovative devices appeared rather abundantly in the 1920s. Florida land speculators were aided by the opportunity to trade in 'binders', negotiable rights to buy which could be obtained by a down payment of 10 percent of the purchase price. The full benefit of the increase in values could be had without owning the property, with only a small amount of money expended (1988, p. 18).

In the practice of allowing stocks to be bought on the margin through brokers' loans to customers, the stock market offered an even better 'design for concentrating the speculative energies of the speculator' (1988, p. 19). While the stocks were held as collateral by the brokerage houses extending the loans, the buyers kept full title to any capital gains as well as to any dividends in exchange for payment of interest on the loan. 'The speculator was willing to pay to divest himself of all of the usufructs of security ownership except the change for a capital gain' (1988, p. 19).

Again in humorous ridicule of conventional institutional poses, Galbraith noted that the purpose, which could not be admitted by Wall Street, of brokers' loans is 'to accommodate the speculator and facilitate speculation'. But that could not be admitted by Wall Street, so by conventional rhetoric margin trading must be defended not on the grounds that it efficiently and ingeniously assists the speculator, but rather that it encourages the extra trading which changes a thin and anemic market into a thick and healthy one. At best, this is a dull and dubious by-product. Even the most circumspect friend of the market must concede that the volume of brokers' loans – collateraled by the securities purchased on margin – is a good index of speculation (1988, pp. 18–20).

Galbraith took special note of the rapid rise in brokers' loans in 1928 and 1929 as an indicator of a speculative binge: 'People were swarming to buy stocks on margin – in other words, to have the increase in price without the costs of ownership' (1988, p. 21). New York banks were rapidly becoming the agents for lenders the country over and even the world over, channeling the funds to the brokerage houses. Galbraith noted why such lending was attractive:

> One of the paradoxes of speculation in securities is that the loans that underwrite it are among the safest of all investments. They are protected by stocks which under all ordinary circumstances are instantly salable, and by a cash margin as well. The money, as noted, can be retrieved on demand. (1988, p. 21)

High rates on these loans attracted lenders: 'A great river of gold began to converge on Wall Street, all of it to help Americans hold common stock on margin. Corporations also found these rates attractive' (1988, p. 22). Some corporations decided to confine themselves to financing speculation rather than producing more output. The New York banks could, in principle, lend funds in the call market for 12 percent which they could borrow from the Federal Reserve Bank at 5 percent (1988, p. 22). This, Galbraith noted, was possibly the most profitable arbitrage operation of all time (1988, p. 22).

Since the Federal Reserve gained the power to set the margin required in the 1930s, low margin requirements were not a parallel feature of the 1980s bull market. But there is a popular view that the ability of speculators to purchase stock index futures contracts (which replicate portfolios of stocks in those indices) on very low initial margins essentially nullified the restrictive effects of the mandated higher margin requirement in the cash market. In its report on the 1987 crash, the Brady Commission concluded that stocks and stock index futures contracts essentially constitute one big market, and recommended that 'Margins should be made consistent to control speculation and financial leverage' (Brady Commission 1989, p. 203).

Pyramiding: Holding Companies and Investment Trusts

While the most important feature of the speculative boom of 1928 and 1929 was the frantic desire of people to buy stocks and the resulting effect on prices, Galbraith argued that the increase in the number of securities to buy was almost as striking and 'the ingenuity and zeal with which companies were devised in which securities might be sold was as remarkable as any' (1988, p. 43). Not all the increase in the volume of securities in 1928 and 1929 was, however, for the sole purpose of accommodating the speculator. Companies could raise funds for general corporate purposes easily without questions from investors.

Reminiscent of the companies that sprang into existence in England during the South Sea Bubble, some new companies were organized in the 1920s for the singular purpose of allowing the promoters to capitalize on public interest in 'industries with a new and wide horizon', however far away that horizon might be (1988, p. 46). But Galbraith noted that '... in the main, the market boom of 1929 was rooted directly or indirectly in existing industries and enterprises. New and fanciful issues for new and fanciful purposes, ordinarily so important in times of speculation, played a relatively small part' (1988, p. 46).

The 1920s was also a time of consolidation and each new merger required some new capital and a new issue of securities to pay for it. This merger movement was different from the previous ones in which the primary motive had been to reduce, eliminate or regularize competition, with each new giant dominating its industry and exercising measurable control over prices and production, and perhaps over investment and the rate of technological innovation. The mergers of the 1920s combined firms doing the same thing in different communities. The purpose was to eliminate the incompetence, somnambulance, naivety or unwarranted integrity of local managements. Central management from New York or Chicago was deemed superior.

For the speculative investor of the 1920s, the two great innovations were the public utility holding companies and the investment trusts. The common feature 'was that they conducted no practical operations; they existed to hold stock in other companies, and these companies frequently existed to hold stock in yet other companies. Pyramiding, it was called' (1987, p. 64). Hailed as financial marvels before the crash, both exemplified what Galbraith described as 'seemingly imaginative, currently lucrative, and eventually disastrous innovation in financial structures' (1987, p. 64).

The holding-company system was utilized to organize the public utilities, issuing securities to buy operating companies: 'Everywhere local power, gas, and water companies passed into the possession of a holding company system' (1988, p. 45). While allegedly organized for the purpose of centralizing management and control of operating companies, the holding companies organized by Samuel Insull and others turned public utilities, traditionally viewed as safe investment outlets for widows, into speculative instruments through the pyramiding process.

Investment Trusts

The most notable piece of speculative architecture of the late 1920s, and the one by which (more than any other device) the public demand for common stocks was satisfied, was the investment trust or company. It did not promote new enterprises or enlarge old ones, but merely arranged that people could own stock in old companies through the medium of new ones. There were limits to the amount of real capital which existing enterprises could use or new ones could be created to employ. The virtue of the investment trust was that it brought about an almost complete divorce of the volume of corporate securities outstanding from the volume of corporate assets in existence. The former could be any multiple of the latter (1988, pp. 46–7).

The volume of underwriting business and of securities available for trading on the exchanges all expanded accordingly. So did the securities to own, for the investment trusts sold more securities than they bought. The difference went into the call market, real estate or the pockets of the promoters (1988, p. 47).

Galbraith commented that it would be difficult to imagine an invention that was better timed or better designed to eliminate the public's anxiety about the possible shortage of common stocks (1988, p. 47). He subsequently compared the investment trusts of the 1920s with the company formed during the South Sea Bubble which did not reveal its purpose, but whose stock was eagerly demanded. As promotions, the investment trusts of 1928 and 1929 were even more wonderful. In 1928, an estimated 186 investment trusts were organized. In 1929, they were being organized at the rate of one per business day, a total of 265 (1988, p. 49).

In nearly all cases the investment trusts were sponsored by another company. A surprising range of companies became involved in bringing trusts into existence – investment banks, commercial banks, brokerage firms, securities dealers and, most important, other investment trusts creating new investment trusts. Ordinarily, the sponsors managed the investment trusts, invested their funds and received fees based on a percentage of capital or earnings. Sponsors that were members of the Stock Exchange received commissions of trading for their trusts. Many were investment banking firms, which meant that those firms were manufacturing securities they could then bring to the market – an excellent way of ensuring an adequate supply of business (1988, pp. 50–51).

The new securities issued by the investment trusts were eagerly demanded by a public willing to pay a sizeable premium over offering prices. The sponsors' promoters received allotments or warrants that allowed them to purchase at offering price and resell at a profit (1988, p. 51). The measure of the public's admiration for the financial genius thought to be associated with investment trusts was the relation between the market value of the trusts' outstanding securities to the value of the securities they owned. Had all the latter been sold, the proceeds would invariably have been less (and often much less) than the current value of their outstanding securities. This premium was in effect the value an admiring community placed on professional financial knowledge, skill and manipulative ability. The special ability, 'the precious ingredient of financial genius', was thought to be able to invoke a whole strategy for increasing the value of securities by joining in pools and syndicates. It was 'in on things', with access to those who really ran Wall Street (1988, p. 54).

Curiously, the development of the investment trusts created 'a golden age' for economics professors. Fully aware of their reputation for omniscience and its importance, the trusts lost no opportunity to enlarge it by having a private, albeit quite tame, economist: 'as the months passed a considerable competition developed for those men of adequate reputation and susceptibility' (1988, p. 55). Galbraith cited several instances in which the tame economists came up lame in their forecasts.

Again, the Factor of Leverage

Knowledge, manipulative skill and financial genius were not the only 'magic' of the investment trusts. There was also leverage. By the summer of 1929, investment trusts were no longer spoken of as such, but rather as high-leveraged, low-leveraged or no-leveraged trusts. Galbraith's analogy for describing the principle of leverage was the game of 'crack-the-whip'. A minor movement near the point of origin is translated into a major jolt on the extreme periphery. In investment trusts, leverage was achieved by issuing bonds and preferred stock, as well as common stock, to purchase, more or less exclusively, a portfolio of common stocks. When the latter rose in value, a tendency that was always assumed, the value of the bonds and preferred stock was largely unaffected. These had a fixed value derived from a specified return. Most or all of the gain from rising portfolio values was concentrated on the common stock of the trust, which rose marvelously. That common stock in turn was frequently bought by another trust with similar leverage. 'In 1929 the discovery of the wonders of the geometric series struck Wall Street with a force comparable to the invention of the wheel' (1988, p. 58).

The miracle of leverage, moreover, made this a relatively costly operation for the ultimate man behind all the trusts. Having launched one trust and retained a share of the common stock, the capital gains from leverage made it relatively easy to swing a second and larger one, which enhanced the gains and made possible a third and still bigger trust. But leverage works both ways, as exemplified by the trust organized by Goldman Sachs.

In association with the speculative mood of euphoria, Galbraith noted that the institutional structures that created the highly leveraged market were surrounded by illusion. Writing months before the 1987 crash, he stated, 'Nothing so gives the illusion of intelligence as personal association with large sums of money' (1987, p. 65). 'The basic fact is that the day will come when it is recognized as illusion, and the burden of debt, triggered by some factor will become insupportable' (1987, p. 65).

Such was clearly the case in 1929, and Galbraith warned that a similar situation had developed in the 1980s. Again, the financial innovations rested on an immense use of leverage in the wave of corporate take-overs, mergers and acquisitions, and leveraged buyouts. 'The mergers, acquisitions, take-overs, leveraged buy-outs, their presumed contribution to economic success and market values, and the burden of debt they incur are the current form of that illusion' (1987, p. 65). Writing after the crash, Galbraith gave the same assessment: 'The manifestation of presumptively innovative corporate finance and design in the 1980s was the corporate mergers and acquisitions mania, the corporate restructuring and leverage buyouts. These presumed innovations, as in the 1920s, involved the substitution of debt for equity; new only was the financing by the admirably denoted junk bonds' (1988, p. xiv). 'The great episode of mergers and acquisitions, leveraged buyouts and junk bonds of recent times was simply a minor variation on the earlier experience. As in 1929, the core of the action was leverage' (1988, p. xv).

Market Manipulation

By the end of the summer of 1929, brokers' bulletins and letters were stating that selected stocks would be 'taken in hand'. The conviction that the market had become the personal instrument of mysterious but omnipotent men was never stronger. This was a period of exceedingly active pool and syndicate operations – in short, of manipulation (1988, p. 79). But Galbraith noted that people did not feel the syndicate operators were shearing them. On the contrary, they viewed the situation as one in which they were being enriched by the actions of the pools as long as they could sense what was going on: 'the public reaction to inside operations was to hope that it might get some inside information on these operations and so get a cut in the profits that the great men ... were making' (1988, p. 80).

The contribution of market manipulation to the fantasy world created by financial illusion propelled by the pure speculative instinct was described by Galbraith's statement that: 'The public at large sensed the attractiveness of these operations, and as the summer passed it came to be supposed that Wall Street was concerned with little else' (1988, p. 80). The consequence was that 'the market came to be considered less and less a long run register of corporate prospects and more and more a product of manipulative artifice' (1988, p. 80).

While manipulation was extensive in the 1920s, it was not a parallel feature of the 1980s market due to the regulations that were implemented in the 1930s. Still, there were those either breaking the laws or stretching the laws:

> The young professionals now engaged in much-admired and no less publicized trading, merger takeover, buy-back, and other deals, as they are called, will one day, we can be sadly sure, suffer a broadly similar fate. Some will go to jail; some are already on the way, for vending, buying, and using inside information. (1987, p. 66)

Tax Policies

Galbraith rejected the 'long accepted explanation that credit was easy and so people were impelled to borrow money to buy common stocks on the margin' as 'obviously nonsense' (1988, p. 169). During 1928 and 1929 most speculation actually occurred on money borrowed at interest rates that would have been considered very high in years before and since. But the Mellon tax cuts of the 1920s and the Reagan tax cuts of the 1980s for the affluent created surpluses that flowed into the stock market rather than into real capital formation or even consumer demand. The financial operations of Wall Street mainly absorbed savings in an inherently sterile activity, with little effect on the productive activity of the companies whose securities were being shuffled. In both cases, the tax cuts sluiced funds into the stock market: 'that is what well-rewarded people regularly do with extra cash' (1988, p. xiv).

In his 1987 article, Galbraith pointed out that in both 1929 and in the 1980s, real capital formation was not stimulated by the tax cuts.

> From the mergers, acquisitions, and buy-backs, it is now reasonably agreed, comes no increase in industrial competence. The young men who serve in the great investment houses render no service to investment decisions, product innovation, production, automation, or labor relations in the companies whose securities they shuffle. They have no real concern with such matters. They do float some issues for new ventures or expanded operations; one concedes this while noting again how dismal is the present showing on real capital investment. Mostly their operations absorb savings into an inherently sterile activity. (1987, p. 66)

In the 1980s, the tax cuts contributed in an indirect way to both the speculative market and the weakening of the economy by the international effects of the huge budget deficits. To check the inflationary effects of those deficits, the Federal Reserve kept interest rates high, which, in Galbraith's view, had the following consequences:

> The high interest rates attracted funds from abroad. These bid up the dollar in foreign exchange markets, and from this came a wonderfully generous subsidy to imports, a marked penalty on exports and a huge deficit in the American balance of trade. Foreign, notably Japanese, goods became lodged in our markets and, unlike old-fashioned commodities, once lodged were not easily dislodged as the dollar fell. The dollars that accumulated in foreign hands also made their way to Wall Street in substantial amount. (1988, p. xvii)

CONSEQUENCES AND CONTROL OF SPECULATIVE MANIAS

What are the consequences of speculative manias in Galbraith's view? And, if the consequences are deemed to be serious, as Galbraith thinks they are, what can be done to control them?

Consequences of Stock Market Crashes

While Galbraith has lightly commented (1994, p. 62) that the tragedy of the 1929 crash can be enjoyed because nothing was lost but money, he actually viewed the economic consequences of stock market crashes in much more serious form. Galbraith argued that any satisfactory explanation of the Great Depression of the 1930s 'must accord a dignified role to the speculative boom and ensuing collapse' (1988, pp. 89–90). Galbraith has severely criticized conventional theory, rejecting as 'high doctrine' the 'accepted view' that the 'stock market is but a mirror which ... provides an image of the underlying or fundamental economic situation' such that 'Cause and effect run from the economy to the stock market, never the reverse' (1988, p. 88).

The inevitability of a crashing end to a speculative bubble was repeatedly emphasized, expressed in typical Galbraithian style in his critique of the tendency for conventional theory to ignore crashes as the inherent results of speculative markets: 'Economic theology is here involved. The market is not only perfect but in some measure sacred. For its own internal dynamic and resulting disaster it cannot be held accountable' (1988, p. xvi). Galbraith's own view was succinctly stated in the following passage: 'If markets are perfect, as much doctrine holds, they cannot incorporate the seeds of their own disaster. In fact, the pure speculative development has a self-contained dynamic. It is programmed to end with a crash' (1988, p. xiii).

What causes the bubble to burst is of no importance. It is only important to understand the inevitability of a crash:

> The collapse in the stock market in the autumn of 1929 was implicit in the speculation that went before. The only question concerning that speculation was how long it would last. Sometime, sooner or later, confidence in the short-run reality of increasing common stock values would weaken. When this happened, some people would sell, and this would destroy the reality of increasing values. Holding for an increase would now become meaningless; the new reality would be falling prices. There would be a rush, pellmell, to unload. This was the way past speculative orgies had ended. It was the way the end came in 1929. It is the way speculation will end in the future. (1988, p. 169)

The above passage appeared in Galbraith's original text written in 1955. But the accuracy of the last sentence was clearly verified by the crash of 1987.

The economic consequences of crashes cited by Galbraith are quite similar to the effects on investment and consumption noted by Keynes. Galbraith argued that 'The Great Crash had a shattering effect on investment and consumer spending and eventually on production and employment, leading to the collapse of banks and business firms' (1987, p. 64). The crash affected first the wealthy and well-to-do, but given the distribution of income they were a vital spending and investing group (1988, p. 186). Unlike Keynes, Galbraith stressed the institutional weaknesses of the economy, especially in the 1920s. The crash was an exceptionally effective way of exploiting the weaknesses of the corporate structure that had developed in the 1920s, ultimately destroying both the ability to borrow and the willingness to lend for investment, which quickly resulted in declining orders and increasing unemployment (1988, p. 187). The crash also led indirectly to reduced exports by bringing foreign lending to an end (1988, p. 187).

While Galbraith cited parallels between the 1929 and 1987 crashes, there were also differences. Galbraith predicted in both the original text of *The Great Crash 1929* and the January 1987 article in the *Atlantic Monthly* that the crash of another speculative stock market would not have the same effect on the economy as the 1929 crash due to the institutional changes that had occurred in the 1930s. In *The Great Crash 1929*, expressing a view from 1955, Galbraith cited a less lopsided distribution of income, SEC regulations of securities markets, bank deposit insurance, 'a modest accretion of economic knowledge' relating to both macroeconomic theory and macroeconomic measurements (the legacies of Keynes and Kuznets), the farm program (however much abused), unemployment compensation, social security, and a tax system that was 'a better servant of stability than it was in 1929' (1988, pp. 191–2). In his analyses of the 1980s in the *Atlantic Monthly* article and in the new Introduction to the 1988 issue of *The Great Crash 1929*, Galbraith reiterated all of these except the tax system as 'a servant of stability'. He added one more important difference: the new certainty that large corporations, if in danger, will be bailed out by the government.

But while cushions now exist to prevent another crash from having the same devastating effects as the 1929 crash, Galbraith argued both before and after the 1987 crash that sufficient protection was not guaranteed. This point was emphasized in the following passage:

> Let no one, however, be wholly certain. A sudden reduction in the nominal wealth of institutions and individuals by a thousand million dollars must have, one can only assume, some depressive effect on investment and

consumer buying. So also on employment – certainly, at least one supposes, employment on Wall Street. As this is written in the days after the crash, there are reports of some changes in upper-income expenditure – that for expensive real estate, exotic automobiles and the more ridiculous of feminine attire. There could be an even larger effect. There is an unlovely saying that when the horse dies on the street, the oats no longer pass through for the sparrows. (1988, p. xix)

Control of Speculative Manias

Given that even with the cushions that are now in place, speculative manias and their inevitable crashes have harmful economic effects, what can be done to control them? In his analysis of the factors that contributed to the speculative bubble that burst in October 1987, Galbraith cautioned that 'Those who warned against past aberration should not now be expected to come up with the perfect solution for the adverse results' (1988, p. xx). But in *The Great Crash 1929*, Galbraith dealt with the problem of controlling speculative manias as involving two elements.

The first of these was the responsibility and will to act. Those with at least nominal responsibility included the President, the Secretary of the Treasury, the Federal Reserve Board, and the Governor and Directors of the Federal Reserve Bank of New York (1988, pp. 25–6). It is virtually impossible to puncture a speculative bubble in such a way that it gradually subsides: 'The real choice was between an immediate and deliberately engineered collapse and a more serious disaster later on' (1988, p. 25). None of the responsible officials in 1929 had the will to act, fearing the blame that would attach. Galbraith was particularly critical of both the intelligence and will of the members of the Federal Reserve Board. He described the Board as 'a body of startling incompetence' (1988, p. 27) that was 'less interested in checking speculation than in detaching itself from responsibility for the speculation that was going on' (1988, p. 35).

The second element of the control problem was what could be done to end the speculative orgy, given the will of responsible officials to act. In reference to 1929, Galbraith argued that the classic instruments of control – open market operations and discount rate increases – were largely useless (1988, p. 29). The Federal Reserve had only a small amount of government securities, although if all had been sold there may have been some positive effect (1988, p. 30). Increases in the discount rate would have hurt everyone except the speculators (1988, p. 31). Interest rates of 20 percent would not have deterred borrowing to purchase stocks if those stocks were expected to appreciate by more than 20 percent in the near future.

But there were other control possibilities. Galbraith suggested both a policy action and an exercise of moral authority. The Federal Reserve

Board could have asked Congress for the power to set margin requirements (1988, p. 32). Since the Board possessed that power in the 1980s, its actual influence may have been questionable in the 1929 case. But, as we noted earlier, new financial instruments, specifically stock index futures contracts, may have served to weaken the influence of margin requirements in the cash market.

In any case, Galbraith argued that such new legislation (or even the threat of it) would not have been necessary if moral authority had been vigorously exercised: 'In 1929, a robust denunciation of speculators and speculation by someone in high authority and a warning that the market was too high would almost certainly have broken the spell. It would have brought some people back from the world of make-believe' (1988, p. 32). Galbraith argued that the Federal Reserve in 1929 feared asking for such legislation and avoided issuing vigorous warnings because 'the very effectiveness of such a measure was the big problem' (1988, p. 33). Many small speculators and some big ones would start selling, and the boom would come to a sudden, and perhaps spectacular, end (1988, p. 32).

There is also the issue of tax policies that contribute to a sluice of funds into speculative stock markets. The speculative binge of the 1920s was helped by the tax cuts that allowed the affluent to keep a much larger portion of their income. This increase in disposable income found its way into the stock market rather than into consumption or real capital formation.

7. Recent Developments in Speculative Markets Theory: Fads, Fashions and 'Rational' Bubbles

In this chapter, several recent developments are examined that lend support, directly or indirectly, to the speculative markets view of stock prices. Robert Shiller's empirical research is of particular importance since it found that stock prices have been more volatile than would be predicted by the efficient market hypothesis. His investigations of popular models of investor behavior explain excess volatility and serve as an alternative to the efficient markets model. In popular models, that is, models used by the broad masses of individual and institutional investors to form their expectations, stock prices are heavily influenced by factors of social psychology, in particular investor fads and fashions.

Substantial indirect support for alternative explanations of stock prices has emerged from within the efficient markets camp. Major concessions have been made to the irrational markets view in the growing literature on 'rational bubbles' which has emerged from efforts to explain deviations of market prices from fundamentals within the efficient markets/rational expectations model. In a closely related development, attempts by some rational markets proponents to explain the October 1987 crash have involved substantial concessions to the irrational markets view.

ORGANIZATION OF THE CHAPTER

The survey of recent developments in speculative markets theory begins with a review of Shiller's conceptual and empirical work that challenges the efficient markets thesis and proposes alternative popular models. An examination follows of the attempts by rational markets proponents to explain bubbles and the crash of 1987 within the context of efficient markets/rational expectations models. These attempts are described as exercises in 'rational irrationality'. Finally, the implications are developed for the speculative markets view of several Post Keynesian critiques of the efficient markets hypothesis, including the 'rational bubbles' models.

FADS, FASHIONS AND POPULAR MODELS

With inflation factored out and a constant discount rate, movements in stock prices in the efficient markets model reflect rational responses to changes in the expected value of future dividends. But in a 1981 *American Economic Review* article, reprinted in his book *Market Volatility* (1989), Shiller reported that stock price volatility relative to dividend volatility for a period of over a century appeared to be far too high to be attributable to new information about future real dividends.

The efficient markets model could explain the observed volatility if it could be attributed to changes in real interest rates or if the true uncertainty about future dividends was under-estimated by the statistical measure of uncertainty. But Shiller argued that neither situation was very likely. While expected real interest rates cannot be measured, changes in real rates would have had to be very large to explain the amount of price volatility. Shiller cast doubt on the supposition that his measure of uncertainty understated the true uncertainty with the observation that such an explanation can only be 'academic' in that it relies fundamentally on unobservables and cannot be evaluated statistically (1981, p. 434).

Social Psychology and Speculative Markets

Shiller's major contribution to the speculative markets view has come from his investigations of alternatives to the efficient market models, the results of which were reported in a series of papers from 1984 to 1990. (Three of those papers, along with the 1981 *American Economic Review* paper, were reprinted with minor editing in *Market Volatility* (1989).) Although Shiller made no reference to Keynes' discussion of stock prices, his investigations have essentially followed the same path. After explaining why changes in stock prices are important in *The General Theory*, Keynes asked 'How then are these highly significant daily, even hourly, revaluations of existing investments carried out in practice?' (1936, p. 151). Similarly, in his research on prices of speculative assets (those held at least in part for their uncertain investment potential), Shiller has attempted to answer the basic question: 'what, ultimately, is behind day-to-day movements in prices?' (1989, p. 1). Those movements can be due to changes in economic fundamentals or to changes in opinion or psychology. Like Keynes, Shiller's work has emphasized the latter: 'Prices change in substantial measure because the investing public en masse capriciously changes its mind' (1989, p. 1).

Fads, Fashions and Bubbles

In a paper entitled 'Fashions, Fads, and Bubbles in Financial Markets', reprinted in *Market Volatility* Shiller stated that 'The speculative markets view that I wish to urge ... is not just a return to the common views of thirty or more years ago; rather my position is, in fact, heavily influenced by the efficient-markets literature' (1989, p. 49). The 'old view of fads' was supported by anecdotal evidence with the common claim that people are sometimes excessively enthusiastic for certain speculative assets and lack sound judgement (p. 50). Shiller's only citation of Galbraith was to quote a brief passage from *The Great Crash 1929* as representative of the 'older view of fads' (p. 51).

Yet Shiller's approach differs from the 'old view of fads', as exemplified by Galbraith's analysis of the 1929 speculative mania, only in its scope. Significantly, he did not reject anecdotal evidence. The anecdotes presented in the 'old view' were chosen for dramatic effect, so they necessarily involved extreme and unusual events where irrationality in investors' judgement would be obvious. Shiller argued that if such extreme cases are accurately reported, it is only natural to suspect that less dramatic fads or fashions are important causes of price variability in the usual course of trading. Thus whereas the 'older' view of speculative markets focused on extreme episodes of highly overvalued stocks, Shiller has presented an expanded view in which fads or fashions can cause stocks to be undervalued as well as overvalued.

The compatibility between Shiller and the 'older view' is clearly evident in his argument that the anecdotal evidence, albeit weak, does suggest that faddish behavior is an important influence in financial markets. Since nothing in theoretical finance implies that changing fashions or fads cannot influence market prices, why have economists ignored this suggestive anecdotal evidence? Shiller did not cite Keynes' comment that conventional theory assumes that professionals will quickly exploit any profit opportunities created by uninformed amateurs. However, he offered essentially the same observation in commenting that some (the efficient markets proponents) seem to think that a theoretical case against fads or fashions exists because profit opportunities for 'smart money' would thereby be created, with the immediate result being that 'smart money' would take over the market and eliminate such profit opportunities. Shiller countered by arguing that fads or fashions may not create spectacular profit opportunities if the future paths of fads or fashions are not very predictable. If only modest and uncertain profit opportunities exist, the tendency for 'smart money' to accumulate wealth through profitable trading may be a slow one and may not keep up with other tendencies that would spread the wealth through the population.

A major problem with the efficient markets models is the absence of any agreed-upon way to define true economic value or abnormal returns. This would seem also to pose a problem for critics, who presumably must show spectacular evidence of market inefficiency to disprove the efficient markets claim. But Shiller argued that such evidence in the form of spectacular profit opportunities is perhaps what would not be expected if fads and fashions exist. The absence of any consensus definition of abnormal returns results in a related problem with respect to the 'anomalies' which are dismissed as small departures from efficiency in the efficient markets literature. But Shiller noted that large valuation errors might generate small abnormal profit opportunities; hence the 'anomalies' may represent large departures from efficiency. Not only may these 'anomalies' occur because fads or fashions dominate the market, but they are exactly the sort that would be expected if fads or fashions did dominate.

Shiller's relationship with the 'older view' of investor fads is further defined by his distinction between fads, fashions and bubbles. While the 'older view' dealt with the more spectacular extreme cases of great bubbles, Shiller has focused on fads or fashions which are more general terms than 'bubble'. A bubble exists if the fad occurs through price, that is, if people are attracted by observed price increases. Because people may react differently to price increases, it is difficult to predict when bubbles will emerge. In some cases, rising prices may encourage people to demand stocks, but in other cases rising prices may be interpreted as indicating the market is overpriced and thus dampen the demand for stocks. Shiller argued that the existence of fashions or fads, which result in less dramatic price effects, can more easily be established by drawing from studies in social psychology which make the anecdotal evidence more plausible. His investigations of links between popular models and social dynamics have provided important insights into the manner in which social movements may affect stock prices.

Popular Models and Social Dynamics

Shiller did not entirely reject the efficient markets model, but views it as an extreme example that may be used selectively to help understand actual markets (1989, p. 3). One of his criticisms of efficient markets studies is that alternative models have not been considered. Rational expectations economic models assume that people know or at least act as if they know the true economic model for the economy. This allows economists to construct simple and elegant models which appeal theoretically and require no collection of data pertaining to what really goes on in the minds of investors. In contrast, popular models in the minds of both individual and institutional investors are not systems of equations, but are usually simple, spontaneous and unsophisticated, consisting of qualitative descriptions of causes, anecdotes suggesting what may happen, and presumed correlations, cycles or other simple patterns of variation of economic variables (1989, p. 3). Associated with the transmission and implementation of popular models are patterns of investor behavior which resemble processes found in social psychology models, for example communications patterns, reaction lags, habits and social norms.

Popular models can affect stock prices in two ways. First, the models can cause people to react incorrectly – overreacting or underreacting – to economic data. Second, the models may be changing; this causes stock price movements that are unrelated to economic fundamentals. At times, the popular models may create feedback loops or vicious circles, with reactions to price causing further price changes, which in turn cause further reactions. Such is the extreme case in speculative bubbles. But popular models do not always create excess volatility. In some cases, they may cause people to underreact to information about fundamentals (1989, p. 4).

To understand popular models, Shiller turned to studies of social dynamics by social psychologists. In his 1984 *Brookings Paper* article 'Stock Prices and Social Dynamics' (1989, pp. 7–48), he presented substantial evidence suggesting that 'social movements, fashions, or fads are likely to be important or even the dominant cause of speculative asset movements'. Shiller conceded that much of the evidence relied on 'the reader's good judgement' since 'no single piece of evidence is unimpeachable' (1989, p. 41). His argument can be summarized in the following way.

Since investing in speculative assets is a social activity, for example people discuss their investments and the market, it is plausible that investors' behavior, and hence prices of speculative assets, will be influenced by social movements. Hence investors' attitudes or fashions regarding investments can change spontaneously or in arbitrary social reactions to some widely noted event (1989, p. 1).

Shiller criticized modern economists for acting as though notions of market psychology have been discredited as unscientific (1989, p. 2). He was especially critical of the efficient markets claim that real prices of stocks are close to intrinsic values because real returns cannot be forecasted, describing that argument for the efficient markets hypothesis as representing 'one of the most remarkable errors in the history of economic thought' (1989, p. 2).

In rejecting the efficient markets model, Shiller contended that mass psychology may well be the dominant cause of movements in the price of the aggregate stock market (1989, p. 2). Since fashions influence many aspects of everyday life, why should fashions not exist in investment choices? Some critics argue that investment is a private affair based on

individuals' perceptions of prospective returns, and therefore not subject to
fads or fashions. But Shiller noted that even the perceptions of expected
returns may represent changing fashions.

The basis for the efficient markets claim is an assumption that
professional investors or 'smart money' controls the stock market. Shiller
argued that while 'smart money' is present, it is very unlikely to dominate.
He dismissed as 'myth' the presumptions on which the supposed
domination of 'smart money' rests – that institutional investors hold most of
the stock and that wealthy investors have delegated authority over their
portfolios to professional investment managers. Moreover, only a portion
of professional investment managements qualifies as 'smart money'. Many
fall into the 'ordinary investor' group (1989, pp. 10–12).

Shiller analyzed the behavior of ordinary investors in terms of the
ambiguity of stock values and social psychology. Although Keynes was
not cited, Shiller's discussion of the ambiguity of values was very similar.
Like Keynes (but with a citation instead of Knight), Shiller described
ordinary investors as faced with 'uncertainty' rather than 'risk' due to lack
of knowledge on which to base probabilities. Added to this is the fact that
it is easier for an individual to decide to change investments than to change
consumption patterns. In the latter case, the impact is felt immediately.
But changing investments has no immediate impact, and the consequence
will become known only over some period of time. Because there is no
'clear sense of objective evidence regarding prices of speculative assets, the
processes by which investors' opinion are derived may be especially social'
(1989, p. 13). Prices of stocks are particularly 'vulnerable to purely social
movements because there is no accepted theory by which to understand the
worth of stocks and no clearly predictable consequences of changing one's
investments' (1989, p. 13).

To model the behavior of ordinary investors, Shiller turned to studies in
social dynamics relating to the influence of group opinion and group
pressure on the attitudes and behavior of individuals, and to studies of the
dynamic processes of diffusion of opinion which borrow from the
contagion models of epidemics. A conceptual model derived from those
sources was applied to the stock market, and yielded indirect evidence
suggesting that a social movement characterized by 'contagious and
increasingly excessive optimism' (1989, p. 16) drove the bull market
between the late 1940s and 1960s but ended in the 1970s. That evidence
related to: (1) the growing number of people participating in the market
interested in the market, or knowing about the market; (2) the changes that
occurred in the relation between investors and agents; and (3) the changes
in attitudes that might plausibly have a great impact on stock prices (1989,
pp. 16–18).

The rising quantity of stocks held by institutional investors indicated the growing number of people in the market. Pension funds, which accounted for a large part of that increase, possibly represented a social movement which has increased demand for stocks. The increase in individual stock ownership appears to correspond to an increase in knowledge about and interest in the market. As evidence of the changing relation between investors and agents, stockbrokers enjoyed a growing reputation throughout the 1950s, in part due to public relations efforts.

Evidence of changing attitudes included surveys that reported declines in the importance of religion in people's lives and declining birth rates which were interpreted as reflecting changing attitudes towards the importance of family, heirs and individual responsibility toward others.

Shiller's description of the most important change in attitude with respect to impact on demand for stocks had a definite Keynesian – Galbraithian ring. The period after the bull market ended was characterized by a pervasive decline in confidence in society's institutions – government, business, other institutions and professions, including stockbrokers. Shiller argued that the pervasiveness of the negative attitudes toward institutions suggested 'prejudice' rather than 'informed judgement'. In the late 1970s, stockbrokers and the entire brokerage industry suffered from a negative image. That, of course, sounds very similar (albeit in the negative) to that element of extraordinary tendency to trust officials and social leaders in Galbraith's speculative mania model. The role of the sense of confidence is clearly reminiscent of Keynes.

An Alternative Model

Shiller noted that the efficient markets model assumes that returns are not forecastable, when in fact they are not very forecastable. That qualification is important because if investor fads exist, stock prices would be somewhat predictable. Thus alternative models that have price determined primarily by fads also imply that returns are not very forecastable.

The alternative model sketched by Shiller included both 'smart money' investors and ordinary investors. Smart money investors respond to rationally expected returns but are limited in their influence on the market by the extent of their wealth. Ordinary investors (everyone not responding to optimally forecasted returns) overreact to news or are vulnerable to fads. If 'smart money' is totally influential, the efficient markets model holds. Alternatively, if ordinary investors are totally influential, prices would be entirely a function of fads, suggestive of the extreme phases of speculative manias described by Galbraith. A Keynesian interpretation suggests where 'smart money' investors exist but are limited by the extent of their wealth, new information becoming public results in a jump in price that reflects both what 'smart money' thinks it means for future dividends but also what 'smart money' thinks it means for the demand for stock by ordinary investors.

Shiller also noted that the random-walk behavior of stock prices may hold up because fashions are inherently rather unpredictable and ordinary investors may overreact to news of earnings or dividends, which may make their demand for stocks relatively unpredictable. Alternatively, ordinary investors may have predictable patterns of behavior which 'are prevented from causing big short-run profit opportunities by the limited amount of smart money in the economy, so the returns may be nearly unpredictable. However, in preventing large profit opportunities, the smart money may not be preventing the ordinary investors from causing major swings in the market' (1989, p. 41) and even being the source of volatility in the market. In addition, an overreaction of prices to dividends may result because firms that set dividends are influenced by the same social dynamics that influence the rest of society.

Portfolio Insurance as a Fad

In one paper, Shiller (1988) examined portfolio insurance, which was identified by the Brady Commission as a factor in the 1987 crash in terms of an investor 'fad'.

> ... the volume of portfolio insurance selling on October 19 may also reflect that stop-loss behavior increased as a result of the publicity that portfolio insurance had received, and of the publicity campaign launched by entrepreneurs who found a new way, by selling portfolio insurance, to profit from such stop-loss behavior. If this is so, then portfolio insurance is best thought of as an investor fad that, like other fads, has caused an important change in investor behavior. Since the change is not best thought of as a technological innovation, its effect is likely to be transient or to be transformed so that it cannot be predicted by the original optimizing models that initially gave rise to the fad. (1988, p. 291)

Drawing on contagion models in which epidemics spread at 'infection rates' and the spread slows at 'removal rates', Shiller used a survey of individual and institutional investors to gain information about the parameters of this process. Based on growth in numbers of references to portfolio insurance in the literature, they found that the rate of infection conformed to the early stages of an epidemic in the contagion models: 'The apparent learning curve in portfolio insurance is hardly what one would expect from models in the finance literature that depict investors as following complicated optimization strategies, and responding instantaneously to information' (1988, p. 291).

Shiller argued that if the growth of portfolio insurance was due to an investors' fad, it should have no more than equal standing, a priori, as a candidate explanation for the crash among all other fads and fashions in investor thinking. Other social trends may have been at work, although it is difficult to pin down exogenous shocks that drive the stock market other than technological innovations.

Collecting Data on Popular Models

While the rational expectations models requires no collection of data about models in the minds of economic actors, such data are essential for understanding popular models. While Shiller did not cite Keynes, this is reminiscent of Keynes' statement that 'There is not much to be said about the state of confidence *a priori*. Our conclusions must mainly depend upon the actual observation of markets and business psychology' (1936, p. 149). Shiller attempted to collect data with respect to popular models immediately after the stock market crash of October 1987 through questionnaire surveys of investors. Several open-ended questions asked respondents to give their interpretation of the crash itself and asked those who thought they could forecast the market to explain why they felt those forecasts could be done.

Shiller reported being struck by how often people, both individual and institutional investors, reported having an intuitive or gut feeling about the future course of the market. He perceived that some personal sense of perspective that they were unable to articulate was behind individual opinions. The frequent commentary in the popular press that the market was overpriced, that the bull market had been going for a long time and that it must end at some point may have had the effect of framing issues so as to suggest that a definitive reversal might come. To test for the role of suggestibility, Shiller included questions to be ranked in relative importance of various news stories on 19 October and the preceding week. The responses plus anecdotal evidence suggested that 'crashes were very much on people's minds just before the crash. A third of individual investors and half of institutional investors who responded to the survey reported thinking or talking about the events of 1929 on the few days before the crash' (1988, pp. 292–3).

Shiller concluded that while the Brady Commission's 'cascade effect' of portfolio insurance may have been a factor, another factor was 'the peculiar mind set of investors, caused partly by the public interpretation of the unusual conformation of price rises over the past five years' (1988, p. 293). The growing fear of a crash may have been an important cause of the popularity of portfolio insurance. Shiller argued that it may be 'that any socially transmitted mental set for interpreting price movements (in particular an increased awareness of the possibility of a crash) marks an important difference between 1987 and earlier years' (1988, p. 294). But he also conceded that 'The importance of social-psychological induced changes in mind set in producing market crashes has not been established because psychological factors have not been properly measured' (1988, p. 294).

Shiller's surveys collected data on the popular models with respect to the crash of 1987 for the purpose of understanding speculative markets. Investors were asked to categorize their theories into either 'a theory about investor psychology' or 'a theory about fundamentals such as profits or interest rates'. Two-thirds of individual and institutional US investors chose investor psychology. Shiller reported being struck by the frequency of 'intuition' or 'gut feeling' mentioned by those respondents who thought they had a pretty good idea of when the rebound would occur. 'It is a striking fact that many investors think they can forecast the market and some of these are eager to take action. The random walk theory of stock prices now has some currency as a popular model, but other theories are still very much around' (1988, p. 57).

Shiller also investigated the emotional environment at the time of the crash by asking respondents whether they experienced any unusual anxiety. While the number responding in the positive was higher than Shiller expected, he was unwilling to conclude that this meant panic feelings since it could simply mean that investors were unusually alert and focused on their investment decisions (1988, p. 58).

He concluded that his research on popular models offers glimpses of the thought processes that underlie speculative booms and crashes. The picture that begins to be revealed is a complicated one – unlike any of the simple stories that have been told of speculative bubbles. A common tendency among the popular models was that investors thought that investor psychology was driving markets.

Shiller sees stock prices as reflecting both popular opinion and facts about fundamental value. Price movements can be reflective of opinion changes generated when a popular model causes people to overreact to some economic indicator, or from opinion changes generated among investors themselves through their communications or through their interaction via price as in the 1987 crash (1989, p. 431).

Related Studies: 'Noise Traders' and Irrational Prices

Shleifer and Summers (1990) suggested as an alternative to the efficient markets model one which rests on two assumptions. The first of these is that some investors are not fully rational and their beliefs or sentiments that are not fully justified by fundamental news affect their demand for risky assets, for example stocks. Second, rather than the perfect riskless arbitrage that is assumed in efficient markets models, Shleifer and Summers assumed that arbitrage is risky and therefore limited. The two assumptions together imply that changes in investor sentiment are not fully countered by arbitrageurs and therefore affect stock prices (1990, pp. 19–20).

Shleifer and Summers divided the market participants into arbitrageurs (or smart money or rational speculators) whose expectations about stock returns are rationally developed, and 'noise traders' or 'liquidity traders' whose opinions and trading patterns are subject to systematic bias. The arbitrageurs face two types of risk. The first is fundamental, that is, fundamentals can change upwards, and fearing the loss of selling short and getting caught will prevent arbitrageurs from short selling to the extent of driving prices down to fundamentals. The second is the unpredictability of the future resale price. Rather than selling short overpriced stocks today, arbitrageurs fear the loss of prices going even higher and their short selling will not drive prices down to fundamentals (1990, pp. 20–21).

'Noise traders' respond to 'pseudo-signals' which they think, incorrectly, convey information. Shiller's popular models describe some forms of this type of behavior. Such changes in demand for stocks may not be related to changes in fundamentals (following technical analysis or market gurus) or may be overreactions to news. When many trading strategies result in correlated directional moves, the entire market becomes affected. Learning and imitation may reinforce irrational behavior. When noise traders realize above average profits by luck and/or by unknowingly taking on more risk, other investors may imitate their behavior without realizing they are taking on more risk. Shleifer and Summers argued that shifts in demand for stocks independent of any news or fundamental factors are likely to affect prices even in the long run (pp. 23–5).

RATIONAL 'IRRATIONALITY'

Financial economists are justifiably reluctant to introduce irrationality into models of market equilibrium. 'Rational models have explained a wide range of economic phenomena. More important, there is no standard framework to constrain the sort of irrationality one might introduce' (French 1988, p. 281).

In the first part of the following section, the responses of proponents of the rational markets view to the rapid rise in stock prices in 1986 and 1987 and the October 1987 market crash are examined. In the second part, the concept of 'rational bubbles' is developed and research on their existence is analyzed.

Rational Markets Proponents and the 1987 Crash

As French (1988, p. 280) noted, 'The most common interpretation of the market crash is that it was the inevitable collapse of a speculative bubble'. Thus many observers thought the October 1987 stock market crash dealt the rational markets view a devastating blow: 'the stock in the efficient markets hypothesis – at least as it has been traditionally formulated – crashed along with the rest of the market on October 19, 1987' (Shleifler and Summers 1990, p. 19). Proponents of the rational markets view responded to the crash in a variety of ways, with some simply choosing to ignore it. Several have argued that no evidence exists to support the popular belief that the great historical bubbles – Tulipmania, Mississippi Company, and South Sea Company – were actually cases of irrational prices. They have contended, overtly or implicitly, that the 1987 crash could be attributed to perceptions of changes in underlying fundamentals. But several others have offered more compromising explanations that allowed for non-rational prices to exist before the market swiftly imposed rational prices.

No Proof of Bubbles?

One indirect response essentially attempts to deny that any evidence exists to support the popular view that great historical price collapses involved manias or bubbles. Garber (1990a, b), for example, argued that 'most of the famous features of the tulipmania are explainable as market fundamentals in the bulb markets' (1990a, p. 4) '... the unexplainable part of the tulipmania was confined to a 2–3 week period ... and to trades in futures markets for common bulbs which established themselves in taverns in the winter of 1636–37' (p. 20). Garber noted that one historian has postulated that the threat of the bubonic plague could have been an external factor that induced a gambling binge among tavern drinkers, but also noted that this may be a false clue (p. 16). According to Garber, the Dutch elite sought to confine the speculation to 'the safe areas of economic activity' which they also happened to control (p. 20). He suggested that the reforms suggested by the SEC report on the 1987 crash similarly represented organizations associated with 'the "safer" spot market in stocks', thus, pinning 'much of the blame on the more "speculative" futures markets' (p. 20): 'From the historical perspective of the tulipmania, it is not surprising that new regulations would have the effect of channeling speculative activity into the "safer area" of the stock market' (p. 21).

In his 1990 article, Garber expanded his analysis to include the South Sea and Mississippi Company bubbles, arguing that neither of these stock market boom/crash episodes should actually qualify as bubbles but could be explained in terms of fundamentals. He contended that the Mississippi Company's price rise and collapse was attributable to investors' thinking that Law's economic policy scheme would work, and that the collapse came because investors lost confidence. The parallel cited was a finance operation in the form of a leveraged buyout or corporate acquisition which must come first before a profitable restructuring can occur, but the project will fail if investors lose confidence before the project can be completed (1990b, pp. 46–7). Similarly, the South Sea project was terminated while still in the finance stage by a liquidity crisis and the withdrawal of parliamentary support (p. 52). But 'the episode is readily understandable as a case of speculators working on the basis of the best economic analysis available and pushing prices along by their changing view of market fundamentals' (1990b, p. 52).

In a similar vein, Santoni and Dwyer (1990) argued that empirical evidence based on long-run data on stock prices and dividends do not support the popular contention that the stock market crashes of 1929 and 1987 were speculative bubbles bursting. 'Rather the data suggest that stock prices followed a random walk which is consistent with a theory that assumes stock prices are largely determined by fundamental factors' (p. 206).

A 'Smart Market' Crash?

But some of those who espouse the more traditional fundamental value analysis approach attempted to explain the crash in terms of models that allowed speculative bubbles to exist for a time before the market reacts by efficiently reducing prices to their proper level based on economic fundamentals. Arbel et al. (1988, p. 124) claimed that 'theories of investor rationality, which have reigned periodically over many years – and also have been vilified and rejected by many scholars over those years – held up reasonably well during the October debacle'. They asserted that:

> The tumultuous stock market crash of October 19, 1987 was almost nothing of what so many analysts, investors, and observers believed it was. Instead of a panic, it was the restoration of sobriety and rationality. Instead of destroying confidence, it restored credibility in the market pricing mechanism ... With sudden swiftness, the crash imposed the rational rules of a remarkable exercise of analytic intelligence. (1988, p. 124)

The Arbel et al. 'smart market crash' argument was based on a rational markets model in which 'rational' prices are those consistent with the calculation of the intrinsic values of stocks using Benjamin Graham's model in a sophisticated process. But the authors conceded that market prices may not always be equal to that intrinsic value, citing Graham's statement that during bull markets investors tend to lose a sense of proportion, with prices becoming 'irrationally' high (1988, p. 124–5). This was what occurred in 1987:

> To a large extent, financial analysts and their sales representatives, the brokers, created and continuously supported the speculative optimism that preceded the crisis. Evidently carried away by the momentum they had helped to create, they were as surprised by the catastrophe as everyone else. (1988, p. 132)

Nor were insiders able to predict the crash, which was a 'macro-generated event' (1988, p. 132).

Thus the market in the months proceeding October was overvalued and a 'rational' correction was due.

> During the early stages of the crash it seems, the market recognized that this 'bigger fool' pricing mechanism was about to melt down. Once it was apparent that the bull market was over, investors put an abrupt end to the cycle of irrationality with a correction that was proportional to the degree of overpricing that preceded the crash. (1988, p. 125)

Arbel et al. contended that the crash was actually a rational correction in prices in proportion to the degree of overpricing (1988, p. 125). The market was 'smart' by quickly correcting prices rather than allowing the prices to decrease over a longer period of time, which would have been more destabilizing: 'By ending the unjustifiably good times, the crash prevented bad times' (1988, p. 124). According to Arbel et al., the Graham valuation model predicted the stock closing prices on Black Monday (1988, p. 133).

Fama (1989) presented a similar view. He argued that the absence of any 'big news' that would provide information that the fundamentals had changed was not sufficient to dismiss the rational markets view. Information that times had simply changed from good to average, while not 'big news', would be sufficient to produce a large price decline. Such information was provided by the dividend/price ratio, which 30 days after the crash was only slightly below its 30-year mean (pp. 74–5). Fama conceded that it was impossible to say for certain whether price behavior during October 1987 was rational, but argued that if the price drop had been followed by a quick reversal, a large irrational component might be suspected (p. 77). But given that the price/dividend ratios after the crash were close to historical averages, it was 'difficult to argue that the drop was an over-reaction' (p. 77).

Fama concluded with an interpretation very similar to Arbel et al.: '... the October price drop has the look of an adjustment to a change in fundamental values. In this view, the market moved with breathtaking quickness to its new equilibrium, and its performance during this period of hyperactive trading is to be applauded' (1989, p. 81).

A 'Learning' Market Crash?

While Arbel et al. proposed a 'smart' market thesis, a thesis suggested by French (1988) and by Romer (1993) could be labeled a 'learning' market scenario in which information is partly 'learned' by individual investors observing directly or indirectly (via market prices) the behavior of other investors. The impetus for this thesis was the problem of explaining such a drastic decrease in market prices in terms of changes in fundamentals in the absence of any large news events that could indicate such changes.

By elimination, French was 'inclined toward the conclusion that prices were above fundamental values before the crash, but that investors did not know they were too high' (1988, p. 281). French noted that standard models of rational information only imply that prices equal fundamental values on the average, leaving ample room for deviations due to 'noise'. But the challenge is to present a plausible model in which traders can infer they have made an enormous error from a small amount of bad news (1988, p. 281). Perhaps the typical investor's private information before the crash was more pessimistic than the information implied by prices, but because the typical investor put too much weight on the market information, he mistakenly believed that he was atypical and that other investors were more optimistic. Consequently, prices before the crash were irrationally high.

The 'trigger events' cited by the Brady Commission corroborated the private information held by investors, and with this confirmation, each one increased the weight placed on his own information and decreased the weight put on the market information. This led to each making a large revision in assessment of fundamentals (which French noted are unobservable) and in the price he was willing to pay for stocks. To each investor's surprise, others were acting similarly, and the large price decreases led investors to conclude that others also had pessimistic private information (1988, pp. 281-3).

This ties in with fundamental values in terms of a procyclical feedback process. A decline in fundamental values lowers stock prices. But the drop in stock prices drives fundamental values down further by the uncertainty created by the falling prices increasing required returns or the sudden reduction in wealth disrupting consumers' spending plans and lowering the market's expectation of future cash flows (1988, p. 283).

Romer (1993) cited two views on stock prices – the efficient markets view in which asset prices are rational assessments of expected future payoffs and the 'fads', 'noise', or 'bubbles' view in which there is a component of prices not tied to fundamentals. In the first, changes in prices reflect the arrival of external news about future payoffs and interest rates, while in the latter, changes in prices can reflect changes in the non-fundamental component as well as the fundamental (1993, p. 1112). Romer conceded that price changes often could not be linked to any identifiable changes in information. Thus, the evidence is weighted in favor of irrationality, so that proponents of the rational markets view 'are reduced to arguing that there are subtle but very important items of news whose significance can be discerned by market participants but not by economists and other outside observers' (1993, p. 1113).

Romer proposed a 'middle way' between these two polar views to suggest 'a possible rational market explanation of the October 1987 crash' (1993, pp. 1112–13). He argued that 'asset prices can change because initially the market does an imperfect job of revealing the relevant information possessed by different investors and because developments within the market can then somehow cause more of that information to be revealed' (1993, p. 1113). Thus there can be rational changes in the market's assessment of fundamentals without the arrival of outside news.

> If each investor recognizes that others possess objectively useful information about value that is not reflected in prices, then changes in the investor's opinion of what others' opinion are will cause the investor to change his or her own estimate of value. Thus Keynes' famous 'beauty contest' interpretation of the stock market, in which market participants are more interested in others' beliefs than in their own estimates of fundamentals, applies even when investors are holding stocks for their fundamental payoffs rather than in the hopes of selling to someone else at a higher price. (1993, p. 1113)

Romer's model of rational movements in asset prices arising from the trading process has two properties – the market's initial reaction to news does not fully reflect investors' assessments of the news' implications for fundamentals, and further trading reveals additional information about those assessments (1993, p. 1113). He argued on basis of that model that:

> ...the process of learning about the quality of other investors' information can lead to sudden shifts in the weight that investors put on their own information and can thus lead to sudden changes in prices. Indeed, this process may have played an important role in the 1987 stock-market crash. (1993, p. 1119)

While Romer made no claim that his highly stylized account of the crash explains it in entirety, he argued that it represents a potentially important element of the crash (1993, p. 1119).

Suppose there were some event whose implications for future profits were uncertain. The event would lead to an initial jump in asset prices in response to the 'conventional wisdom' about the event's implications and to any trading by informed investors. In addition, however, the gradual appearance of investors who had not yet traded in response to that information, many of whom possessed estimates of the implications of that information that differed from the market's, would lead to additional changes in prices. Thus, the market, rather than information about the fundamentals, would be the source of price movements, and asset prices would respond to news that was already publicly available. Yet those phenomena would reflect rational revisions of fundamentals. (1993, p. 1127)

How could rational changes in the market's estimates of fundamentals without the arrival of any new information other than that conveyed by the market itself explain the size of decline in stock prices as occurred on 19 October 1987? Romer cited Shiller's survey data as indicating that market participants and analysts appear to believe that the market does not completely process public information immediately and that the trading process gradually conveys information about investors' beliefs. Thus, investors reporting that they considered the price declines in the week before 19 October and the initial decline that morning as the most important proximate 'news' triggering the crash fit the modeled scenario (1993, p. 1128).

Romer seems to be challenging Keynes in arguing that if price movements were irrational, rational investors' estimates of fundamentals would often differ substantially from market prices, so that 'fads' suggest large profit opportunities which would be taken advantage of (1993, pp. 1127–8). Both the incentives to exploit this information and the size of the resulting trades would be large. Romer apparently did not consider the Keynesian case of professionals who have the greatest potential for being rational, that is, informed about fundamentals, still having incomplete information and finding it more profitable to simply 'beat the mob'. Nor did he explicitly suggest that the sell-off on 19 October was due to rational investors who estimated lower fundamentals than prices suggested exploiting that opportunity for gain by selling overvalued stocks.

Romer moved away from what he termed 'an extreme "efficient-markets" view of the functioning of financial markets' where 'asset markets mechanically process all information and effortlessly arrive at optimal estimates of fundamentals'. Instead, Romer argues that his model is a rational one because 'market participants are groping toward reasonable estimates of fundamentals, and price movements, even when they are unrelated to outside news, generally represent improvements in assessments of underlying fundamentals' (1993, p. 1129).

Rational Bubbles

> Rationality both of behavior and also of expectations often does not imply that the price of an asset be equal to its fundamental value. In other words, there can be rational deviations of the price from this value – rational bubbles. (Blanchard and Watson 1982, p. 295)

Adams and Szafarz (1992) have noted the rapidly expanding literature on 'rational' bubbles. Beginning with the pioneering work of Flood and Garber (1980), they have examined the theoretical formulation and increasingly sophisticated empirical testing procedures for detecting the existence of bubbles. For several years after the emergence of rational expectations, it was thought that traditional bubbles would not arise in rational pricing markets. Flood and Garber (1980) stated: 'The possibility of a market's launching itself onto a price bubble exists when the expected rate of market price is an important factor determining current market price' (p. 745). They went on to say that under rational expectations 'the arbitrary, self-fulfilling expectations of price changes may drive actual price changes independently of market fundamentals; we refer to such a situation as a price bubble' (p. 746).

Flood and Hodrick (1990) noted that 'The possibility that movements in prices could be due to the self-fulfilling prophecies of market participants has long intrigued observers of free markets. Such self-fulfilling prophecies are often called "bubbles" or "sunspots" to denote their dependence on events that are extraneous to the market' (p. 85). They claim that 'The widespread adoption of the rational expectations hypothesis provided the required underpinning for theoretical and empirical study of the issues' (p. 86). Many rational expectations models have an indeterminate aspect because current decisions of agents depend on both the current and future prices. Since the current price depends partially on the expected future price because capital gains are part of the expected returns, a number of price paths emerge as possible sequences of prices. Only one sequence is the market fundamental price path, and the others will have price bubbles. Flood and Hodrick referred to the literature that has developed on the subject as 'empirically-oriented literature concerning rational dynamic indeterminacies, by which we mean a situation of self-fulfilling prophecy within a rational expectations model' (p. 86).

In their 1980 article, Flood and Garber concluded by questioning the existence of price-level bubbles but stated no strong opinions about price bubbles in specialized asset markets. In their 1982 paper, Flood and Garber argued that 'the recent adoption of the rational-expectations assumption has clarified considerably the nature of price bubbles and has focused wide-spread professional attention on the problem' (p. 745). 'The rational-expectations assumption has stimulated progress because its application imposes a precise mathematical structure on the relationship between actual and expected price movements' (p. 745).

Blanchard and Watson (1982) argued that 'Rationality both of behavior and also of expectations often does not imply that the price of an asset be equal to its fundamental value. In other words, there can be rational deviations of the price from this value–rational bubbles' (p. 295). But they stated that 'There is little question that most large historical bubbles have elements of irrationality' (p. 295) and cited Kindleberger's descriptions of many of those bubbles. Their justification for focusing on rational bubbles was that: 'it is hard to analyze rational bubbles. It would be much harder to deal with irrational bubbles' (p. 296).

Blanchard and Watson (1982) argued that rational bubbles have real effects.

> A bubble on the price of any asset will usually affect the prices of other assets, even if they are not subject to bubbles. The increase in the price of the asset that is subject leads initially to both an increase in the proportion of the portfolio held in that asset and an increase in total wealth. The first effect will, if assets are not perfectly substitutable, require an increase in the equilibrium expected return on the asset with a bubble and a decrease in the equilibrium expected return on most other assets. The second effect will, by increasing the demand for goods and possibly for money, lead to an increase in the equilibrium average expected return. The net effect is ambiguous, but it is likely to be a decrease in the price of most of the other assets together with a further decrease in the fundamental value of the asset experiencing the bubble. (p. 302)

A rational bubble must be expected to grow exponentially, which may imply that the effects on other markets mean that some other prices may be expected to grow or decrease exponentially as well. Their response to the question of whether negative prices or some such impossibility rules out the existence of a rational bubble in the initial market was 'it depends' – because it is possible to construct general equilibrium models in which bubbles cannot be ruled out (p. 303).

Miller (1991) identified two views of 'rational' bubbles. First, movements in stock prices that reflect both rational consideration of fundamentals and irrational bubbles may be 'rational' in the specific sense that over the long run and allowing for both ups and downs, the real return to the investor from holding shares is exactly the same as it would have been if prices had been based entirely on the economic fundamentals. Price fluctuations only have a redistributive effect on wealth holdings of participants in the market in zero-sum games, without creating or destroying lasting values.

Second, the combined process might be 'rational' also in the sense that investors cannot be considered to be acting foolishly or irrationally if they choose to participate in the process even if aware that they may be riding a bubble doomed someday to burst. At any point in time, thanks to the inner dynamics of the bubble process, the prospect of loss on a sudden collapse would be balanced exactly by the prospect of continued supernormal returns before cashing in. Thus, looking back, everyone always seems to stay in too long, except, of course, for the annoying few who did manage luckily to get out in time and who never cease reminding others of their prescience (pp. 90–91).

The notion of rational bubbles is clearly an appealing one, combining ingeniously two lines of explanation for price movements that seem at first to be antithetical. But Miller argued that surveys provided evidence of rational elements in valuations, but raised questions as to whether any real evidence of bubbles existed. He cited two strands of constrained research. The first was Shiller's claim of excess volatility, which Miller criticized as 'still unproven' (1991, p. 94). The second strand of research is whether stock prices systematically overreact to news. Dismissing anecdotal evidence and folklore, Miller conceded that serious statistical analysis seems to point in that direction, but claimed that 'the extent to which these findings can support the case for bubbles still remains very much in dispute' (1991, p. 96).

Thus, Miller argues that 'the positive evidence in the data suggestive of bubbles, rational or irrational, is far from compelling' (1991, p. 98) but notes that many regard the absence of news that could have caused the 1987 crash as precluding anything other than the bursting of a bubble. His response was that a small change in expectations about the future could trigger large changes in prices, and that the 'long-sought missing "fundamental" explanation of the Crash of 1987' was simply that investors simultaneously believed based on the same information that the very favorable political and economic climate for equities was changing and hence, came to the same conclusion that they were holding too large a share of their wealth in risk equities and not enough in safer instruments such as bonds (1991, pp. 100–102).

This is reminiscent of a change in Keynes' 'animal spirits'. Miller cited Keynes' discussion of the fallacy of composition in the stock market in which liquidity is provided for the individual but not for the entire group of investors (1991, p. 97). He also recognized Keynes' paradox of liqudity and discussed regulations to reduce liquidity (1991, pp. 103–5) but the psychological aspects of animal spirits were not mentioned.

Adams and Szafarz (1992) have noted that two large sets of phenomenon exist – traditional or popular bubbles and rational bubbles – of which intersection is not necessarily large. 'Rational' bubbles lack general definition. Instead, bubbles are model specific, and rational expectations have multiple equilibria solutions with no best criteria for selecting unique solutions. The economic interpretation raises important questions. Traditional or popular bubbles have a particular shape – rapid rise in price and ending in a burst – and an economic interpretation in terms of self-fulfilling prophecies and agent expectations of rivals' expectations. Many belong to non-rational category. Rational expectations bubbles, however, can have infinite shapes, many of which do not correspond to popular economic intuition of bubbles. Deterministic bubbles, for example, expand to infinity. Although 'rational' bubbles end in these scenarios, the question of how they start is not answered.

POST KEYNESIAN CRITIQUES OF EFFICIENT MARKETS

A curious relationship between the efficient markets hypothesis and Keynes' speculative markets theory has been noted by Andersen (1983/84) who showed that 'a situation similar to that described by Keynes can be generated from the assumptions of the efficient capital markets hypothesis' (p. 282). The model developed by Andersen:

> ... shows that with heterogeneous expectations it is rational for agent to devote resources to anticipating the expectations of other agents ... since the expected period t + 1 is an important factor determining the current asset price. A possible limit of the expectations process described by Keynes, i.e., expectations process of infinite degree, is the rational expectations equilibrium concept since this captures the situation where agents know the expectations of all agents (since they are the same) and all agents know this to be the case. The situation envisaged by Keynes is thus perfectly consistent with the assumptions underlying the efficient capital markets hypothesis, and implies in the limit that the asset price become indeterminate. (p. 285)

Since information sets are informative if information is provided on other agents' information/expectations, this is equivalent to Keynes' argument that market participants are concerned not with the real worth of assets to someone buying to hold over the long term but rather with what the market will value them in a short while under the influence of mass psychology (p. 287). One consequence of the analysis was to show that speculative mania 'may arise even if the market works perfectly and agents form expectations rationally. Thus, if financial markets become too perfect/efficient they may become liable to speculative manias' (p. 288).

Glickman (1994) emphasized the difficulties encountered in conceptualizing information in a world of intractable uncertainty and reiterated Keynes' emphasis on investors attempting to assess average opinion. Information does not exist in objective form waiting to be discovered but must be interpreted from events. Financial information has an essentially dual nature in that financial events are subject to interpretation at two levels – information about real underlying conditions and information about possible changes in behavior of market participants (p. 325). Consequently, 'information becomes a problematic concept within the efficient markets theory since the information to be gleaned from a particular financial 'event' is not objectively determinable and is in particular dependent on interpersonal dynamics operating between traders in the market' (p. 347).

Glickman's Post Keynesian analysis emphasized the highly contingent and problematic relationship between past experience and future expectations in a world of intractable uncertainty and the liquidity of stock market securities as a characteristic of critical importance. Short-run expectations of market behavior are thus shown to be the key and proximate determinant of share prices (p. 326); 'irrational market outcomes are seen as quite consistent with signal rationality on the part of individual investors' (p. 348). He showed that 'the efficient markets theory rests on the conceptual mistake of imagining that financial information is the type of entity that can unambiguously be characterized as being used either "efficiently" or "inefficiently"' (p. 348).

Intrinsic value cannot be known because of the intractable uncertainty of the future. While long-run expectations will be an influence on short-term price movements and recognized as such by market sentiment, their influence on the average short-term opinion will frequently be swamped by other considerations because the future in not calculable and because economic conditions are constantly changing (p. 335).

Glickman argued that Post Keynesian views impute 'a rich and sophisticated rationality' to the average voter (p. 336) and that rational action by individuals requires attempting to assess average opinion in the Keynesian model because it is known that market prices depend on average opinion and that there is no 'hard' information. But the notion that universal individual rationality necessarily produces market rationality is rejected (p. 337). There can be no market rationality because there can be no intrinsic value (p. 339). Glickman (1994) defined a rational bubble as follows:

> A 'rational' bubble in the current price of a given share will arise if 'rational' agents believe there is a probability of a positive deviation from intrinsic value in next period's share price. This belief will be impounded into today's price, causing it to rise above intrinsic value today by an

amount equal to the expected value of the next period's deviation. Of course, the next period's deviation can only arise if there is the prospect of an even larger deviation in the period following, and so on, into the indefinite future. (p. 339)

Glickman rejects rational bubbles since there is no explanation of why they occur, which reduces their real-world value, and because they cannot be informationally efficient because they are not a response to any information in any meaningful sense of the word (p. 341). Since intrinsic value cannot be known, bubbles as deviations from intrinsic values are meaningless. But he also dismisses investors' fads because they suggest a deviation from an intrinsic value with a return when the fad ends (pp. 341–2). In the Post Keynesian view, share prices are volatile not due to rationality or irrationality but simply as the outcome of the behavior of individual agents in organized markets seeking their own short-term advantage under conditions of intractable uncertainty and the opportunity to enter/leave by virtue of liquid markets (p. 346).

8. Current Prospects for Speculative Markets Theory

Efficient markets models have dominated recent analyses of stock markets in neo-classical books, mainstream journals and papers presented at economics and finance meetings. However, a popular perception persists that stock markets are heavily influenced by speculative psychology, as evidenced by the frequent commentaries to that effect in financial journalism and by market professionals in interviews and speeches. Of greater significance, however, is the combination of the robust critiques of the efficient markets hypothesis by Shiller and other economists and the concessions from within efficient markets enclaves in academia that stock prices in real-world markets tend to have an irrational component.

The current environments in both the real-world stock markets, which were described in the Preface and the academic world of financial economics, seem particularly ready for a broad-based and robust speculative markets model. But what can be said about the current prospects for speculative markets theory? From the perspective of this investigation of the development of speculative markets theories, the critical question is whether the analyses of Keynes, Veblen, Galbraith and Shiller can provide the basis for a plausible conceptual model of speculative markets. In the first section of this chapter, it is shown that Keynes provided the essential structural framework for a general model, that the analyses by Galbraith and Shiller illuminate and expand upon elements in Keynes' analysis, and that Veblen's analysis provides an important complementary element.

Several features indicate the robustness of this conceptual model of speculative stock markets, which for convenience may be labeled the KVGS model. Most importantly, the model explains varying degrees of speculative influence on stock prices, ranging from mild cases of chronic speculation (speculation as relatively harmless bubbles on streams of enterprise) to intense speculative manias that culminate in great market crashes (whirlpools of speculation in which enterprise is a bubble).

A related feature is that the KVGS model recognizes that speculative demand for stocks can derive indirectly from speculative expectations about profits of corporations or emanate directly from purely psychological

147

expectations about responses of the mass of investors to rising stock prices. A speculative movement may start as the former, then ultimately become a case of the latter. Hence the KVGS model has relevance not only to the infrequent cases of manias that produce booms and crashes, such as in 1929 and 1987, but also to the less frantic bull and bear movements that occur over a number of months or even years.

An immediate test of a general model of speculative markets is whether it can offer a plausible explanation of the historically uncharacteristic strong performance of the stock market over the decade following the October 1987 crash. The aftermath of the worst one-day crash in history, which was reviewed in the Preface, might seem to suggest that a 'new era' really has emerged, one in which stock market crashes can be shrugged off as insignificant events about which investors need not be concerned (or perhaps seen as golden opportunities for buying stocks) and from which the economy is almost totally insulated. Recent stock market developments are considered within the context of the KVGS model in the second part of this chapter.

THE KVGS MODEL OF SPECULATIVE MARKETS

In addition to explaining that the pricing of stocks has an important influence on the level of investment through the marginal efficiency of capital and on the level of consumption through the marginal propensity to consume, Keynes dealt with the institutional features of stock markets. Specifically, he considered how investments are made liquid for individuals but not the masses, the role of expectations, the psychology involved in the formation of expectations under the inevitable conditions of uncertainty, and the conventional rules governing the sense of confidence that have evolved to guide the behavior of stock market participants.

With very tenuous ties to any real knowledge of the underlying economic fundamentals that affect long-term corporate yields, expectations which guide investors' stock market activities are subject to frequent changes as the mass psychology of the crowd may suddenly and drastically change. The consequence is an inherent instability in stock prices that is unrelated to any changes in economic fundamentals. But because stock prices affect both consumption and investment, the instability of stock prices can contribute to fluctuations in the underlying real economy where the economic fundamentals are determined.

The expectation that speculation will be an inherent behavioral tendency in modern investment markets draws implicit support from Keynes' more ubiquitous phenomenon of 'animal spirits' as a recurring psychological mood of general optimism. But the instability of stock prices need not always be severe. Speculation does not always dominate enterprise, although the tendency for that to happen increases as the organization of modern stock markets improves. Keynes noted that 'the state of long-term expectation is often steady, and, even when it is not, the other factors exert their compensating effects' (1936, p. 162). The prospective yield on many investments 'is legitimately dominated by the returns of the comparatively near future' (1936, p. 163). Indeed, it is because of this steadiness that the influence of the interest rate on investment is relevant. In addition, Keynes recognized the presence of investors who attempt to forecast long-term yields, although he argued that they were too few to influence the market seriously.

Since we reviewed Keynes' analysis in considerable detail in Chapter 5, our remaining task is to explain how the analyses of Veblen, Galbraith and Shiller either illuminate certain elements of Keynes' analysis or provide complementary elements that serve to expand the general framework. An explicit examination is due in part to a curious absence of acknowledgements by Keynes, Galbraith and Shiller of the relevant work(s) of predecessors. Perhaps it is not too surprising that Keynes indicated no familiarity with Veblen's earlier analysis of speculative stock markets, given the fundamental differences in their methodologies and normative positions. But neither Galbraith nor Shiller cited Keynes' analysis of speculative stock markets, and Shiller's only citation of Galbraith was a short descriptive passage from *The Great Crash 1929*.

As an overview, general agreement exists on two major points. First, stock markets have an important influence on the level of business investment, and hence on the level of prosperity in the general economy. Second, stock prices will be influenced by psychological and sociological factors. On this point, Galbraith and Shiller have made major contributions by extending the analysis much deeper: Galbraith by focusing on speculative manias and Shiller by drawing upon social psychology.

In addition, Veblen and Shiller complement and expand Keynes' analysis by allowing stock prices to reflect both expectations about corporate profits and expectations about the psychological mood of the crowd of investors. In this respect, Veblen's focus on speculative demand for stocks as derived from speculative expectations about corporate profits and Shiller's inclusion of both 'smart money' and 'ordinary investors' in his popular models add important insights.

Veblen and Keynes

The compatibility between Keynes' and Veblen's analyses of speculative stock markets, and especially the complementariness of certain differences in their analyses, may not be readily apparent. Indeed, in view of the very deep fundamental differences in methodologies and normative positions between Keynes and Veblen, it might seem futile to expect to find any substantive degree of compatibility in either the specific content of their general theories or the policy implications derivable from those theories. Those differences are amply reflected in Keynes' statement that

> To put the point concretely, I see no reason to suppose that the existing system seriously misemploys the factors of production which are in use. There are, of course, errors in foresight; but these would not be corrected by centralizing decisions. When 9,000,000 men are employed out of 10,000,000 willing and able to work, there is no evidence that the labour of these 9,000,000 men is misdirected. The complaint against the present system is not that these 9,000,000 men ought to be employed on different tasks, but that tasks should be available for the remaining 1,000,000 men. It is in determining the volume, not the direction, of actual employment that the existing system has broken down. (1936, p. 379)

The claim by Harvey (1994) that elements of Veblenian institutionalism can be identified in Keynes' work in *The General Theory* may be disputable. But as the focus is narrowed to specific elements in their economic analyses, compatibility between Veblen and Keynes on certain points becomes much easier to see. In particular, several scholars have noted similarities in Keynes' and Veblen's cycle theories (see Vining 1939 and Brockie 1958). But the greatest degree of compatibility emerges when the focus is concentrated tightly on their analyses of stock markets within those cycle theories.

At a more fundamental level in socio-economic analysis, there is an intractable major difference in their stock market analyses that reflects the fundamental differences in their methodologies and normative positions relating to the role of stock markets as institutional arrangements for allocating capital. Veblen completely rejected the neo-classical presumption that stock markets allocate real capital goods to their most socially beneficial uses because he rejected the notion that business values reflect social values. As much more of a mainstream economist, Keynes was willing to accept, at least for methodological purposes, the assumption that a socially beneficial allocation of capital occurs if investors correctly forecast long-run yields and all investment decisions are based on those yields. He was primarily concerned with explaining why stock prices would not be based on long-term yields, so that stock markets could not be expected to allocate capital efficiently.

Regardless of how much Keynes and Veblen may have differed on the fundamental nature of social values and the allocative functions of stock markets, they both dealt analytically with the existing economic order as a business enterprise system and, accordingly, explained the functioning of the stock market as a vital institution within that system. Important commonalties appear in their explanations of how stock prices are determined. And where differences exist, they are either inconsequential with respect to the compatibility of those explanations or serve to make the explanations complementary. The most obvious such difference is Veblen's extensive discussion of manipulation of stock prices, a practice which was scarcely mentioned by Keynes. But manipulated markets are not incompatible with Keynes' theory of speculative markets. Moreover, Veblen's rather lengthy discussion of periods of speculative inflation implied situations in which manipulation of stock prices was not a factor.

Another difference of some significance is the lack of any explicit counterpart in Keynes' analysis of capital and stock markets to the emphasis that Veblen placed on loan capital. Likewise, there is certainly no Keynesian counterpart to Veblen's assertion that bonds represented effective claims to corporations' tangible capital and common stock represented the present market value of corporations' goodwill. However, as we noted in Chapter 4, Veblen specifically stated that the processes by which stock prices are determined during episodes of 'speculative inflation' did not depend upon credit expansion. And he claimed that the asset values of bonds and common stock were the result of a process that was amplified by credit expansion through use of rising market values of stocks as loan collateral. Moreover, Keynes hinted at several points that credit was important. His discussion of borrower's risk and lender's risk with respect to the marginal efficiency of investment was repeated in his discussion of 'the state of credit' and speculators: 'A collapse in the price of equities, which has had disastrous reactions on the marginal efficiency of capital, may have been due to the weakening either of speculative confidence or the state of credit' (1936, p. 158).

An important complementary difference relates to the nature of speculative demand for stocks. While demand for stocks based purely on speculative expectations of rising stock prices was clearly evident in his analysis, Veblen emphasized speculative demand for stocks as derived from speculative expectations of corporate profits. In contrast, Keynes dealt almost exclusively with speculative demand for stocks based on speculative expectations about how other investors would respond to short-run price movements. We will return to this complementary difference shortly, but first the commonalties that make Veblen's and Keynes' basic explanations compatible must be presented.

The economic importance of stock markets
On the fundamental question of why stock markets have economic importance, both Veblen and Keynes recognized that an important function of stock markets is to place current values on business capital via the

establishment of prices of stocks, and that these valuations affect rates of return, and hence, with constant interest rates, levels of investment. For that reason, it is important to understand the institutional processes and psychological tendencies involved in the establishment of stock prices. Once again, there are important commonalties in Keynes' and Veblen's analyses.

Formation of expectations

Like Keynes, although certainly less explicitly and less completely, Veblen explained investors' behavior in terms of expectations formed under conditions of uncertainty. He seemed to anticipate Keynes in his comment about 'an imperfect, largely conjectural, knowledge of present earning-capacity and on the still more imperfectly known future course of the goods market and of corporate policy' (Veblen 1904, pp. 155–6). In the framework of Keynes' more extensively developed analysis, investors rely on a conventional rule of assuming that the present and recent past are approximately correct and will continue. Veblen seemed more inclined to a random-walk view in his statement that a forecast on which presumptive earnings will be based 'retains the character of a forecast based on other grounds besides the computation of past results' (Veblen 1904, pp. 153–4). Yet he implies that investors tend to follow something along the lines of Keynes' conventional rule of assuming the present will continue in his explanation of stock prices rising based on expectations of rising corporate profits on a general basis because profits in one sector increase on a rise in product demand.

Importance of psychological factors

The essential commonality in Keynes' and Veblen's analyses is in the psychological factors that shape expectations under conditions of uncertainty. It is true that Veblen seemed to rule out Keynes' suggestion that speculative stock markets resemble casinos with his comment that only the earlier commercial speculation was of a gambling nature. Modern speculative inflation that takes the form of speculative expectations of rising corporate profits is not of that nature. Even so, stock prices in Veblen's analysis are frequently driven by the 'psychological phenomena of crowds' especially 'in times of panic or speculative inflation' (Veblen 1900, pp. 310–11). But even on a daily basis, Veblen attributed changes in stock prices to 'folk psychology'; dependent on 'the indeterminable, largely instinctive, shifting movements of public sentiment and apprehension' rather than material fact (1904, p. 102).

Complementary differences

These commonalities establish a substantial degree of compatibility between Keynes' and Veblen's explanations of how stock prices are determined. But with Keynes providing a much more developed explanation of the nature of uncertainty and the psychology of investors' behavior, the real significance of that compatibility is in establishing the complementariness of differences in relative emphasis on the nature of the speculative demand for stocks. Much of Veblen's discussion of stock prices suggested that the fundamental value view of stock prices reflected the present value of 'putative' corporate earnings. And his analysis of 'speculative inflation' concentrated largely on rising stock prices based on speculative expectations of rising corporate profits, although it is clear that pure speculation, that is, specultation based on expectations of short-run changes in stock prices.

An interesting consequence of this emphasis is that it makes Veblen's analysis seem similar to the qualified version of rational markets that has appeared in recent 'rational bubble' models in which individuals act 'rationally' on irrational information. Stock prices rise in Veblen's analysis because the market acts 'rationally' in responding to what is thought to be 'rational' expectations about corporate profits. In fact, that similarity only indicates how closely the 'rational bubbles' models have come to the general speculative markets model. This is best seen in Glickman's (1994) explanation that Post Keynesian theory allows individual investors to act rationally in the constrained sense while rejecting the claim that investors form correct expectations about economic fundamentals that affect corporate profits.

Veblen's recognition of speculative demand for stocks based on speculative expectations of corporate profits complements and expands Keynes' analysis in several ways. While Keynes said little directly about this type of speculative demand, dealing mostly with speculation in the form of expectations about the psychology of the market, the influence of his 'animal spirits' would seem capable of producing such episodes. The extra-rational feeling of optimism causes people to expect business successes, and hence stock prices would be expected to reflect those expectations of profits. In that light, historical movements of stock prices over periods of several years might be largely explained in terms of 'animal spirits'. Since Veblen perceived, at least in *The Theory of Business Enterprise* (1904), chronic depression as 'normal' to the modern situation, Keynes' more optimistic view of the buoyancy provided by 'animal spirits' suggested greater likelihood of stock price fluctuations based on speculative expectations of rising business profits.

It is particularly noteworthy that both Keynes and Veblen described the influence of speculative psychology as ranging from very mild to very intense. Keynes' reassurance at the end of Chapter 12 of *The General Theory* that everything does not depend on 'waves of irrational speculation', that 'the state of long-term expectation is often steady', that when it is not steady 'the other factors exert their compensating effect' and that 'certain important factors ... somewhat mitigate in practice the effects of our ignorance of the future' (1936, pp. 162–3) can be compared with Veblen's indication that except in times of speculative prosperity or the crises that end such periods, stock prices tend to reflect expected earnings. Because of his theory of chronic depression, there is a strong expectation in Veblen's analysis that stock prices will be relatively free much of the time from 'speculative buoyancy'. A parallel in Keynes' analysis would seem to be his statement that a rising stock market may be necessary to ensure a sufficient level of consumption.

A relative degree of stability was suggested also in Veblen's comment that profit margins tend to return to normal after a crisis in 'modern' times because (1) new firms with new cost-reducing technology and (2) reorganized firms that have experienced liquidation but have now written down and simplified their capital structures can both realize normal profit margins at the current prices in the goods markets. Since new firms with new cost-reducing technologies do not appear only after crises, their competitive presence would tend to reduce any tendency toward speculation before it can build to crisis levels. The pressure put on prices in the goods markets would depress profit margins of existing firms.

It must be noted, however, that this corollary would have little significance with the price rigidity assumption in the general Keynesian model. The new firms could realize above-average profits if they could find buyers, but in the absence of any expansion in overall demand (since prices remain constant) there is no reason to expect the new firms to be able to pull customers away from the existing firms. While Veblen's theory of business enterprise includes heavy reliance on advertising to create demand, competitive advertising outlays would tend to eliminate the cost differentials and hence, profit margins would not change. Also, in Veblen's larger theory, large corporations tend to restrict output levels to keep prices high. Still, there is much in Veblen's discussion that explicitly indicates that prices are set in competitive markets and tend to fall rather easily.

Keynes and Galbraith

Although Galbraith did not mention Keynes' discussion of speculative stock markets, the high degree to which his analysis expands upon Keynes' analysis is readily apparent. Although Keynes clearly suggested the possibility of great bubbles that end in crashes, he said relatively little about the intense psychological nature of those bubbles. Rather, he portrayed speculation as an inevitable presence that creates instability in investment and hence in the aggregate economy. The speculative presence at times may be very mild but occasionally may become very strong. Keynes noted that average opinion can change very quickly, but said relatively little about what happens when the change is one that produces an intense speculative mania. Galbraith's model of speculative manias focuses directly on the extreme cases.

There is little to suggest that Galbraith perceived the problem of uncertainty as contributing to the speculative tendency. On the contrary, like Veblen, Galbraith seems to accept that stock prices will reflect expected profits in the absence of the speculative mood that gives rise to speculative manias. In addition, there is at least an element of Veblen's speculative demand for stocks based on speculative expectations of corporate profits in the early phase of the emergence of a speculative mania. But the emergence of the psychological mood that turns a 'normal' market rise into a speculative mania seems very suggestive of an extreme case of the mood of spontaneous optimism that Keynes termed 'animal spirits'.

In addition to giving closer attention to the psychology of speculative manias, Galbraith's analysis complements Keynes' analysis by directing much more attention to the role of institutional contributors to a speculative mania. In particular, while tax cuts that substantially increase the disposable income of the well-to-do and leverage do not cause speculative manias, they are certainly important contributors to the extent to which a speculative mood can influence the market.

On two points, Galbraith and Keynes expressed very similar views. Galbraith essentially echoed Keynes' explanation of how stock prices, especially when experiencing drastic fluctuations, affect investment and consumption. And both were critical of efforts by the monetary authorities to curb a speculative stock market mania by raising interest rates. Galbraith, however, said a little more than Keynes about other possible measures, namely warnings by the Chairman of the Federal Reserve Board.

Keynes and Shiller

Although Shiller did not mention Keynes, his analysis of speculative stock markets, pointing to mass psychology as the likely dominant cause of fluctuations in the general level of stock prices, is very similar to Keynes'. In particular, the attention that Shiller devotes to fads, fashions, suggestibility, group pressure and social movements expands upon points that were only suggested in several of Keynes' comments. Shiller's observation about the ambiguity of stock values and the effect of that ambiguity upon investor behavior is very Keynesian. Shiller's popular models as alternatives to the efficient markets models are similar to

Keynes' explanation of how investors behave under conditions of uncertainty. Popular models are usually simple, unsophisticated and spontaneous, consisting of qualitative descriptions of causes, anecdotes as suggestions of what may happen, and presumed correlations, cycles or other simple patterns of variation of economic variables. The patterns of investor behavior associated with the transmission and implementation of popular models suggest both Veblen's 'folk psychology' and Keynes' conventional rules that rest on fragile psychological footings.

Shiller's citation of a popular model relating to the sequence of price movements surrounding the 1929 crash is strikingly similar to Keynes' explanation of investor behavior. People using this popular model think that these price movements might repeat themselves, in a similar sequence, at a later date. The easiness of this model allowed investors to ignore any economic variables that may be different. Thus this popular model received considerable attention just before the 1987 crash, creating impressions that the past will repeat itself.

But Shiller argued that popular models tend to ignore less dramatic movements, such as the fairly steady increases in prices between 1924 and 1929 and 1982 and 1987. Where popular models forget or overlook certain patterns that end in large downturns, the rise in prices is likely to continue longer, as would be expected under Keynes' conventional rule of not expecting the near future to be much different than the present or recent past, which is regarded as being 'normal'.

In addition to expanding upon the psychology of speculation in Keynes' analysis, Shiller joined Veblen in providing complementary insights by leaving room for stock prices to reflect expectations of fundamentals. His alternative model, which included 'smart money' and 'ordinary investors', provides an elaboration on Keynes' observation that there are a few who attempt to assess the long-run yield but most do not. In Shiller's model, 'smart money' considers both fundamentals and expected reactions of ordinary investors.

The most noticeable difference between Shiller and Keynes is that Shiller attempts to investigate the psychology of investors by drawing upon social psychology and by field research. But on a conceptual basis, Shiller is more cautious than Keynes in ruling out the possibility that fundamental values will not influence prices. Consider, for example, his observation that some people seem to think that fads or fashions could play no role because 'smart money' would recognize profit opportunities that it would eliminate by profitable trading. Shiller suggests that this may happen to the extent of ruling out spectacular profit opportunities. In contrast, Keynes virtually ruled it out because professionals do not have sufficient information and, moreover, it is more profitable for them simply to 'beat the mob'. Shiller's argument about the ambiguity of the value of stocks weakens any interpretation that 'smart money' can really be very 'smart'. But in allowing 'smart money' to anticipate reactions of ordinary investors in his alternative model, Shiller comes quite close to Keynes' description of the behavior of professionals.

EXPLAINING THE POST-1987 CRASH STOCK MARKET

Speculative markets theory faces the challenge of explaining the performance of the stock market since the 1987 crash. Questions abound: If 19 October 1987 was the bursting of a speculative bubble, why did the worst single-day crash in history fail to restore a more lasting sobriety and traditional sense of caution on the part of market participants? In Galbraithian terms, why did the crash have such a weak immunizing effect? Was the Brady Commission correct in blaming the crash on a market mechanism failure rather than the bursting of a speculative bubble? Can the new bull market be a speculative mania in the absence of several institutional contributors specified in Galbraith's model, namely, the bull market started while the economy was still in recession rather than after a period of prosperity, taxes on the affluent were raised by the Clinton administration rather than lowered, and leverage has been a less conspicuous factor?

If the Brady Commission's interpretations were correct, several rational markets explanations would be invalidated. The arguments by Fama (1989) and Arbel et al. (1988) that the market had swiftly moved prices to new equilibria consistent with economic fundamentals with the crash would have to be expanded to contend that the subsequent price recovery to the old level in 1989 meant that those fundamentals had improved. Romer's (1993) 'learning' market explanation would similarly be jeopardized.

Those who argued that the prices were essentially rational before the crash, and that the crash was actually due to panic selling, could argue that the circuit breakers which were implemented removed the fear of panic selling, and thus investors returned to their pre-crash 'rational' behavior. Miller (1991, p. 245) suggested that the primary contribution of circuit breakers would be to free the mass of investors from 'the fear that computer-driven markets are thrashing about, like some mad Golem, totally out of human control'. When prices dropped, circuit breakers kicked in, and panic selling did not ensue (see French 1988, p. 279).

The market mechanism failure interpretation, however, encounters the difficulty of little evidence that program trading was sufficient to cause the crash. Panic selling out of fear of the unknown consequences of program-driven selling is an interpretation that better fits the scenario. Arguments that prices returned to rational levels and that prices since the crash have been rational reflections of fundamentals are lacking in light of such technical indicators as price/dividend and price/earnings ratios which suggest that the market was as overpriced in the early 1990s as before the October 1987 crash. Thus the new bull market would have to be explained in terms of the psychology of investors.

In seeking to explain why investor expectations exhibited such a strong resistance to any immunizing effect of the crash, three factors seem to warrant attention by virtue of their dominance in the new environment. First, both individual and institutional investors seem to have accepted a higher degree of risk in their portfolios. Second, actions by the Federal Reserve on the morning after the 1987 crash and subsequent expansionary policies seem to have contributed to the increased willingness of investors to accept greater risk because of a general sense of confidence that the Fed will not allow the market to crash. Although the huge flows of retirement funds into stock mutual funds is the overt explanation of the continued market boom, these psychological changes would explain why a greater proclivity for risk has occurred. The absence of any serious economic consequence of the 1987 crash and the observation that large financial institutions will be bailed out by the federal government undoubtedly contributed to that sense of confidence.

Empirical evidence of a growing willingness by investors to take on greater risk was provided by a study intended to identify the determinants of stock prices in the 1980s (Lowenstein 1991). Some 38 percent of the rise in stock prices could not be statistically attributed to either economic fundamentals or over-optimistic expectations of corporate earnings. The author of the study suggested that this 'X' factor could be attributed to 'changing social attitudes' with respect to willingness to accept risk.

An alternative would be to view the new developments as a sea change, with investors becoming more inclined to invest for the long haul. That would not be inconsistent with Keynes' argument that if the longer view prevailed – if speculation is only a bubble on a pool of enterprise – the natural rate of interest would be lowered. Since higher stock prices in *Treatise* had the same effect on investment as a lower natural rate of interest if stock prices were sustainable at those higher levels, this might be argued to represent a new development. Toporowski (1993) argued that the compulsory flows of contributions into pension funds have been a major contributor to the market's performance.

The current sense of confidence in the Fed's ability to keep the market on an upward course seems to suggest Veblen's view in *Absentee Ownership* that the Federal Reserve had effectively stabilized the financial markets. That view, of course, proved to be wrong in 1929! Keynes' comments about the pressures on institutional fund managers to avoid investing for the long run seem to be borne out in the 1990s by the numerous references in the financial press to the pressures on fund managers to do what other fund managers are doing, for example the *Wall Street Journal* of 30 December: 'Despite Rising Doubts, Mutual-Fund Officials Pour Cash Into Stocks' (1995, p. 1A). While the margin requirement has been higher than during the 1920s, the tax deferment on pension contributions has somewhat the same effect.

In Galbraith's analyses of the 1920s and the 1980s, he drew attention to the mergers. As the *Wall Street Journal* (26 February 1997, p. 1) reported, another merger movement is occurring in the 1990s. The article noted that this movement is bigger than those of the 1920s and 1980s, and that the forces behind it are different. The parallel cited was to the larger movement of the late 1800s that Veblen had observed. Among other factors cited was 'A roaring stock market that has given acquiring companies an ever-more-valuable currency – their own shares – with which to pay for acquisitions' (p. 1).

In the next millenium, corporate equity buyers will have many factors to consider. Stock market investors will have to decide whether the value of their shares is driven primarily by the rational estimation of future corporate earnings or whether mass psychology and speculative mania drive the value of their investments. In the latter scenario, investors will have to expend more resources to determine the 'mood of the crowd' and, then, time the market correctly. Certainly, forecasting future earnings for corporations will continue to be important to the long-term investor. However, in volatile, manic financial markets where stock prices can exceed all historical measures of reasonable value, an understanding of human psychology will become increasingly important to investors. The speculative market theories developed by Keynes, Veblen, Galbraith and Shiller can provide valuable guidance in this new era.

Bibliography

Adams, M.C. and A. Szafarz (1992), 'Speculative Bubbles and Financial Markets', *Oxford Economic Papers*, 626–40.

Allen, Fredrick Lewis (1931), *Only Yesterday*, New York: Harper & Brothers.

Allen, Robert Loring (1993), *Irving Fisher*, Cambridge, Mass.: Blackwell.

Andersen, Torben M. (1983/84), 'Some Implications of the Efficient Capital Markets Hypothesis', *Journal of Post Keynesian Economics*, Winter, 281–94.

Arbel, Avner, Steven Carvell and Erik Postnicks (1988), 'The Smart Market Crash of October 19', *Harvard Business Review*, May–June, 124–36.

Arrow, Kenneth (1986), 'Thorstein Veblen as an Economic Theorist', in Michael Szenberg (ed.), *Essays in Economics*, Boulder: Westview Press, 47–56.

Bagehot, Walter (1880), *Economic Studies*, London: Longmans, Green and Co.

Baldwin, William (1992), 'The Crazy Things People Say to Rationalize Stock Prices', *Forbes*, 27 April, 140–50.

Balogh, Thomas (1930), 'Absorption of Credit by the Stock Exchange', *American Economic Review*, December, 658–63.

Barsky, Robert B. and J. Bradford De Long (1989), 'Bull and Bear Markets in the Twentieth Century', *NBER Working Paper Series*, Working Paper No. 3171.

Baumol, William J. (1965), *The Stock Market and Economic Efficiency*, New York: Fordham University Press.

Bernstein, Peter L. (1992), *Capital Ideas: The Improbable Origins of Modern Wall Street*, New York: Free Press.

Black, Fischer (1988), 'An Equilibrium Model of the Crash', in Stanley Fischer (ed.), *NBER Macroeconomics Annual 1988*, Cambridge: The MIT Press, 269–75.

Blanchard, Olivier J. and Mark W. Watson (1982), 'Bubbles, Rational Expectations, and Financial Markets', in Paul Wachtel (ed.), *Crises in the Economic and Financial Structure*, Lexington: Lexington Books, 295–315.

Brady Commission. (1989), 'The Brady Report', in R.J. Barro, E.F. Fama, D.R. Fischel, A.H. Meltzer, R.W. Roll and L.G. Telser (eds), *Black Monday*, Homewood: Irwin, 127–201.

Brockie, Melvin D. (1958), 'The Cycle Theories of Veblen and Keynes Today', in Douglas F. Dowd (ed.), *Thorstein Veblen: A Critical Appraisal*, Ithaca: Cornell University Press, 113–28.

Browning, E.S. (1996), 'Is It Still a Stock Market, or Just a Launch Pad?', *Wall Street Journal*, 13 June, C1.

Burtchett, Floyd F. (1937), 'Unorganized Speculation: The Possibility of Control', *American Economic Review*, March, 263–95.

Cameron, Rondo (1993), *A Concise Economic History of the World*, 2 edn, Oxford: Oxford University Press.

Case, Karl E. and Ray C. Fair (1996), *Principles of Economics*, Upper Saddle River, NJ: Prentice Hall.

Clews, Henry (1908), *Fifty Years in Wall Street*, New York: Irving Publishing Company.

Clough, Shepard B. and Charles W. Cole (1952), Economic History of Europe, Boston: D.C. Heath.

Cnnfn.com (1997), 'Greenspan Roils Market', 26 February.

Cnnfn.com (1997), 'Greenspan Backs Remarks', 5 March.

Cnn.com (1997), 'Fed Not Trying to Hit Stocks', 6 March.

Cootner, Paul H. (1964), 'Introduction: Origins and Justification of the Random Walk Theory', in Paul H. Cootner (ed.), *The Random Character of Stock Market Prices*, Cambridge: MIT Press, 1–6.

Cormier, Frank (1962), *Wall Street's Shady Side*, Washington, DC: Public Affairs Press.

Crutsinger, Martin (1996), 'Greenspan Frightens Markets', *Tuscaloosa News* (New York Times News Service), 7 December: A1.

Dirlam, Joel B. (1958), 'The Place of Corporation Finance in Veblen's Economics', in Douglas F. Dowd (ed.), *Thorstein Veblen: A Critical Appraisal*, Ithaca: Cornell University Press, 199–220.

Dorfman, Joseph (1934), *Thorstein Veblen and His America*, New York: Viking Press.

Edie, Lionel (1922), *Principles of the New Economics*, New York: Thomas Y. Crowell Company.

Edwards, G.W. (1938), *The Evolution of Finance Capitalism*, London: Longmans, Green and Co.

Eiteman, Wilford J. (1932), 'The Economics of Brokers Loans', *American Economic Review*, March, 66–77.

Ely, Richard (1896), *Outlines of Economics*, New York: Eaton and Mains.

Ely, Richard, et al. (1930), *Outlines of Economics*, rev. 5th edn, New York: The Macmillan Company.

Ely, Richard and Ralph H. Hess (1937), *Outline of Economics*, 6th edn, New York: The Macmillan Company.

Emery, Henry C. (1915), 'Speculation on the Stock Exchanges and Public Regulation of Stock Exchanges', *American Economic Review*, March, 69–85.

Emshwiller, John R. (1996), 'Manipulations of NASDAQ-Listed Stocks are Rising, but Investors Keep Buying', *Wall Street Journal*, 13 September, C1.

Fama, E.F. (1970), 'Efficient Capital Markets: A Review of Theory and Empirical Work', *Journal of Finance*, May, 17–40.

Fama, E.F. (1989), 'Perspectives on October 1987, or, What Did We Learn from the Crash?' in *Black Monday and the Future of Financial Markets*, Homewood: Irwin, 71–82.

Fama, E.F. (1991), 'Efficient Capital Markets II', *Journal of Finance*, December, 1575–617.

Fetter, Frank (1913), *Source Book in Economics*, New York: Century Co.

Fisher, Irving (1912), *Elementary Principles of Economics*, 3 edn, New York: Macmillan.

Fisher, Irving (1930), *The Stock Market Crash — and After*, New York: Macmillan.

Fisher, Irving Norton (1956), *My Father, Irving Fisher*, New Haven: Yale University Press.

Flood, Robert P. and Peter Garber (1980), 'Market Fundamentals versus Price Level Bubbles: The First Tests', *Journal of Political Economy*, August, 745–70.

Flood, Robert P. and Peter Garber (1982), 'Bubbles, Runs, and Gold Monetization', in Paul Wachtel (ed.), *Crises in the Economic and Financial Structure*, Lexington: Lexington Books, 275–93.

Flood, Robert P. and Robert J. Hodrick (1990), 'On Testing for Speculative Bubbles', *Journal of Economic Perspectives*, Spring, 85–102.

Fraser, Lindley M. (1932), 'The Significance of the Stock Exchange Boom', *American Economic Review*, June, 193–202.

French, Kenneth (1988), 'Crash Testing the Efficient Markets Hypothesis', in Stanley Fischer (ed.), *NBER Macroeconomics Annual Edition 1988*, Cambridge: MIT Press, 277–85.

Friend, Emil (1908), 'Stock-Exchange Regulation in Germany', *Journal of Political Economy*, June, 369–74.

Froot, Kenneth A. and Maurice Obstfeld (1991), 'Intrinsic Bubbles: The Case of Stock Prices', *American Economic Review*, December, 1189–214.

Galbraith, John Kenneth (1952), *American Capitalism*, Boston: Houghton Mifflin.

Galbraith, John Kenneth (1958), *The Affluent Society*, Boston: Houghton Mifflin.

Galbraith, John Kenneth (1971), *The New Industrial State*, 2 edn, Boston: Houghton Mifflin.

Galbraith, John Kenneth (1987), 'The 1929 Parallel', *Atlantic Monthly*, January, 62–6.

Galbraith, John Kenneth (1988), *The Great Crash 1929*, Boston: Houghton Mifflin.

Galbraith, John Kenneth (1990), *A Tenured Professor*, Boston: Houghton Mifflin.

Galbraith, John Kenneth (1994), *A Journey Through Economic Time*, Boston: Houghton Mifflin.

Garber, Peter M. (1990a), 'Who Put the Mania in Tulipmania?', in Eugene N. White (ed.), *Crashes and Panics*, Homewood: Dow Jones-Irwin, 3–32.

Garber, Peter M. (1990b), 'Famous First Bubbles', *Journal of Economic Perspectives*, Spring, 35–54.

Glickman, Murray (1994), 'The Concept of Information, Intractable Uncertainty, and the Current State of the Efficient Markets' Theory: A Post Keynesian View', *Journal of Post Keynesian Economics*, Spring, 325–49.

Graham, Benjamin and David L. Dodd (1934), *Security Analysis: Principles and Techniques*, New York: McGraw-Hill.

Hardy, Charles O. (1937), 'Recent Developments in the Theory of Speculation', *American Economic Review*, March, 254–62.

Harrison, J. Michael and David M. Krebs (1978), 'Speculative Investor Behavior in a Stock Market With Heterogeneous Expectations', *Quarterly Journal of Economics*, May, 323–36.

Harvey, John T. (1994), 'Circular Causation and the Veblenian Dichotomy in the General Theory: An Introduction to Institutionalist Method', *Journal of Post Keynesian Economics*, Fall, 69–89.

Hollander, Jacob H. (1910), *David Ricardo*, New York: Augustus M. Kelley.

Hume, David in Eugene Rotwein (ed.) (1955), *Writings on Economics*, Madison: University of Wisconsin Press.

Kansas, Dave (1996), 'Taking Stock', *Wall Street Journal*, 'A Century of Investing', 28 May, R1.

Kaufman, Henry (1996), 'Today's Financial Euphoria Can't Last', *Wall Street Journal*, 25 November, A18.

Keynes, John Maynard (1936), *The General Theory of Employment, Interest and Money*, New York: Harcourt, Brace and Co.

Keynes, John Maynard (1971a), *A Treatise on Money*, Vol. I, 'The Pure Theory of Money', *The Collected Writings of John Maynard Keynes*, Vol. 5. London: Macmillan.

Keynes, John Maynard (1971b), *A Treatise on Money*, Vol. II, 'The Applied Theory of Money', *The Collected Writings of John Maynard Keynes*, Vol. 6. London: Macmillan.

Keynes, John Maynard (1973a), *The Collected Writings of John Maynard Keynes: The General Theory and After, Part I, Preparation*, Vol. 13, London: Macmillan.

Keynes, John Maynard (1973a), *The Collected Writings of John Maynard Keynes: The General Theory and After. Part II, Defence and Development*, Vol. 14, London: Macmillan.

Keynes, John Maynard (1981), *The Collected Writings of John Maynard Keynes: Activities 1929–1931: Rethinking Employment and Unemployment Policies*, Vol. 20, London: Macmillan and Cambridge University Press.

Keynes, John Maynard (1982), *The Collected Writings of John Maynard Keynes: Activities 1931–1939: World Crises and Policies in Britain and America*, Vol. 21, London: Macmillan and Cambridge University Press.

Keynes, John Maynard (1983), *The Collected Writings of John Maynard Keynes: Economic Articles and Correspondence on Investment and Editorial*, Vol. 12, London: Macmillan and Cambridge University Press.

Kindleberger, Charles P. (1989), *Manias, Panics, and Crashes: A History of Financial Crises*, New York: Basic Books.

Kregel, J.A. (1992), 'Some Considerations on the Causes of Structural Change in Financial Markets', *Journal of Economic Issues*, September, 733–47.

Kuhn, Susan E. (1996), 'How Crazy is this MARKET?' *Fortune*, 15 April , 79–83.

Lavington, F. (1913), 'The Social Interest in Speculation in the Stock Exchange', *Economic Journal*, March, 36–52.

Lindbeck, Assar (1992), 'Presentation of James Tobin' and 'Presentation of Markowitz, Miller, and Sharpe', in Karl-Goran Maler, *Nobel Lectures: Economic Sciences 1981–1990*, Singapore: World Scientific, 3–41, 271–2.

Lowenstein, Roger (1991), 'Goldman Study of Stocks' Rise in '80s Poses a Big Riddle', *Wall Street Journal*, 6 June, C1.

Lowenstein, Roger (1996), 'A Common Market: The Public's Zeal to Invest', *Wall Street Journal*, 9 September, A1, A11.

Machlup, Fritz (1940), *The Stock Market, Credit and Capital Formation*, New York: Macmillan (1931).

Malkiel, Burton G. (1989), 'Efficient Markets Hypothesis', in John Eatwell, Murray Milgate and Peter Newman (eds), *The New Palgrave: Finance*, New York: W.W. Norton, 127–34.

Malkiel, Burton G. (1990), *A Random Walk Down Wall Street*, New York: W.W. Norton.

Markowitz, Harry M. (1991), 'Foundations of Portfolio Theory', *Journal of Finance*, June, 469–78.

Marshall, Alfred (1907), *Principles of Economics*, 5th edn, London: Macmillan.

Marshall, Howard D. (1967), *The Great Economists*, New York: Pitman.

Marx, Karl H. (1906), in F. Engels (ed.), *Capital*, Vols 1–3, Chicago: Charles H. Kerr & Co.

McGeehan, Patrick (1996), 'A Shaken Wall Street Reaches for the History Books', *Wall Street Journal*, 29 July, C1.

Mill, John Stuart (1873), *Principles of Political Economy*, London: Longmans, Green, Reader and Dyer.

Miller, Merton H. (1991), *Financial Innovations and Market Volatility*, Cambridge: Blackwell.

Moore, Gregory C. (1996), 'The Practical Economics of Walter Bagehot', *Journal of the History of Economic Thought*, Fall, 229–49.

Murphy, Antoin E. (1986), *Richard Cantillon, Entrepreneur and Economist*, Oxford: Oxford University Press.

Pigou, A.C. (1913), 'Independence of Sources of Supply and Demand', *Economic Journal*, March: 19–24.

Pratten, Cliff (1993), *The Stock Market*, Cambridge: Cambridge University Press.

Raines, J. Patrick and Charles G. Leathers (1992), 'Financial Innovations and Veblen's Theory of Financial Markets', *Journal of Economic Issues*, 433–40.

Raines, J. Patrick and Charles G. Leathers (1994), 'The New Speculative Stock Market: Why the Weak Immunizing Effect of the 1987 Crash?', *Journal of Economic Issues*, September, 733–53.

Raines, J. Patrick and Charles G. Leathers (1996), 'Veblenian Stock Markets and the Efficient Markets Hypothesis', *Journal of Post Keynesian Economics*, Fall, 137–51.

Ramirez, Anthony (1995), 'Cue from the Q: Dow Looks High', *The Tuscaloosa News* (New York Times News Service), 3 December, 4E.

Ricardo, David (1951), in P. Sraffa (ed.), *The Works and Correspondence of David Ricardo*, Vol. 1, Cambridge: Cambridge University Press.

Ricardo, David (1955), in P. Sraffa (ed.), *The Works and Correspondence of David Ricardo*, Vol. 10, Cambridge: Cambridge University Press.

Romer, David (1993), 'Rational Asset-Price Movements Without News', *American Economic Review*, December, 1112–130.

Ross, Stephen A. (1989), 'Finance', in John Eatwell, Murray Milgate and Peter Newman (eds), *The New Palgrave: Finance*, New York: W.W. Norton, 1–34.

Rutherford, Malcolm (1980), 'Veblen on Owners, Managers, and the Control of Industry', *History of Political Economy*, Fall, 434–40.

Samuelson, Paul A. (1965), 'Proof that Properly Anticipated Prices Fluctuate Randomly', in R.C. Merton (ed.), *The Collected Scientific Papers of Paul A. Samuelson*, Vol. 3, Cambridge: The MIT Press, 782–89.

Samuelson, Paul A. (1979), *The Collected Scientific Papers of Paul A. Samuelson*, in H. Nagatani and K. Crowley (eds), Cambridge: MIT Press.

Santoni, Gary J. and Gerald P. Dwyer, Jr. (1990), 'Bubbles or Fundamentals: New Evidence from the Great Bull Markets', in Eugene N. White (ed.), *Crashes and Panics*, Homewood: Dow Jones-Irwin, 188–210.

Schwert, G. William (1989), *Business Cycles, Financial Crises and Stock Volatility*, Cambridge: National Bureau of Economic Research, Working Paper No. 2957.

Scott, Peter (1996), 'The New Alchemy: Veblen's Theory of Crisis and the 1974 British Property and Secondary Banking Crisis', *Journal of Economic Issues*, March, 1–12.

Sease, Douglas R. (1992), 'Black Monday Taught Investors to Lose Fear', *Wall Street Journal*, 16 October, C1.

Shiller, Robert J. (1981), 'Do Stock Prices Move Too Much to be Justified by Subsequent Changes in Dividends?', *American Economic Review*, June, 421–36.

Shiller, Robert J. (1984), 'Stock Prices and Social Dynamics', *Brookings Papers on Economic Activity*, (2), 457–98.

Shiller, Robert J. (1988), 'Portfolio Insurance and Other Investor Fashions as Factors in the 1987 Stock Market Crash', in Stanley Fischer (ed.), *NBER Macroeconomics Annual 1988*, Cambridge: MIT Press, 287–95.

Shiller, Robert J. (1989), *Market Volatility*, Cambridge: MIT Press.

Shiller, Robert J. (1990), 'Speculative Prices and Popular Models', *Journal of Economic Perspectives*, Spring, 55–65.

Shleifer, Andrei and Lawrence H. Summers (1990), 'The Noise Trader Approach to Finance', *Journal of Economic Perspectives*, Spring, 19–33.

Smith, Adam (1976), *An Inquiry Into the Nature and Wealth of Nations*, Indianapolis: Liberty Classics.

Sobel, Robert (1965), *The Big Board*, New York: The Free Press.

Stigler, George J. (1964), 'Public Regulation of the Securities Markets', *Journal of Business*, April, 117–42.

Stigler, George J. (1966), *The Theory of Price*, 3rd edn, New York: Macmillan.

Tanner, Michael (1996), 'It's Time to Privatize Social Security', *Challenge*, November–December, 19–20.

Teagarthen, Timothy (1996), *Microeconomics*, New York: Worth Publishers.

Telser, Lester G. (1990), 'October 1987 and the Structure of Financial Markets: An Exorcism of Demons', *Black Monday and the Future of Financial Markets*, Homewood: Irwin, 101–12.

Thomas, D.L. (1967), *The Plungers and the Peacocks*, New York: G.P. Putnam's Sons.

Toporowski, Jan (1993), *The Economics of Financial Markets and the 1987 Crash*, Cambridge: Edward Elgar.

Twain, Mark (1949), *A Connecticut Yankee in King Arthur's Court*, New York: Basic Books.

Untermeyer, Samuel (1915), 'Speculation on the Stock Exchanges and Public Regulation of the Exchanges', *American Economic Review*, March, 24–68.

USAToday.com (1997), 'Fed Chief Waves Caution Flag at Racing Stocks', 27 February.

Veblen, Thorstein (1900), 'Industrial and Pecuniary Employments', reprinted in *The Place of Science in Modern Civilization*, New York: Russell & Russell, 1961.

Veblen, Thorstein (1904), *The Theory of Business Enterprise*, New York: Charles Scribner's Sons.

Veblen, Thorstein (1908), 'On the Nature of Capital', reprinted in *The Place of Science in Modern Civilization*, 324–86.

Veblen, Thorstein (1923), *Absentee Ownership*, New York: Viking Press.

Vining, Rudledge (1939), 'Suggestions of Keynes in the Writings of Veblen', *Journal of Political Economy*, October, 692–704.

Walker, Donald A. (1977), 'Thorstein Veblen's Economic System', *Economic Inquiry*, April: 72–96.

Walras, Leon (1874), *Elements of Pure Economics*, translated by William Jaffe, London: George Allen and Unwin Ltd. (1954).

Weatherall, David (1976), *David Ricardo*, The Hague: Martinus Nijhoff.

Weiner, John M. (1964), 'The London Stock Exchange and Other Stock Markets in Great Britain', in D.E. Spray (ed.), *The Principal Stock Exchanges of the World*, Washington, DC: International Economic Publishers, 175–209.

Werner, W. and S.T. Smith (1991), *Wall Street*, New York: Columbia University Press.

Wessel, David (1996), 'The Outlook: Worried Fed Watches Stock Market's Climb', *Wall Street Journal*, 25 November, A1.

West, Richard R. and Sheha M. Tinic (1971), *The Economics of the Stock Market*, New York: Praeger.

White, Eugene N. (1990), 'The Stock Market Boom and the Crash of 1929 Revisited', *Journal of Economic Perspectives*, Spring, 76–83.

White, Horace (1909), 'The Hughes Investigation', *Journal of Political Economy*, March, 528–40.

Wicksteed, Phillip H. (1910), *The Common Sense of Political Economy*, New York: Augustus M. Kelley (1966).

Wilson, Jack W., Richard E. Sylla and Charles P. Jones (1990), 'Financial Market Panics and Volatility in the Long Run, 1830–1988', in Eugene N. White (ed.), *Crashes and Panics*, New York: Dow Jones-Irwin.

Williams, J.B. (1938), *The Theory of Investment Value*, Cambridge: Harvard University Press.

Wysocki, Bernard Jr. (1996), 'Do Investors Confuse Price With Quality?', *Wall Street Journal*, 4 December, A2.

Index